CW01184273

HIS

This book should be returned or renewed on
before the last date stamped below

THE ORIGINS AND DEVELOPMENT OF
FOOTBALL IN IRELAND

'Football in Ireland may be said to consist of three parts – Rugbeian, Associationist, and Gaelic. The rule of play in these organisations has been defined as follows: In Rugby, you kick the ball; in Association, you kick the man if you cannot kick the ball; and in Gaelic, you kick the ball if you cannot kick the man. This puts the present procedure and position of the rival devotees into a nutshell.'

From Rev. F. Marshall (ed.)
Football: the Rugby Union Game
(London, 1892) p. 222.

ASSOCIATION - RUGBY - GAELIC

THE ORIGINS AND DEVELOPMENT OF
FOOTBALL IN IRELAND

being a reprint of R.M. Peter's
Irish Football Annual
of 1880

WITH AN INTRODUCTION BY
NEAL GARNHAM

ULSTER
HISTORICAL FOUNDATION

Published 1999
by the Ulster Historical Foundation
12 College Square East, Belfast, BT1 6DD

All rights reserved. No part of this publication may be reproduced, stored in a retrieval system or transmitted in any form or by any means, mechanical or otherwise without permission of the publisher.

© 1999 Ulster Historical Foundation

ISBN 0-901905-93-3

Typeset by the Ulster Historical Foundation
Printed by ColourBooks Ltd, Dublin

Cover and design by Dunbar Design

CONTENTS

ACKNOWLEDGEMENTS	vi
ORIGINS AND DEVELOPMENT OF IRISH FOOTBALL BY NEAL GARNHAM	
In the beginning...	1
The Birth of Organised Football: A More Gentlemanly Affair	3
Rugby: The Early Days	5
A Rival Code: The Dribbling Game	7
Something Old, Something New: The Gaelic Game	9
The Progress of Rugby	12
The 1890s: Great Changes	13
1900-1914: Success and Failure	17
Football and the Great War	23
Post-war Problems and Progress	25
Extra Time	29
INTRODUCTION TO *THE IRISH FOOTBALL ANNUAL 1880* BY NEAL GARNHAM	31
REPRINT OF *THE IRISH FOOTBALL ANNUAL 1880* EDITED BY RICHARD M PETER	35
STRANGE BUT TRUE! BY NEAL GARNHAM	171

ACKNOWLEDGEMENTS

For their help in the writing of the introduction to this book I would like to thank everyone who has discussed the project with me, but speical thanks are due to Bill Crawford, Ray Gillespie, Trevor Parkhill and Dawson Simpson. Sean Connolly, David Hayton and all the other members of the School of Modern History at the Queen's University of Belfast have also helped both directly and indirectly. Shane McAteer at the Ulster Historical Foundation has been a model of patience during production. I would also like to thank all those who have given permission for the reproduction of illustrations in their possession. Publication was generously assisted by a grant from the Community Relations Council. Last but not least I remain indebted to the Leverhulme Trust, who have co-funded my present post, and who kindly agreed to support my research into sport in Ireland.

IN THE BEGINNING...

The urge for young men to kick, throw and catch a ball in play seems to be an ancient and almost universal one. From China to the chilly wastes of the arctic, and from Ancient Greece to Medieval France, the playing of some form of football was almost a primeval urge. In this respect the inhabitants of Ireland were no different from those elsewhere. Perhaps the earliest surviving written reference to the playing of the game in Ireland is one from 1308, when a man was accidentally stabbed while 'playing at ball' in County Dublin. More specific, if isolated, reports of the playing of football continued to be made over the following centuries. For example, in 1518 an order of the Archbishop of Dublin made it clear that clergymen in the diocese of Ossory were to refrain from playing the game, and to pay for any damages that they caused to church property should the urge to indulge become too great. Bye-laws made for the city of Galway in 1527 aimed at controlling the activities of the city's inhabitants placed a ban on hurling and handball, but excluded playing with 'the great foote balle' from its provisions. In 1706 a naval press gang used the pretext of a challenge match against the townsmen of Waterford to capture a dozen fit but unwilling recruits. Exactly what form these games took is not certain, but they were certainly vigorous, physical and potentially dangerous. In 1780 an attempt by the city's watchmen to prevent a game being played in Dublin's streets resulted in the shooting dead of one player and the conviction of a watchman for his murder. However, from the end of the eighteenth century, the social, economic and political situations in Ireland all conspired to ensure an apparent decline in the existing folk practice of football. During the troubled years of the 1790s and beyond the government was reluctant to allow any large gathering of young men and football, along with bull-baiting and cock-fighting, was opposed by the country's authorities. In the following years the churches of all denominations became eager to see their members reform their manners, and conform to a more strict public and personal morality. Football, as well as the drunkenness and the celebration of popular festivals and fairs which often went along with it, was discouraged as morally degrading and ethically unacceptable. Finally, from the 1820s the worsening economic conditions in the country ensured that fewer men were able to devote the amount of time they once had to recreations and amusements of any sort. For example, in one County Antrim parish in 1838 it was noted that the fall in linen prices had meant that 'the taste for amusements' had 'declined as the pressure of the times has increased.' In another the common people found that 'now all their industrious exertions and energies are called forth to meet the pressure of the times', leaving them little time or inclination to engage in the less necessary activities of life. By the time of the Great Famine in the 1840s many of the existing social practices in rural Ireland were under threat. The resultant depopulation, and the alienation of the remaining population from many of what were deemed the old, failed ways seems to have more or less ensured their practical disappearance. Amongst them were the old, often riotous and sometimes threatening, forms of football.

A sketch of an Irish football match in 1805. Note the two players brawling in the foreground.

National Library of Ireland

THE BIRTH OF ORGANISED FOOTBALL: A MORE GENTLEMANLY AFFAIR

At the same time as Ireland was seeing her traditional sports and pastimes decline almost into oblivion, quite different developments were taking place in the public schools on the other side of the Irish Sea. From the 1830s the elite schools of England saw sports and games become an integral part of their curriculum. The ideologies behind the promotion of such activities were various. Sports did, of course, lead to a greater physical development and sense of well-being among pupils. At the same time, they were also seen as morally improving and character forming. Competition on the sports field made young men value team-work and discipline, and impressed on them the importance of respecting authority and codes of behaviour. Such ideals, and the games to which they were attached, were almost inevitably transported to Ireland in the following years. As far as football is concerned, the first concrete evidence of this transmigration came in 1854. In that year a number of former pupils of the Rugby and Cheltenham schools in England, who were now students at Trinity College in Dublin, formed a football club there. The subsequent growth of the game was far from meteoric. Over the next five years all the reported games played by the Trinity club were internal ones. Students divided themselves into makeshift teams along lines of counties of birth, places of schooling, and even alphabetically. Not until 1860 did the Trinity side take on outside opposition, and even that year's game against a side known as 'Wanderers' was essentially an all-Trinity affair, with most of the opposition side apparently being former Trinity students. Football in Ireland seems to have continued to involve only very small numbers of men, most of whom had some link to Trinity and the club there. Occasional matches between the students and outside opposition did occur, such as those against the masters and pupils of St. Columba's College, at Rathfarnham or the Royal School Dungannon, but even these matches seemed to have relied upon some link to Trinity, with masters at the relevant schools being graduates of Trinity. In fact, the wider spread of the game in Ireland actually came to rely as much upon the continued influence of later generations of Irishmen educated in England, and the deliberate importation of English public school ethics, as upon football missionaries from Trinity. For example, the North of Ireland Football Club was founded in Belfast in 1868 as an adjunct to the already prospering cricket club, by a number of young local men who had studied at Rugby School in Warwickshire and Cheltenham College in Gloucester. Football at the Catholic Clongowes College near Dublin owed its origins

Members of Dublin University Football Club pictured in 1867. This is the earliest known photograph of a formal football club in Ireland.

Dublin University

to the fact that the college modelled itself so closely on the Jesuit school at Stonyhurst in England. In this way both football and cricket at Clongowes were played under the distinctive 'Stonyhurst rules.'

In October 1868 however, the Trinity club made a crucial contribution to the development of Irish football, when two of its members formulated a set of rules under which the previously informal games in the college would henceforth be conducted. The rules were simple and relatively straightforward. They allowed for players to 'call a mark' when they caught a ball cleanly; they also established an offside law. Players could run with the ball, but were prohibited from lifting it off of the ground. A goal was to be scored when the ball was kicked over a cross-bar between the two upright goal posts. The tripping of players was legal, though 'hacking', that is kicking an opponent in the shins, along with the practices of 'holding' and 'throttling', were not. In many of their particulars these rules were similar to those adopted by the Blackheath Football Club in London from 1863. It was this club that headed a group of dissidents who decided in that year not to join the newly-founded Football Association in London, but to continue to play their games along their own lines. Eventually it was the members of these clubs who were to found the Rugby Union in England. A fateful decision had been made with regard to Ireland's immediate footballing future. For the time being at least, the game in Ireland was to take the form that was soon to be known as Rugby football.

RUGBY:
THE EARLY DAYS

The publication of the Trinity rules in the next edition of John Lawrence's *Cricket Annual* may have given the game something of a new impetus over the following years. The cricket annuals produced by the Dublin sports outfitter John Lawrence were widely available in Ireland, and the inclusion of football rules did at least potentially provide a common basis on which Irish football teams could compete. Games outside Trinity remained informal however and, even if the new rules were adhered to, they were imprecise enough to allow for a certain level of local interpretation. For example, when the North of Ireland club played the team from the Queen's College in Belfast in January 1870, the match took place over three consecutive Saturdays. Perhaps partly as a result of the fact that their team outnumbered the opposition by eighteen to fifteen, Queen's ran out the eventual winners by two clear goals. For the most part though, participation in the game was still limited. Few working men could afford the luxury of regularly taking time off work to play sports for amusement. The attitudes of the day ensured that the educated elites who had overseen the growth of the game to date were generally no more eager to mix with their social inferiors on the football field than elsewhere. Nonetheless, by October 1874 the geographic spread of football in Ireland was certainly much wider than it had been for many years. Clubs had been established in, amongst other places, Queen's College Cork, Carlow, Ballinasloe and Dungannon. This growth in the number of clubs meant that games could also now be played more frequently. Led by the North of Ireland club in Belfast, and Trinity College in Dublin, Irish clubs also began to forge sporting links with clubs outside Ireland. In December 1871 a West of Scotland team visited Belfast, while two years later the Trinity club crossed the Irish sea to play in Liverpool. The next logical step was a full international fixture between teams representing Ireland and England.

The first-ever recognised international football match had taken place in 1871, when an English team organised by the recently formed Rugby Football Union had played a Scottish team in London. Subsequent efforts to arrange a similar fixture between English and Irish teams had foundered, primarily due to the lack of a central representative body within Irish football. Primarily with this in mind, in December 1874 several members of the Trinity club arranged a meeting of representatives from the leading clubs in the country. On 14 December 1874 the initiative came to its initial fruition, and the Irish Football Union was formed. Eight clubs were initially affiliated. Five, including the Dublin University club, were based in the Dublin area. The remaining three, Portora, Dungannon and Monaghan, were from Ulster. Each paid their £1 subscription, and undertook through the Union, 'to promote and foster the game of rugby football in Ireland.'

Within a month the Belfast clubs, none of whom had attended the earlier Dublin meetings, but who were eager to protect their own interests and honour, had founded their own organisation, the Northern Football Union of Ireland. However co-operation rather than confrontation seems to have been the aim. In the event, the first Irish team was selected jointly by the two Unions, and the team that was eventually defeated by England at the Oval in February 1875 had members from clubs in both Belfast and Dublin. Later that year the Irish Football Union proposed an amalgamation with the Belfast based body, but this was rejected as too inconvenient at that juncture. The first interprovincial match, in which Ulster defeated Leinster, followed in November 1875. An English national team paid a victorious first visit to Ireland the following month. Both matches were now apparently accepted as annual fixtures. In February 1877 Scotland came to Ireland for the first time, defeating the home side in Belfast.

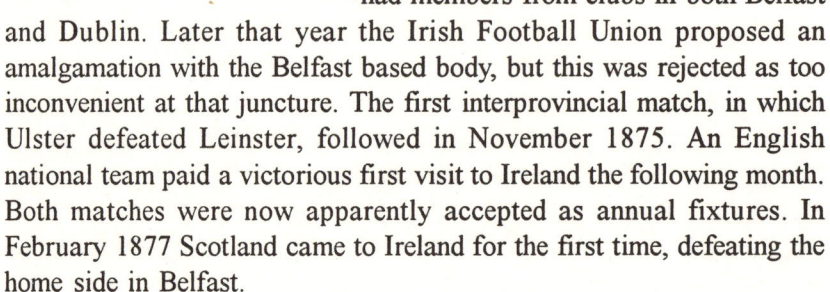

The co-existence of the two Unions in Ireland was at times cumbersome, but there was initially little real antagonism. International team selection was carried out jointly, and fixtures rotated. However, a further attempt at a merger came in November 1877. The terms offered by the Irish Football Union were seen as unacceptable by their northern counterparts though, and relations between the two bodies became strained. Just over a year later the conditions for amalgamation were finally agreed. This

As this cartoon from 1901 shows, physical strength and sheer size were important attributes for a rugby player.

Ireland's Saturday Night

time the Northern Football Union was more compliant, apparently prompted at least in part by the threat that the Munster clubs might break away from the Irish Football Union and form their own organisation. This would have further diluted the influence of the Northern Union, and possibly presented the prospect of the two southern organisations combining to defeat any initiatives the Belfast men might make. However, the story was not yet quite at an end. Despite the announcement in the Irish press in January 1879 that the Irish Rugby Football Union had now been founded as the sole body representing and controlling football in Ireland, the Northern Football Union's representative subsequently informed his counterparts from Dublin and Munster that they considered that the agreement should not be implemented until the following season. The whole project now seemed in doubt. A further meeting followed in Belfast in February 1879, at which rules for the IRFU were finally drawn up to the satisfaction of all those involved. The season closed, the Irish Football Union held its final meeting in Dublin on 28 October 1879, and the IRFU was eventually convened for the first time on 5 February 1880. From humble beginnings, and after some struggle, rugby football and its governing body in Ireland had emerged in recognisably modern forms.

A RIVAL CODE: THE DRIBBLING GAME

From 1878, however, organised football in Ireland had ceased to be a monolithic entity. In October of that year two Scottish association football clubs played a demonstration game in Belfast. The reaction was initially mixed. Despite the fact that the association game was becoming increasingly popular in England and Scotland, public opinion was against it succeeding in Ireland. One Dublin newspaper noted that the players were prone to head the ball 'like a pack of young goats'. Some in Belfast were more optimistic, but here too scepticism initially prevailed. In early 1879 however, the first association football club in Ireland, Cliftonville FC of Belfast, was founded. In November 1880 a meeting was held in a Belfast hotel at which representatives of three Belfast clubs, Cliftonville, Knock and Avoniel, agreed to form an association to promote the new game in Ireland: the Irish Football Association was formed.

Many of the early problems that had beset the organisations that were eventually to become the IRFU were avoided by the IFA. At their second meeting, rather than draft their own rules, the IFA agreed to adopt 'the Scotch rule book.' Opposition was more easily come by for teams, as many established sports clubs were eager to try their hand at the new game. At various times cricket, swimming and even lacrosse clubs in the Belfast area all fielded association teams. Several clubs, like Knock, who were already playing the rugby game, also began fielding association teams. The IFA was indirectly benefiting from the pioneering work of Ireland's earlier footballers.

At the same time other circumstances also coincided to help encourage the game in Ulster. Migrants to the area were vitally important in promoting and fostering the game. It was a happy coincidence for the IFA that the Belfast shipyards attracted skilled men to the city from Glasgow and the north-east of England: both were hotbeds of association play in Britain. The Avoniel side, who were one of the original members of the IFA, was formed by Scottish workers employed in the building of a new distillery in Belfast. The passing of the Factory and Workshops Act in 1878 effectively limited the hours worked by industrial workers, and ensured that most men were free from the burden of toil on Saturday afternoons. For the first time in Ireland working men had the time, and in some cases the inclination, to take part in organised sports. At the same time, many of the ideologies that had ensured the success of sports in the public school arena were also now being transferred to the wider community. Involvement in sports of any kind was seen as promoting a healthy body, and encouraging a healthy mind. Within a very short time football was being seen as a possible antidote to those twin scourges of the Irish working man: drink and the public house.

Progress for what was almost invariably known as 'the dribbling game' was to be slow but steady. The IFA Challenge Cup competition, the first domestic trophy, was established in January 1881; and Ireland's first association international, again against England, was played in February 1882. A match against Wales followed later in the same year, and one against the Scottish national side in 1884. By 1890, 124 active clubs were affiliated to the IFA, most were in the Belfast area, but centres were also emerging in Dublin, Londonderry, North Armagh and County Antrim. Local competitions and Associations affiliated to the IFA had also sprung up. The first two Associations were the Mid-Armagh FA, later known as the Mid-Ulster, and the County Derry FA, both formed in 1887. The former quickly established a Cup competition for local teams. The County Antrim FA was established in 1888, and began its own Shield competition in the same year. From very modest beginnings, soccer was becoming a footballing force to be reckoned with in Ireland.

On the international scene, though, Ireland were clearly novices and this showed in their lack of success. A first international victory came in 1887, in Belfast against an under-strength Welsh side; but this was to be the only bright spot in a decade which saw double figures defeats at the hands of Wales and Scotland, and a total of 54 goals conceded in eight games against England. Despite the team's failings however, the Irish administrators enjoyed rather more success. Most important amongst these was the Irish contribution in 1882 to the formation of the International Board, consisting of representatives from the four national Football Associations then in existence. The Board took on the responsibility of creating a common set of rules for the association game from the various sets then in existence. Eventually it was to oversee the creation of the modern game of soccer, and still enjoys the lead in formulating and developing the game's laws. Despite the initial scepticism of the Irish delegates, and the less-than-impressive playing record of the national side, Irish soccer was now integrated into an emerging international system.

SOMETHING OLD, SOMETHING NEW: THE GAELIC GAME

Gaelic football was to become the third form of football to be codified in Ireland. It owes its modern roots to a meeting that was held in Hayes's Hotel in Thurles in November 1884. This meeting, largely organised by the Dublin-based schoolmaster Michael Cusack, and the renowned Irish athlete Maurice Davin, followed the publication of a series of articles in the Irish press concerning the future of athletics in Ireland. In the event the meeting went further than this simple remit, and the Gaelic Athletic Association for the preservation and cultivation of national pastimes was formed. A great deal has been written concerning the subsequent development of the Association, the importance both of the political situation in

An advertisement for Hayes's Hotel in Thurles, which provided the venue for the first meeting of the GAA in 1884.

Limerick Chronicle

Ireland to its growth, and its own contribution to the world of Irish politics. However, in the context of Irish football, it must be stressed that the game of Gaelic football was, at least initially, a relatively unimportant part of the GAA's activities. In fact, circumstances conspired to ensure that Gaelic football remained a minority interest, both for the GAA and the public, for the first decade of the game's existence. For the most part athletics, which was then the most popular spectator sport in Ireland, along with the revival of what was seen as the uniquely Irish game of hurling, were the primary concerns of the GAA. Football, in any form, was not perceived as truly Irish enough to warrant much attention from the GAA. This was made clear in 1888 when a GAA 'invasion' of America was planned, with the twin ideas of raising funds and promoting Irish games. The force consisted of most of Ireland's leading athletes, and two hurling teams, but no footballers. At the same time, the rules of Gaelic football, first published in February 1885, did the game few favours. Scoring was to be accomplished by propelling the ball under a cross bar, but few other provisions were so precise. Teams could number from 15 to 21 players. The size of the pitch, stipulated as at least 120 yards long, meant that the game needed comparatively large areas for play. Partly as a consequence of the rules the general nature of the play left a great deal to be desired. Two styles soon emerged. In one, players simply gathered in a group and followed the ball around the pitch. In the other they attempted to keep a rigid formation, moving together in semi-military fashion. Neither generated much enthusiasm from players or spectators.

Simultaneously, the new football code had trouble establishing for itself a niche and an identity within Ireland. Amongst existing football players it had to compete with the comparatively well-established rugby game, and the novelty of the association code which was already seen as the popular game in England and Scotland. For sportsmen more eager to take up a game that had the image of the Irish hero more closely attached to it, hurling was the obvious choice. In fact, many of the early rule changes in Gaelic football seem to have been aimed primarily at ensuring the game was not simply another form of rugby. These came too late for one man, however. J. F. Murphy, an early GAA official, was expelled from the Association in February 1886 for promoting a form of the game in Munster that was simply too much like rugby. In September of the same year the GAA resolved to ban all individuals from its ranks who played any sport under non-GAA rules. Changes were to be made in Gaelic football's rules however, some of which at least would make the game more attractive to players and spectators alike. From late 1886 'wrestling' between players was banned, as was lifting the ball from the ground with the hand; pushing or striking the ball was legalised, however. The hand pass, a crucial and distinctive part of the Gaelic game, was emerging.

Yet if the game on the pitch was eventually to change for the better, as in the case of the association game, other circumstances also aided in the growth of Gaelic football's popularity. Crucially important was the decision to hold all Gaelic games on Sundays. Although this alienated many Protestants from the Association, it ensured that rural workers, and urban white-collar workers such as shop assistants, who could not be assured of a day of rest on Saturdays, were able to participate. At the same time, the atmosphere in which matches were played made sure that as spectacles they were quite different from those of the other two codes. Many matches were accompanied by political and patriotic displays it is true, but there were also other attractions. Games often became centres for more general cultural festivities, including Irish dancing and even Irish poetry recitals. Major games also tended to be played consecutively rather than simultaneously. This meant that for a single entrance fee to a ground spectators might see as many as three matches. Subsidiary attractions also included beer tents and bookmakers, neither of which were openly tolerated at rugby or association matches.

Growth was nonetheless initially slow. The initial county championships in 1887 saw only seven counties represented, none of which were from

Limerick Commercials, all-Ireland gaelic football champions in 1887. The name of the club gives away the social and economic background of its members.

Private Collection

Connaught or Ulster. Although by 1890 there were 777 GAA clubs in Ireland, the previous year's football championship saw only six counties enter. Gaelic football was, at least for the time being, very much a minority interest even in footballing and general sporting terms.

THE PROGRESS OF RUGBY

While the 1880s had been the years of genesis for association and Gaelic football in Ireland, for the rugby code the decade was one of continued advancement, consolidation and qualified success. The game within Ireland was to see a steady progression in the numbers of players involved in the game, as well as the development of new clubs and competitions. Most important amongst these were the various provincial cups that were established. The Leinster Senior Cup was the first, being competed for from 1882. Ulster followed suit in 1884, and Munster in 1885. The various provincial authorities also recognised the importance of encouraging the game amongst the nation's youth. The very first Irish rugby trophy had been established in the north in 1875, when the Ulster Schools Cup was first set up. A Leinster equivalent came in 1887. Although a plan in 1882 to establish an IRFU Challenge Cup for competition between Irish clubs came to nothing, the domestic game was taking on a new competitive edge.

At the time of the final formation of the IRFU, the Irish national team had neither won a match, nor even scored a point against international opposition. The latter situation was amended in 1880, when the Irish side scored a try against England though they went on to lose the match. Ireland's first international victory came against Scotland in Belfast in February 1881. A year later a draw was secured against England in Dublin, though a controversial refereeing decision was blamed for robbing the home side of victory. It was also in 1882 that Ireland played her first ever game against Wales. Regular international matches and an effective home championship had to wait a few years yet, however, as the respective Unions quibbled over venues, dates, administrative arrangements, and the rules of the game they were engaged in. It was this situation which in December 1885 prompted the IRFU to take a crucial initiative, and call on the four Unions to form an International Board to govern the contests between the nations. A conference followed in Dublin in February 1886, and despite continued disputes the seeds had been sown for the essential supervising body. The IRFU had made a contribution to international competition off the field of play that was far greater than any to date that

A group from the Wanderers RFC c1888. The founding of this club saw rugby in Dublin move out of the confines of Trinity College for the first time.

Wanderers RFC

it had made on it. Yet playing success was not far behind. The long-awaited victory over England finally came at Lansdowne Road in February 1887. A first win against Wales came a year later. The decade was to close with a further victory over the Welsh, this time in Swansea. It was Ireland's first triumph on foreign soil. On an international level at least, the decade ended on a victorious note.

THE 1890s
GREAT CHANGES

If its patriotic image and nationalist connections had served the GAA well during the initial years of its existence, they were to have an opposite effect in the first half of the 1890s. The schism within the Irish Parliamentary Party and the eventual fall of Charles Stewart Parnell from its leadership in the first two years of the decade had profound consequences for the GAA and the sports it governed. Against the stance of the Catholic church, and more importantly contrary to general nationalist opinion, the GAA opted to support its patron Parnell. The split in political nationalism was re-enacted in the GAA. Outside of the counties of Cork, Dublin and Galway the GAA largely ceased to function between 1892 and 1896.

However, it was during this apparent lapse of sporting activity that Gaelic football underwent fundamental changes which were to shape its future development as a sport. From 1892 rules were introduced restricting teams to between 17 and 14 players. Three years later, at the instigation

John Peden, who received 24 caps for Ireland 1887-99, was also the first Irishman to be connected with Manchester United. He was transferred to the Newton Heath club, the predecessors of United, in 1893.

Ulster Football and Cycling News

Robert Gibson, a linen merchant, and the President of the Linfield club, was the man primarily responsible for raising the issue of professionalism in Irish soccer.

Ulster Football and Cycling News

of Richard Blake, the Chairman of the Co. Meath GAA, crucial rules were introduced which banned carrying the ball and throwing it. Physical contact between players was also reduced to a minimum. Recognisably modern and distinctive styles of play could now begin to emerge, which were clearly distinguishable from the existing rugby and soccer codes. Gaelic football was establishing its own unique sporting identity. Even the ban on players involving themselves in the rival codes was dropped in 1896.

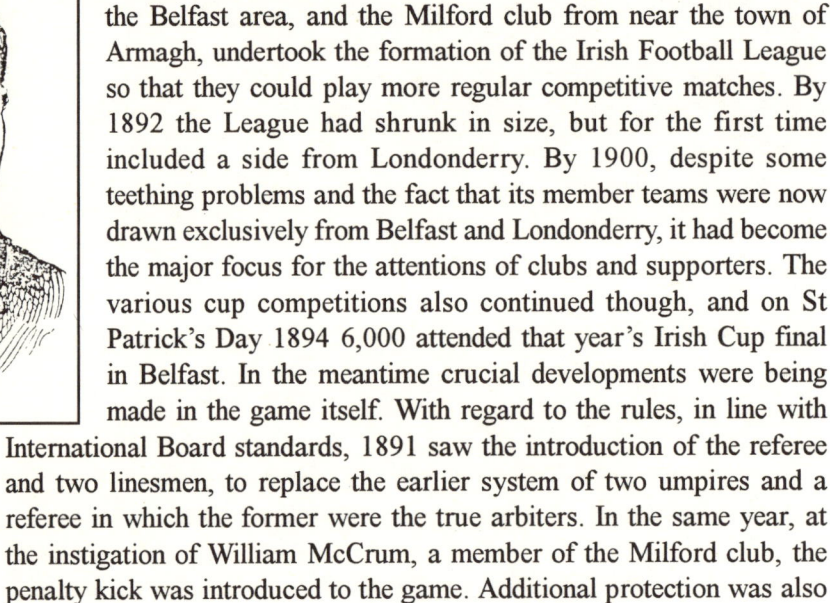

The 1890s opened on an optimistic note for the followers of the association game in Ireland. In that year seven clubs from the Belfast area, and the Milford club from near the town of Armagh, undertook the formation of the Irish Football League so that they could play more regular competitive matches. By 1892 the League had shrunk in size, but for the first time included a side from Londonderry. By 1900, despite some teething problems and the fact that its member teams were now drawn exclusively from Belfast and Londonderry, it had become the major focus for the attentions of clubs and supporters. The various cup competitions also continued though, and on St Patrick's Day 1894 6,000 attended that year's Irish Cup final in Belfast. In the meantime crucial developments were being made in the game itself. With regard to the rules, in line with International Board standards, 1891 saw the introduction of the referee and two linesmen, to replace the earlier system of two umpires and a referee in which the former were the true arbiters. In the same year, at the instigation of William McCrum, a member of the Milford club, the penalty kick was introduced to the game. Additional protection was also given to goalkeepers from barging by opposing players.

Internally, however, one of the most important decisions ever to be made by the IFA was taken at the 1894 AGM. Since 1890 various motions had been put forward to legalise professionalism amongst the game's players. Rumours had circulated for some time that illegal payments were being made, usually to prevent star players migrating to England where professionalism had been legalised in 1885. Finally, despite the misgivings of many smaller clubs, by a majority of more than thirty votes the meeting voted to ratify professionalism in Ireland. A whole new dimension to the game, and one that was not always to be welcome, had emerged.

At the same time, the game was finally emerging on a more regular footing in the country's capital. The various Dublin clubs of the 1880s, including one from Trinity College, had proved to be rather transient affairs, and the standard of play was apparently always lower than that amongst the Belfast teams. That all changed in 1890, when a number of students from the Catholic Medical School in the city, several of whom had attended Clongowes College together, founded the Bohemians Football Club in the gate lodge at Phoenix Park. Four years later the Shelbourne club was formed in a pub in the city's northern outskirts. A great rivalry was born, and the fortunes of association football took a turn for the better in Dublin. In 1895 the Bohemians reached the final of the Irish Cup, serving notice on the Belfast clubs of the rise of soccer outside of the northern metropolis. Three years earlier an important step had been taken to regularise the sport in Dublin when the Leinster Football Association had been formed, to promote and encourage the game in the Dublin area.

Yet if the domestic game was blossoming, the national side was not. Parity had been reached with the Welsh, with the 1890s seeing Ireland secure five wins and two draws against the principality. Against Scotland, however, only a draw in Belfast in 1896 upset a solid run of defeats, while against the English the record was identical, with the draw coming in 1894. Followers of the national side, and the game's administrators, were perplexed and disillusioned. Action had to be taken.

Despite this situation, by the end of the nineteenth century soccer was played more regularly and more widely in Ireland than ever before. For some players it actually provided a reasonable living. For many spectators, who came to matches in often surprisingly large numbers, it now provided a staple element in their weekly routines.

As the 1890s opened, rugby in Ireland, with a new administrative structure in place and a wider spread of adherents then ever before, was in a comparatively strong position. Eventually this was to be reflected on the field of international competition. Between 1890 and 1893, despite playing a dozen

SCOTLAND V. IRELAND AT GLASGOW
AN AWFU' BLOW.

Cartoonists had to deal with international failure more frequently than success. But even a 9-1 defeat for the Irish soccer side in Glasgow could generate some humour.
Ireland's Saturday Night

Louis Magee, the Irish captain and the inspiration for their Triple Crown victory of 1899.
Belfast Telegraph

games, the Irish national side recorded only a single victory, against Wales in Dublin in 1892. This lack of success in part reflected the changing nature of the game. Led by Wales, the national teams were now starting to implement a system of four running three-quarters, rather than relying on older tactics such as short rushes by heavy forwards, and long kicking. The 1893/4 season was the first to see the Irish national side use the new methods, and with instant success. Victories over England at Blackheath, and Scotland and Wales in Dublin and Belfast, saw Ireland take her first ever Triple crown. In truth however, this first triumph relied more upon peculiarly Irish methods than the new-fangled running backs. A modified form of forward play, incorporating dribbling the ball with sheer physical force, was the real reason for the Irish victories. Two years later, although the game with Scotland ended in a draw, the same methods again proved successful as Ireland once more took the home championships. A second triple crown followed in 1899, though by now the backs were playing a more prominent role in the team. This was in no small part due to the abilities of Samuel Lee, a Belfast man and a formidable Irish half-back between 1891 and 1896, and the Dubliner Louis Magee, the captain of the side in 1899, and the winner of 27 Irish caps between 1895 and 1904. Both men were recognised in their day as gifted and innovative players, and crucial members of the Irish side.

On the domestic front, some initial decline in activity in the early years of the decade was first halted and then sharply reversed. Although club numbers were falling in Munster, in 1896 the Connaught championship was established for the first time, and won by Galway Town. The four consecutive victories over England from 1896 gave a major fillip to the game in Leinster, and new clubs were founded there

The 1899 Triple Crown was celebrated across Ireland, and provided great material for the cartoonists of the day.

Ireland's Saturday Night

while others converted to the rugby code from the Gaelic and association ranks. In a wider context, the controversies over the establishment of the Rugby League in England and Wales largely passed Ireland by. Arguments over payments to players were almost irrelevant in a country where rugby remained largely a game for gentlemen. There was involvement in the wider rugby world, however, and in 1896, for the first time, Irish players were invited to join a combined British tour. In the end nine Irishmen travelled to South Africa as representatives of the best of home nations rugby.

As the new century opened, Irish rugby was perhaps at the pinnacle of its achievements. At home the game enjoyed a new popularity and esteem. Abroad the national side was triumphant, and its players recognised for their individual skill and flair. It looked like being a brave new rugby world for the Irish adherents of the game.

Ireland take on Wales at Balmoral Showgrounds in 1894. Primarily an agricultural showground, Balmoral also hosted international soccer and rugby matches, air displays, and cycle racing prior to the Great War
Belfast Telegraph

1900–1914:
SUCCESS AND FAILURE

Despite the success and promise of the 1890s, the following decade and a half did not live up to the expectations of Ireland's rugby aficionados. Individual victories were recorded by the national side, including a further six over English sides, but Ireland remained the only one of the home nations not to win the Triple Crown between 1900 and 1914. New dimensions were given to the game by the visits of New

Zealand to Dublin in 1905, and of South Africa to Belfast and Dublin in 1906 and 1912 respectively, but these games too ended in defeat. Only the commencement of annual matches, and a string of victories, against France from 1909 offered much solace. This lapse into mediocrity seems to have had at least two causes. In the first place, new players of the calibre of the men who had been so successful in the 1890s were simply

> **RUGBY INTERNATIONAL**
> **ENGLAND v IRELAND**
> at Lansdowne Rd · DUBLIN ·
>
> HIBERNIAN VICTORY.
> CLOSE AND DETERMINED STRUGGLE.
> ULSTERMAN SCORES WINNING TRY.
> BRILLIANT IRISH FORWARDS.
> LLOYD IN FINE FORM.

What success Ireland's rugby side experienced prior to the Great War depended upon her powerful forwards, such as in this game against England in 1911.
Ireland's Saturday Night

not coming forward. Simultaneously it was suggested that Ireland were now lagging behind the other nations tactically.

More hopeful, though less spectacular, news was however being generated within the domestic game. In May 1904 Connaught received full provincial recognition under the IRFU, giving the game there something of a new impetus, and more fully integrating the west's players and administrators in the Irish rugby fraternity. Rugby was at last a truly national game in Ireland. In 1907 a perhaps even more important development took place. Following the death of the treasurer of the IRFU, Harry Sheppard, in the previous year, the Union managed to acquire from his estate the lease to the Lansdowne Road ground. An extension to this was negotiated with the owner Lord Pembroke, and within a year a major redevelopment had been completed. The IRFU, and rugby in Ireland, now had a permanent home. If for the time being success eluded the sport on the field of play, it had been seized in the arena of administration.

It was to be the first year proper of the twentieth century, rather than the end of the nineteenth, which heralded a sea-change in the fortunes of Gaelic football in Ireland. Two county finals were played in 1901, the first for the 1899 season and the second for 1900. The gate money collected provided a welcome influx of capital for the cash-starved GAA. By 1908, largely due to football related income, the GAA would also be able to secure itself a permanent home, by purchasing the then Jones's Road sports field, later to be renamed Croke Park. Later in 1901 though, more profound changes began to occur. Due to a number of deaths and resignations, the Association's administration now fell into the hands of a younger and more dynamic body of men. Many were members of the revolutionary Irish Republican Brotherhood, but for the time being at least, their energies were overwhelmingly directed into the sporting arena.

THE DOINGS OF LARRY O'HOOLIGAN

Larry Cheers the Canadians.

Gaelic football was to both aid in, and benefit from, the rejuvenation of the GAA. From 1901 Provincial Councils were established, making the sports administration less cumbersome. Further rule changes were also introduced. The most important of these was the provision that players could 'hop the ball' for any distance: in effect toe-tapping, which allowed players to make swift runs while maintaining control of the ball, was legalised. The ban on players engaging in soccer or rugby was also reinstated in 1901, becoming a permanent part of the rules, in an expanded form, from January 1905. It was to remain in force for almost another seven decades. What was in effect international competition was established for the first time, with the inauguration, for a four year period, of county championships that included teams from London and Scotland.

Touring Rugby parties from the colonies, such as the Canadians of 1902 who are celebrated by this cartoon, generated a great deal of excitement and meant that the idea of the Empire came into the lives of many who would never travel beyond their own shores.

Ireland's Saturday Night

The 1903 football finals, actually played in 1905 due to the backlog of fixtures, set new standards of play, and generated a whole new level of popular interest in the sport. Played between Kerry and Kildare, the contest went to two replays. The apparent hostility between the teams and their supporters, the reports of the preparations being made by the teams and their players, as well as the reported quality of the play, saw the press offer extended coverage to a Gaelic football fixture for the first time. Popular interest in the game as a spectator sport was finally being aroused. At the other end of the scale, 1905 also saw the first schools competitions being established under GAA auspices. In May the Great Southern and Western Railway, in apparent gratitude for the business that the GAA sponsored sports provided them with, donated two shields for competition between the hurlers and Gaelic footballers of the four provinces. However, Gaelic football was still in some disarray with regard to its championships, and though the 1907 GAA Convention required all championship matches to be played within certain deadlines, it was not until 1910 that the football fixtures were finally brought up to date. In the meantime the Railway Shield had been won outright by Munster, and rules were passed requiring teams to start matches more promptly. The game itself continued to evolve in ways that made it more acceptable to players and spectators alike. Distinctive regional styles of play had been emerging from the late 1890s, when Kildare sides perfected the long hand pass. Kerry sides now became renowned for their quick passing and effective combination, while Antrim and Louth teams took to what became known as 'ground football': that is, a soccer-style game of kicking the ball from man to man. Fundamental rule changes were still to be made though. From 1910 the scoring system was modified to give a recognisably modern system incorporating the scoring of goals under the cross-bar, and points above it. Goal nets were required, and the goal

IRELAND WINS—HURROO!!

The victory of the Irish rugby side over the Scots in Belfast in 1902 inspired this drawing in a local newspaper. It was to be a brief moment of joy during a period of limited success.

Ireland's Saturday Night

itself was enlarged. From 1913 teams were limited to 15 players and a basic off-side rule was introduced to prevent goal-mouth congestion. The game was largely complete, and only relatively minor changes would follow in later years. By 1915 20,000 spectators would attend the final championship tie, and give testimony to the game's popularity. In a comparatively short time Gaelic football had moved from being the least important of its parent organisation's interests, and had become the mainstay of its grip on the popular imagination.

As Irish rugby secured its position in the country at large, and Gaelic football reached new heights of popularity, Irish soccer was to experience both failure and, for the first time, real triumph in the decade and a half prior to the Great War. The international side was largely responsible for the latter. In 1903 Ireland recorded their first-ever victory over Scotland, with a 2–0 triumph in Glasgow. As they also defeated Wales by the same score in Belfast, for the first time the Irish side shared the Home Championship, even if it was with both the English and the Scots. Unfortunately disputes between the IFA and some key players, as well as injuries and unavailability, meant that the success could not be followed up. The 1910 Championship did see the Irish draw with the English and defeat the Scots, but on this occasion a defeat by the Welsh denied them the title. Revenge finally came in the two seasons before the outbreak of war. In the first, the English were finally defeated, in Belfast. The following year the feat was repeated in Middlesborough. A victory over Wales, and a draw against the Scots in Belfast in 1914 gave Ireland the Championship outright for the first, and effectively only, time.

All three codes recognised the importance of involving Irish youth in their sports, and as a consequence established schools' competitions. Pictured here are the pupils of Patrick Pearse's St Enda's school, the 1911 winners of the Dublin Schools Gaelic football championship.

National Library of Ireland

International success was accompanied, at least initially, by domestic expansion. In October 1901 the Munster Football Association was formed and affiliated to the IFA. Three years later the Fermanagh and South Tyrone Association, later the Fermanagh and Western, was recognised by the IFA. Soccer bodies with a remit to support and encourage the game right across Ireland now existed. Marks of the continued expansion of the game in Dublin came in 1902 when Bohemians became the first Dublin club to compete in the Irish League. They were joined in 1904 by Shelbourne, who in April 1906 became the first Dublin side to take the Irish Cup to the capital. Only three times between 1900 and 1912 was there no Dublin side in the Irish Cup final. In 1904 the IFA figures showed that for the first time ever there were more clubs affiliated in the Leinster area than in Antrim. By 1910 there were 420 soccer clubs across the country as a whole. The following year however, the domestic game entered a two year period of turmoil and trouble. The 1911–12 season saw a dispute arise between the major clubs and the IFA about the division of gate monies, and the rents paid for the use of club facilities in the latter stages of the Irish Cup. The outcome was the formation of a rival 'New Football Association' and the playing of only a single Irish Cup tie that season. Although the rift was eventually healed, the following League season saw a match between the Belfast Celtic and Linfield sides, generally seen as representing the Catholic and Protestant communities of West Belfast, conclude in a riot and an exchange of gunfire. At least sixty men, including four policemen, needed hospital treatment. Crowd disturbances were not unknown at soccer games, or for that matter Gaelic football matches, but the use of firearms was a wholly new development. Sporadic firing at various games occurred throughout the season, but no injuries were reported. This mattered little to many observers, however, as the soccer game had now been lastingly tarnished. Not least amongst those who offered scathing comments were the game's authorities in Dublin.

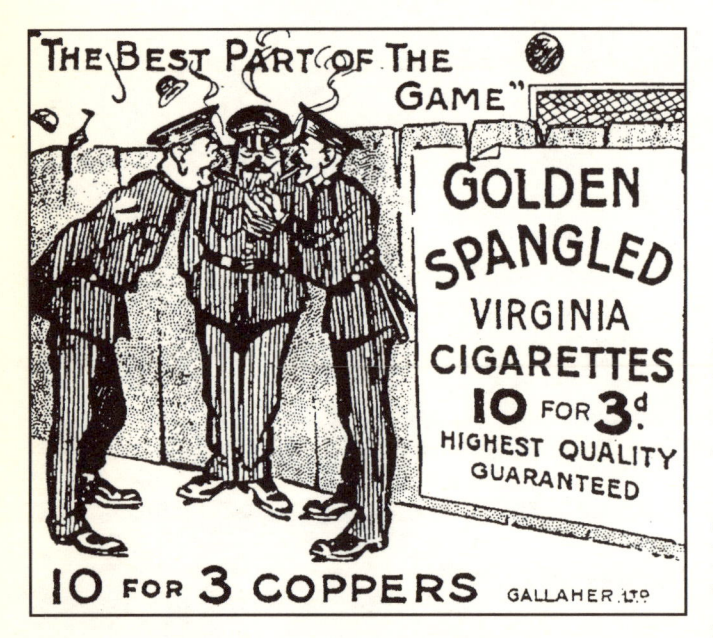

The readiness of manufacturers to use soccer in their advertisements, such as in this one from the Irish Times *in 1912, shows the level of popularity the game had achieved by the immediate pre-war years.*
Irish Times

Internal dissension, on one level or another, was beginning to show through.

FOOTBALL AND THE GREAT WAR

On the outbreak of the Great War in August 1914 Ireland had a very lively football culture. The three codes were all now well established and relatively widespread. Rugby was played in most of the great educational institutions across the country, and the university students and public schoolboys who engaged in the game often took it with them into the wider world. Dublin, Belfast, Cork and Limerick all had more than one thriving club, and in the provinces many smaller towns had successful teams. At international level the glories of the 1890s were still remembered, and the Irish XV were looked upon by their opposition as providing stiff competition. Soccer had its main centres in Belfast and Dublin, where the working classes provided the bulk of those who both played and watched the game. Despite the scepticism of some following the 1912 riot in Belfast, the long-awaited Irish victory in the 1914 Home Championships had elevated the game to new heights of achievement. Gaelic football was probably now the most widely played of the three games, and the evolution of the game's rules had finally led to a game that could satisfy the demands of players and spectators. It had not of course spread onto the international stage, but in itself this fact acted to promote the image of the game as one that was uniquely the property of, and suited to, the Irish. Football of all kinds was to be overtaken by events however, and by 1923 the situation had in many ways changed fundamentally, while remaining remarkably similar.

The advent of the War placed Ireland's footballing authorities in something of a quandary. The IRFU reaction was simple: sports must be suspended for the duration to allow for the all-consuming war effort. As a result all games other than schoolboy matches and charity games were abandoned. It was to be four years before a rugby ball would again be kicked in anger. The effect of the War itself on the game's adherents was spectacular. It was typified by the fate of the Irish Rugby Football Union Volunteer Corps. Within a fortnight of the outbreak of the War this body of men had been raised by Frank Browning, the then President of the IRFU, from the members of the rugby clubs in the Dublin area. Their intention was to seek service in what it was reckoned would be a short and glorious war. By mid-September 110 of the Corps's members had enlisted in the Royal Dublin Fusiliers. Many of those too old or infirm to enlist remained in Dublin, but took on voluntary duties in support of the garrison there. Provided with olive green uniforms and red armbands, they assisted in guiding men to their billets and running errands for the regular troops in the city. In the event, both groups of Volunteers came to unhappy ends. Those who had enlisted became part of the ill-fated expedition to Gallipoli in 1915, and were involved in some of the bloodiest battles of the entire war. The men who were left behind suffered an even crueller fate. Nominally part of the Irish garrison forces, once a month they were required to engage in a day's military training. Usually this took the form of a brisk march out of the city for a picnic lunch, before a return in the afternoon. It was just this format that the training took on Easter Monday 1916. The Volunteers, carrying rifles and equipment, but without ammunition, and headed by a brass band, marched back into the city, and the Easter Rising. Five men, including Browning, were shot by the enthusiastic insurgents, and subsequently died. Several others were injured. The war had come to the very heart of Irish rugby.

The IFA also considered the option of suspending all their activities, but eventually decided to continue the game on a limited basis. The prevailing argument was that continued soccer would be useful in maintaining morale at home, and provide a continued wholesome alternative to the public house. Internationals were not played however, and amateur soccer was eventually almost to cease, but local league competitions were established in Belfast and Dublin to replace the suspended Irish Football League, and the Irish Cup was played on a restricted basis. The game was to maintain its presence, even if it was on a reduced scale. In fact the War eventually resulted in something of a boom in Irish soccer. Though many players were to be lost to the game on the battlefields, at home the economic upturn in the war industries, especially in Ulster, meant that crowds at games reached new heights. On several occasions, in excess of 20,000 individuals were reported as witnessing matches in Belfast, and soccer does indeed seem to have provided an escape for some from the hardships and miseries of the War.

With regards to Gaelic football, a third approach emerged. The advent of the war saw the GAA attempt to avoid any major split along political grounds, such as that which had so nearly destroyed the Association in the 1890s. As late as mid-1915 Gaelic football matches were being played in some areas to raise money for wounded servicemen and the war charities, but at the same time GAA members were noted as working to discourage recruitment into the armed forces. By and large the GAA, at least initially, was attempting to stand aloof of wider developments.

However, a crucial development came with the 1916 rising. Up to this time many branches of the GAA, and the Gaelic football clubs associated with them, had been regarded as potentially subversive by the state. The parliamentary commission convened to enquire into the rising was less circumspect in its assessment of the situation, and the GAA as a whole was condemned as a bastion of anti-government feeling and near-treasonous sympathies. The evidence to support this assertion apparently came in July 1916, when the County Kerry champion Gaelic football club withdrew from the Irish championships as most of their team had been interned. The conduct of the game also became increasingly difficult. The imposition of martial law in certain areas increased travel restrictions across the country, and new censorship provisions all combined to make the staging of Gaelic games a complex task. A final burden was the introduction of an entertainment tax on ticket sales from late 1916. In the light of these developments all junior competitions were suspended from the following year, though in 1916 and 1917 the senior championship finals were played, resulting in two wins for Wexford. Pressure on the continuance of Gaelic football continued however. The wartime demands of the state were met with little co-operation as the Gaelic authorities withheld entertainment tax revenue, and many club and Association members agitated against any possible introduction of conscription. The imposition in July 1918 of an order requiring military authority permits for any large gathering brought the whole situation to something of a head. The 4 August 1918 was declared 'Gaelic Sunday' by the GAA, and players and supporters were encouraged to collect to play the various sports administered under the GAA banner, in defiance of the government ruling. Most games, including several Gaelic football contests, went ahead unimpeded. Gaelic football was now merging, along with its other allied sports, as a means of expressing not only one's physical prowess, and Irish identity, but also political opposition to the government.

POST-WAR PROBLEMS AND PROGRESS

The end of the War in 1918 came as a relief to all. Irish football, in all its modes, looked to return to normality. Ireland itself was not, however, returning immediately to the relative calm of the pre-war years. The overwhelming victory of Sinn Fein in the 1918 election, and the murder of two policemen at Soloheadbeg in January 1919 both heralded a new period of largely domestic turmoil.

On the Gaelic football field the end of the war had little real effect.

1919 saw the holding of both that year's and the delayed 1918 football finals, and partly as a result that year was the most profitable ever in the GAA's existence. By the summer of the following year the increasing number of attacks on the Crown forces in areas of Munster and the midlands made it necessary for the authorities to place some regions again under martial law. This was also the heartland of Gaelic football activity outside Dublin, and again it became very difficult for clubs to fulfil their fixtures. Little competitive Gaelic football was played anywhere in Ireland that season. It was in Dublin on 21 November 1920 however, that perhaps the most long-remembered incident on a Gaelic football pitch took place. Following the killing of a number of suspected British intelligence agents by IRA members that morning, a party of Auxiliary Police Cadets arrived at Croke Park that afternoon to search the crowd for suspects. In the ensuing gunfire more than a dozen people were killed, including Michael Hogan, a player in the Tipperary side taking part in the match. Gaelic football had given up a martyr for Ireland.

The eventual declaration of a truce between the government and the IRA in July 1921, and the subsequent establishment in December that year of the Irish Free State, did not allow much of a respite. Only in June 1922 were the 1920 championships decided, and these against the background of civil war. The war itself again threatened to split the GAA, and with it Gaelic football. In the event, such damage was kept to a minimum. The civil war ended in May 1923. Within nine months the undecided Gaelic football championships of the previous three seasons were played up to date. Ireland, now partitioned into two states, was settling down into some sort of political normality. Gaelic football was also doing the same thing.

Meanwhile, the timing of the armistice in 1918 had meant that the IRFU were unable to see an immediate return to normality. However, by the advent of the 1919–20 season some sense of order and purpose had returned. Internationals against all the home nations took place, and the French side were entertained in Dublin, though in each case Ireland suffered a defeat. Club competitions in all the provinces were now also restarted. In 1921 international success returned when the Irish XV triumphed over the Scots in Dublin, though sustained victories were to have to wait some time. At club level the main development was the donation by Mr Robert Bateman of a trophy for competition between the champion club of each province, in memory of his son who had been killed in the Great War. The great achievement of the Union, however, was its re-emergence as an effective and united sporting body. In the charged political atmosphere of the day the IRFU trod carefully, and was able not only to maintain its own position, but also to avoid the conflicts that were now going on around it. As the War of Independence dragged on into the Civil War, questions would be asked in the press and the Dail concerning the failure of the Rugby Union to fly the Irish flag at Lansdowne Road. The erection of a war memorial at the stadium also raised some eyebrows, as did the decisions in 1922 and 1923 not to play international matches in Belfast. However the IRFU weathered the storms, emerging intact on the far side.

Of the three footballing codes in Ireland, it was to be soccer which would undergo the most noticeable and lasting changes in the years immediately after the Great War. The wartime suspension of the game in Britain meant that the international programme was slow to be re-established. Two victory internationals were played against Scotland in 1919 to raise funds for charities, but both were fairly undistinguished events. A full international programme recommenced in 1920, but the Irish supremacy of 1914 had passed. The only positive result of the first series was a draw with Wales. The following season saw Ireland defeated in all three of her matches. The triumphs of the immediate pre-war period seemed a long way off.

In the shorter term, the domestic game came under a different form of pressure. A combination of wartime inflation, followed by the post-war slump in Irish industries, left the game in economic turmoil. Crowd numbers fell, and the demands of the professional players rose. By early 1919 the Belfast professionals were threatening a strike and it was alleged their union organiser was dropped from the national side for fermenting trouble. Developments of a more lasting importance were also taking place however.

Differences already existed between the game in Belfast and Dublin in 1914. The origins of the game in the two centres had been radically different. This was to some extent perpetuated in the social classes of the games adherents: in Belfast soccer was the game of the industrial working man; in Dublin it was most popular amongst white-collar workers and the lower middle classes. Professionalism was more widespread and better accepted in the north, while in Dublin the sport remained as much one for participators as spectators. The 1912 riot, and the consequent disturbances, were seen by the game's administrators in Dublin as highlighting the incompetence of the Belfast dominated IFA, and marking out the most unsavoury aspects of the game in Ulster. The air of mutual suspicion that these differences engendered had been encouraged by the practical partition of the game necessitated by the scaling down of activities in wartime. With the outbreak of peace new challenges emerged.

By 1921 the relations between the authorities and the clubs in Belfast and Dublin were somewhat strained. The decisions of the IFA to go back on an earlier resolution to hold the final of the Intermediate Cup in Dublin, and to abandon the Junior Cup entirely due to the general disorder then present in the capital, alienated many Dublin-based clubs. A similar decision that a replay of the Irish Cup final must also be held in Belfast rather than Dublin, had a comparable effect on the senior sides in the capital. Accusations were also made in the Dublin press, though they were refuted by those allegedly involved, that IFA officials had objected to the display of Irish tricolours at an amateur international in Paris. Politics had not only reared its head in Irish soccer, it was winking and smiling at most of those involved in the game. Both the long term antagonisms, and the immediate sporting and political difficulties in Irish soccer, came to a head in May 1921 when the secretary of the Leinster FA sent a circular letter to his Association's members and the IFA in Belfast. It announced simply that the Leinster FA were severing their links with the IFA, and would seek to establish a new governing body for soccer in Ireland. A meeting was subsequently held on 1 June 1921 at the Molesworth Hall in Dublin, and the Football Association of Ireland was formed. Over the next two years threats, conciliatory gestures, and meaningful sacrifices were made. Negotiations were entered into that came within a hair's breadth of re-unifying Irish soccer. In 1923 however, the new Association won international recognition as the Football Association of the Irish Free State. The IFA, despite its own efforts and those of many in Dublin, was left as the effective ruling body

The post-war failure of the Irish international Rugby and soccer sides were greeted by dismal headlines.

Ireland's Saturday Night

only within the new state of Northern Ireland. The pattern and divided nature of Irish soccer that survives to this day had been set.

EXTRA TIME

Between 1880 and 1923 Ireland endured prolonged periods of civil strife; political decay and regeneration; involvement in the Great War; and two essentially civil wars, which together resulted in more than 2,000 deaths. By the close of the period the face of the country had been changed in some ways almost beyond recognition. Over the same four and a half decades, influenced by the political, social and economic changes that surrounded them, the country's three footballing codes were also changing. Rules were more clearly defined; distinctive styles of play emerged, and the sporting allegiances of various groups in Irish society were defined and re-defined. By 1923 football in Ireland had emerged largely as the entity we know today. It was undoubtedly very different to the game that the players and administrators of 1880 had known. Yet at the same time, the game itself, in its various forms, had outlasted not only the early personalities but many of the institutions and attitudes that had initially made its potential development possible.

THE IRISH FOOTBALL ANNUAL 1880

The *Irish Football Annual's* original editor, Richard Milliken Peter, as the *Annual* itself shows, was the Honorary Secretary of the IRFU and a former player with the Leinster provincial side, and the Wanderers club of Dublin. His sporting interests were not confined solely to football however, and he later became prominent in amateur rowing and swimming circles in Ireland. In his working life he was a civil servant, spending most of his career with the Commissioners of Church Temporalities in Dublin, overseeing the administration and maintenance of the Church of Ireland's property. At various times he also acted as an insurance agent, and had an interest in a sports outfitting business. Though born in Ireland, he had been prepared for this life by his education at Blackheath School near London.

His involvement with the IRFU was comparatively short however. Despite his prominence in the early years of the IRFU's predecessor, the Irish Football Union, and his obvious enthusiasm for the game, Peter parted company with the IRFU in 1882. The cause seems to have been the publication in the *Irish Times* of a rather critical article by Peter. It was probably the departure of the dynamic Honorary Secretary that ensured the *Irish Football Annual* never went to a second edition.

The short life of the *Annual*, along with several other circumstances, have conspired to make this publication a truly unique one. In the first place, the probable perception that this was to become a regular publication ensured very few subscribers kept their copies. Only two originals are now known to exist. By 1900 at least two Irish newspapers, *Ireland's Saturday Night* and *The Ulster Football and Cycling News*, were producing football annuals, but these seem to have been little more than glorified fixture lists, and a project on the scale of Peter's, including details of clubs and players, was never tried again. The time of its publication also insured that the *Irish Football Annual* was to become a vitally important document for those interested in the development of sport in Ireland. As we have already seen, the IRFU had just been established as an effective all-Ireland body, and the formation of the Irish Football Association was imminent. The *Annual* came at a critical juncture in Ireland's footballing history. The Rugby game was now well established; soccer was emerging in Belfast, and several men who were to be prominent in the early years of the Gaelic Athletic Association, including Michael Cusack, were cutting their footballing teeth on the Rugby field.

The mass of details which the *Annual* includes makes it not only of interest to those concerned with the early history of Irish sport, but also a potentially important source for the local and family historian. The details given of more than 600 individuals and the clubs to which they belonged, makes it possible to identify the educational and employment backgrounds of players and administrators, as well as the sporting preferences of some men most notable for their activities off the sports field. Amongst the notable sportsmen are, of course, Michael Cusack, the founder of the GAA but described here simply as 'a heavy, hard-working forward.' Less well known, though still distinguished in their own way, are the likes of John MacDonald and William McWha. MacDonald, of the Methodist College and Queen's College clubs, was to become the first ever Irishman to win ten international Rugby caps, and captained the side in his last season. In 1880 McWha was playing rugby for Knock FC, though he went on to gain seven caps as an Irish soccer international and score Ireland's first ever goal against England. Having later qualified as a doctor, he travelled to India where he became a District Medical Officer, before eventually being accidentally drowned while out duck shooting. Men listed who were to be more notable for their non-sporting activities include Fred Warden, the long-time manager of Belfast's Theatre Royal, and the city's leading theatrical impresario. Arthur Gaussen, again a future soccer international, became a successful business entrepreneur in County Londonderry, and was eventually appointed as the Sheriff of the County.

In short, Richard Milliken Peter's one and only *Irish Football Annual* is not simply a formidable publishing achievement. It has now become an incomparable source of information for those interested in

Fred Warden, Belfast theatre impressario, rugby player and leading cricketer.
Belfast Telegraph

the early history of any form of football in Ireland; the nature of society in Victorian Ireland, and local and family history. It is also capable of providing an extremely interesting and stimulating read for anyone prepared to leaf through its pages.

R M PETER

FIRST YEAR OF PUBLICATION.

THE

IRISH FOOTBALL ANNUAL.

EDITED BY

RICHARD M. PETER,

Honorary Secretary, Irish Rugby Football Union.

Published for the Proprietor by

THE DUBLIN STEAM PRINTING COMPANY,

MIDDLE ABBEY STREET.

1880.

Price, 1s. 6d.

CONTENTS.

	PAGE
INTRODUCTION,	39
THE RUGBY UNION LAWS,	42
THE PAST SEASON—1879-80,	47
THE RUGBY GAME,	51
FOOTBALL IN IRELAND,	59
FOOTBALL IN MUNSTER,	65
IRISH RUGBY FOOTBALL UNION,	66
RULES OF THE IRISH RUGBY FOOTBALL UNION,	67
LIST OF FOOTBALL CLUBS, WITH NAMES AND ADDRESSES OF HON. SECRETARIES,	68
IRISH RUGBY FOOTBALL CLUBS, WITH NAMES OF OFFICERS AND REPORTS OF THE PAST SEASON,	70
DIARY OF MATCHES PLAYED DURING THE PAST SEASON,	104
FOOTBALL STATISTICS—1879-80,	124
THE MUNSTER TOUR IN WALES,	125
REPORTS OF MATCHES—ENGLAND v. IRELAND,	129
,, ,, SCOTLAND v. IRELAND	134
LIST OF IRISH FOOTBALL PLAYERS, WITH NAME OF CLUB, AND REMARKS ON STYLE OF PLAY, ETC.,	138
THE ASSOCIATION GAME,	161
FOOTBALL STATISTICS (ASSOCIATION RULES),	170

INTRODUCTION.

To my Friends the Football Players of Ireland.

GENTLEMEN,

At the conclusion of last season—a brilliant one in the annals of football—it occurred to me that if the records of the past six months could by any means be collected, they might make an interesting volume, and one that would be appreciated by all followers of the noble game. Accordingly I at once issued the following circular letter to all the Hon. Secs. of Irish Football Clubs:—

"PETER'S IRISH FOOTBALL ANNUAL."
24 UPPER MERRION STREET, DUBLIN,
March, 1880.

DEAR SIR,

As one who has taken a warm interest in the progress and development of Rugby Football in Ireland during the past nine years, it has occurred to me that the game would become more popular, and its interests be much advanced, if the doings of the several Clubs could be collected together and published at the end of the season.

Having mentioned the matter to several of the leading football players in Ireland, and from the numerous offers of support promised me from various quarters, I have undertaken the task of editing the first IRISH FOOTBALL ANNUAL. I have concluded arrangements with the proprietors of the University Press to print the book, which is a guarantee that the work will be creditably executed.*

I must now ask you to kindly grant me all the assistance in your power, and, by so doing, you will serve the interests of your Club.

I consider by the close of this month all Football will be over for 1879-80, and I would ask you, as soon after that date as possible, to return me the enclosed forms filled up with the required information. Feeling sure you will accord me these particulars,

I remain,
Faithfully yours,
R. M. PETER.

The result of this letter was, that communications flowed in on all sides—North, South, East, and even West, promising me every facility and all manner of support.

* Since this letter was written the "University Press," owing to partnership arrangements and press of business, could not undertake the printing, &c., so I have arranged for the publication with the Dublin Steam Printing Company.

I was bold enough to announce, in March last, that I thought by the 1st May I would have the ANNUAL ready, but indeed I little dreamed of the many difficulties that bestrewed my path, and the voluminous correspondence I would have before I could obtain the required information.

The unforeseen delay which has prevented the publication of the ANNUAL until this date may still have a good effect on the cause we have at heart—Football in Ireland; and I only trust that it will stimulate our players to increased exertion in the future.

That this, the first IRISH FOOTBALL ANNUAL, is very incomplete, I freely acknowledge; but I know my friends will readily overlook all its shortcomings.

I cannot withhold my best thanks to the numerous gentlemen who have so readily, at much personal loss of time and inconvenience, assisted me in the production of this book. To name them would be invidious, but any one can easily see that many of the reports and statistics were not prepared without great labour and much self-sacrifice.

Respecting the ANNUAL itself, I would wish to make a few remarks.

It may be noticed that I have expunged all titles of distinction, such as "Esq.," "L.R.C.S.I.," "B.A.," "M.A." "R.I.C.," "Capt.," and numerous other appendices; and I would feel much obliged if Hon. Secretaries would note this for future returns.

In giving the results of matches in the diary form, I would be saved great trouble if matches were simply recorded thus:— "Won by ——," or "Lost by ——," or "Drawn," instead of the terms, "Victory for ——," "Beaten by ——," "Suffered defeat," or "Drawn in favor of ——." It should also be borne in mind that *when a goal is kicked from a try, the try does not count.*

Hon. Secretaries and Captains would save themselves much trouble if they would enter up each week the diary of the Club according to the prescribed form.

In the "*List of Irish Football Players,*" I have endeavoured to make the list as complete as possible, and so, instead of restricting it to only International and Interprovincial men, have included the names of many whom I hope yet to see on future "Irish Fifteens." Of course, in preparing this list, I have had to invoke the assistance of the Captains and Secretaries of the various Clubs, as it is hardly possible I could know all the players. Some of the criticisms are a little severe, but men must not be angry on that score. If any player finds his name omitted, he must look to the Secretary of his Club for explanation; but as to any remarks on the style of play, I alone am responsible. In future years I would feel obliged, if, in furnishing the "Chief Players," the initials were always given, as well as the record of having played in any Interprovincial or International match.

In conclusion, I must say I do not see any reason why an IRISH FOOTBALL ANNUAL should not be published within one month after the close of the season. The matter is entirely in the hands of the Committees of the several Clubs; the required particulars are simply—(1) Name of Club; (2) Ground; (3) Colours; (4) Hon. Secretary's name and address; (5) Hon. Treasurer; (6) Committee; (7) Report of the season; (8) Diary of matches played; (9) Chief Players; (name and initials, with remarks on style of play. Many returns did not reach me until June and July, and, in fact, I attribute my inability to publish by the appointed time, viz., 1st May, to this fact, as I was anxious to make the ANNUAL somewhat complete. I regret extremely that many Clubs—even good Clubs—have withheld from me the information I respectfully asked for; and although several letters were written to many of them, no reply has ever been received. I do not attribute it to any personal motives, but more to the desultory movements of the Clubs in question. However, I again thank those of my friends who have helped me, and if I have, even in a small way, succeeded and met their approval, and if the advancement of the game will be strengthened by the fact that its doings will for the future be recorded, I will feel fully recompensed for my endeavours to start an IRISH FOOTBALL ANNUAL.

I am,

Faithfully yours,

R. M. PETER.

THE RUGBY UNION LAWS.

1. A DROP KICK or DROP is made by letting the ball fall from the hands, and kicking it the *very instant* it rises.

2. A PLACE KICK or PLACE is made by kicking the ball after it has been placed in a nick made in the ground for the purpose of keeping it at rest.

3. A PUNT is made by letting the ball fall from the hands and kicking it, *before* it touches the ground.

4. EACH GOAL shall be composed of two upright posts, exceeding 11 feet in height from the ground, and placed 18 feet 6 inches apart, with a cross-bar 10 feet from the ground.

5. A GOAL can only be obtained by kicking the ball from the field of play direct (*i.e.*, without touching the ground or the dress or person of any player of either side) over the cross-bar of the opponents' goal, whether it touch such cross-bar, or the posts, or not; but if the ball goes directly over either of the goal posts it is called a *poster*, and is not a goal. A goal may be obtained by any kind of kick except a *punt*.

6. A TRY is gained when a player touches the ball down in his opponents' goal.

7. A match shall be decided by a majority of goals; but if the number of goals be equal, or no goal be kicked, by a majority of tries. If no goal be kicked or try obtained the match shall be drawn.

8. The ball is *dead* when it rests absolutely motionless on the ground.

9. A TOUCH DOWN is when a player, putting his hand upon the ball on the ground in touch or in goal, stops it so that it remains dead or fairly so.

10. A TACKLE is when the holder of the ball is held by one or more players of the opposite side.

11. A SCRUMMAGE takes place when the holder of the ball being in the field of play, puts it down on the ground in front of him, and all who have closed round on their respective sides endeavour to push their opponents back, and, by kicking the ball, to drive it in the direction of the opposite goal line.

A scrummage ceases to be a scrummage when the ball is in touch or goal.

12. A player may *take up* the ball whenever it is rolling or bounding, except in a scrummage.

13. It is not lawful to take up the ball when dead (except in order to bring it out after it has been touched down in touch or in goal) for any purpose whatever; whenever the ball shall have been so unlawfully taken up it shall at once be brought back to where it was so taken up and there put down.

14. In a scrummage it is not lawful to touch the ball with the hand under any circumstances whatever.

15. It is lawful for any player who has the ball to run with it, and if he does so, it is called a RUN. If a player runs with the ball until he gets behind his opponents' goal line, and there touches it down, it is called a RUN IN.

16. It is lawful to *run in* anywhere across the goal line.

17. The goal line is in goal, and the touch line is in touch.

18. In the event of any player holding or running with the ball being tackled, and the ball fairly held, he must at once cry *down*, and immediately put it down.

19. A MAUL IN GOAL is when the holder of the ball is tackled inside goal line, or being tackled immediately outside, is carried or pushed across it, and he, or the opposite side, or both, endeavour to touch the ball down. In all cases the ball when so touched down, shall belong to the players of the side who first had possession of it before the maul commenced, unless the opposite side have gained entire possession of it.

20. In case of a *maul in goal*, those players only who are touching the ball with their hands when it crosses the goal line, may continue in the maul in goal; and when a player has once released his hold of the ball after it is inside the goal line, he may not again join in the maul, and if he attempts to do so, may be dragged out by the opposite side.

But if a player when *running in* is tackled inside the goal line, then only the player who first tackled him; or if two or more tackle him *simultaneously*, they only may join in the maul.

21. TOUCH IN GOAL (see plan). Immediately the ball, whether in the hands of a player (except for the purpose of a *punt out*—see Rule 29) or not, goes into touch in goal, it is at once *dead*, and out of the game, and must be brought out as provided by Rules 41 and 42.

PLAN OF THE FIELD.

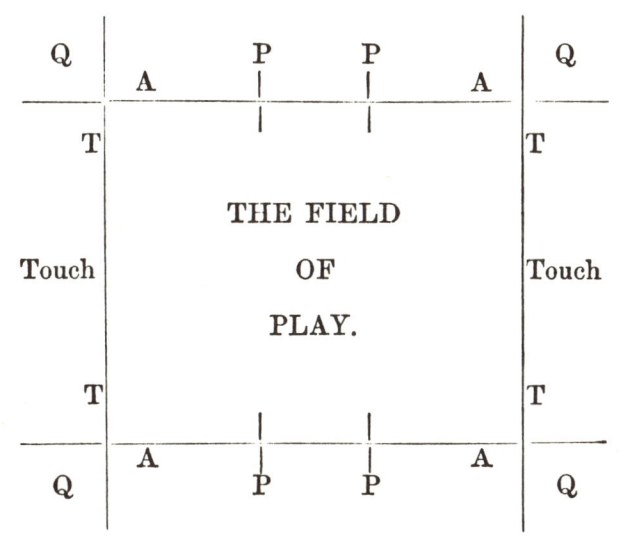

Q	A	P	P	A	Q
T					T
Touch		THE FIELD OF PLAY.			Touch
T					T
Q	A	P	P	A	Q

AA. AA. Goal Lines. *PP. PP.* Goal Posts.
TT. TT. Touch Lines. *QQ. QQ.* Touch in Goal.

The Touch Lines and Goal Lines should be cut out of the Turf.

22. Every player is on side, but is put off side if he enters a scrummage from his opponents' side, or being in a scrummage, gets in front of the ball, or when the ball has been kicked, touched, or is being run with by any of his own side behind him (*i.e.*, between himself and his own goal line). No player can be off side in his own goal.

23. Every player when *off side* is out of the game, and shall not touch the ball in any case whatever, either in or out of touch or goal, or in any way interrupt or obstruct any player, until he is again *on side*.

24. A player being *off side* is put *on side* when the ball has been run five yards with, or kicked by, or has touched the dress or person of any player of the opposite side, or when one of his own side has run in front of him either with the ball or having kicked it when behind him.

25. When a player has the ball, none of his opponents who at the time are *off side* may commence or attempt to run, tackle or otherwise interrupt such player until he has run five yards.

26. THROWING BACK. It is lawful for any player who has the ball to throw it back towards his own goal, or to pass it back to any player of his own side who is at the time behind him, in accordance with the rules of *on side*.

27. KNOCKING ON, *i.e*, deliberately hitting the ball with the hand, and THROWING FORWARD, *i.e.*, throwing the ball in the direction of the opponents' goal-line, are not lawful. If the ball be either *knocked on* or *thrown forward* the captain of the opposite side may (unless a fair catch has been made as provided by the next rule), require to have it brought back to the spot where it was so *knocked* or *thrown on*, and there put down.

28. A FAIR CATCH is a catch made direct from a kick or a *throw forward*, or a *knock on* by one of the opposite side, or from a *punt out* or a *punt on* (see Rules 29 and 30), provided the catcher makes a mark with his heel at the spot where he has made the catch, and no other of his own side touch the ball. (See Rules 43 and 44.)

29. A PUNT OUT is a *punt* made after a touch-down, by a player from behind his opponents' goal-line, and from touch in goal if necessary, towards his own side, who must stand *outside* the goal-line and endeavour to make a fair catch, or to get the ball and *run in* or *drop* a goal. (See Rules 49 and 51.)

30. A PUNT ON is a *punt* made in a manner similar to a *punt out*, and from touch if necessary, by a player who has made a fair catch from a *punt out*, or another *punt on*.

31. TOUCH. (See Plan). If the ball goes into *touch*, the first player on his side who touches it down must bring it to the spot where it crossed the touch line; or if a player, when running with the ball, cross or put any part of either foot across the touch-line, he must return with the ball to the spot where the line was so crossed, and thence return it into the field of play in one of the modes provided by the following rule.

In cases when boundaries beyond the touch-lines are used, the ball, on going over or touching either boundary, shall belong to the side opposite to that of the *player who last touched it in the field of play*.

32. He must then himself or by one of his own side either (1) bound the ball in the field of play, and then run with it, kick it, or throw it back to his own side; or (2) throw it out at right angles to the touch-line; or (3) walk out with it at right angles to the touch line, any distance not less than *five*,

nor more than *fifteen* yards, and there put it down, first declaring how far he intends to walk out.

33. If two or more players holding the ball are pushed into *touch*, the ball shall belong *in touch* to the player who first had hold of it in the field of play, and has not released his hold of it.

34. If the ball be not thrown out straight, the opposite side may at once claim to bring it out themselves, as in Law 32, sec. 3.

35. A catch made when the ball is thrown out of touch is not a *fair catch*.

36. KICK-OFF is a place-kick from the centre of the field of play, and cannot count as a goal. The opposite side must stand at least *ten yards* in front of the ball until it has been kicked. If the ball pitch in *touch*, the opposite side may claim to have it kicked off again.

37. The ball shall be *kicked off* (1) at the commencement of the game; (2) after a goal has been obtained; (3) after a change of goals at half-time.

38. Each side shall play from either goal for an equal time.

39. The captains of the respective sides shall toss up before the commencement of the match. The winner of the toss shall have the option of choice of goals or the kick-off.

40. Whenever a goal shall have been obtained, the side which has lost the goal shall then kick off.

When goals have been changed at half-time, the side which did not kick off at the commencement of the game shall then kick off.

41. KICK OUT is a drop kick by one of the players of the side which has had to touch the ball down in their own goal or into whose touch in goal the ball has gone (Rule 21), and is the mode of bringing the ball again into play, and cannot count as a goal.

42. KICK OUT must be a *drop kick*, and from not more than *twenty-five yards* outside the kicker's goal line; if the ball, when kicked out, pitch in touch, *the opposite side may claim to have it kicked off again*. The kicker's side must be behind the ball when kicked out, *and the opposite side may not obstruct such kicker within twenty-five yards of his own goal-line*.

43. A player who has made and claimed a *fair catch*, shall thereupon either take a *drop kick* or a *punt*, or *place* the ball for a place kick.

44. After a *fair catch* has been made, the opposite side may come up to the catcher's mark, and (except in cases under Rule 50) the catcher's side retiring, the ball shall be kicked from such mark, or from a spot any distance behind it, in a straight line parallel with the touch-line.

45. A player may touch the ball down in his own goal at any time.

46. A side having touched the ball down in their opponents' goal, shall *try at goal* either by a *place kick* or a *punt out*.

47. If a TRY at GOAL be made by a *place kick*, a player of the side who has touched the ball down shall bring it up to the goal line (subject to Rule 48), in a straight line from and opposite to the spot where the ball was touched down, and there make a mark on the goal line, and thence walk straight out with it at right angles to the goal line such distance as he thinks proper, and there place it for another of his side to kick. The kicker's side must be behind the ball when it is kicked, and the opposite side must remain behind their goal line until the ball has been placed on the ground. (See Rules 54 and 55.)

48. If the ball has been touched down between the goal posts, it may be brought out in a straight line from either of such posts; but if brought out from between them, the *opposite* side may *charge* at once. (See Rule 54.)

49. If the *try at goal* be by a *punt out* (see Rule 29), a player of the side which has touched the ball down shall bring it straight up to the goal-line, opposite to the spot where it was touched down, and there make a mark on the goal-line, and then *punt out* from touch in goal, if necessary, or from any part behind the goal-line not nearer to the goal post than such mark, beyond which mark it is not lawful for the opposite side (who must keep behind their goal-line) to pass until the ball has been kicked. (See Rules 54 and 55.)

50. If a *fair catch* be made from a *punt out* or a *punt on*, the catcher may either proceed as provided by Rules 43 and 44, or himself take a *punt on*, in which case the mark made on marking the fair catch shall be regarded (for the purpose of determining as well the position of the player who makes the *punt on*, as of the other players of both sides), as the mark made on the goal-line in the case of a *punt out*.

51. A catch made in touch from a *punt out* or a *punt on* is not a fair catch; the ball must then be taken or thrown out of touch as provided by Rule 32; but if the catch be made in touch in goal, the ball is at once dead, and must be *kicked out* as provided by Rules 41 and 42.

52. When the ball has been touched down in the opponents' goal, none of the side in whose goal it has been so touched down shall touch it, or in any way displace it, or interfere with the player of the other side who may be taking it up or out.

53. The ball is *dead* whenever a goal has been obtained; but if a *try at goal* be not successful, the kick shall be considered as only an ordinary kick in the course of the game.

54. CHARGING, *i.e.*, rushing forward to kick the ball or tackle a player, is lawful for the opposite side, in all cases of a *place-kick* after a *fair catch* or upon a *try at goal*, immediately the ball touches or is placed on the ground; and in cases of a *drop-kick* or *punt* after a *fair catch*, as soon as the player having the ball commences to run or offers to kick, or the ball has touched the ground; but he may always draw back, and unless he has dropped the ball or actually touched it with his foot, they must again retire to his mark (see Rule 56). The opposite side in the case of a *punt out* or a *punt on*, and the kicker's side in *all* cases, may not *charge* until the ball has been kicked. *Except in a scrummage, it is not lawful for a player to charge against or obstruct any opponent, unless such opponent is holding the ball, or such player is himself running at the ball.*

55. If a player, having the ball when about to *punt it out*, goes outside the goal-line, or when about to *punt on*, advances nearer to his own goal-line than his mark, made on making the fair catch, or if after the ball has been touched down in the opponents' goal or a fair catch has been made, more than one player of the side which has so touched it down or made the fair catch, touch the ball before it is again kicked, the opposite side may *charge* at once.

56. In case of a *fair catch*, the opposite side may come up to and *charge* from anywhere on or behind a line drawn through the mark made by the player who has made the catch and parallel to their own goal-line; but in the case of a *fair catch* from a *punt out* or a *punt on*, they may not advance

further in the direction of the touch line nearest to such mark than a line drawn through such mark to their goal line and parallel to such touch line. In all cases (except a *punt out* and a *punt on*) the kicker's side must be behind the ball when it is kicked, but may not *charge* until it has been kicked.

57. No HACKING, OR HACKING OVER, or tripping up shall be allowed under any circumstances. No one wearing projecting nails, iron plates, or gutta percha on any part of his boots or shoes shall be allowed to play in a match.

58. *In the case of any law being broken, or any irregularity of play occurring on the part of either side, not otherwise provided for, the opposite side may claim that the ball be taken back to the place where the breach of law or irregularity of play occurred, and a scrummage formed there.*

59. Unless Umpires be appointed, the Captains of the respective sides shall be the sole arbiters of all disputes, and their decision shall be final. If the Captain of either side challenge the construction placed upon any rules, he shall have the right of appeal to the Rugby Union Committee.

60. Neither half-time nor no side shall be called until the ball is fairly held or goes out of play, and in the case of a try or fair catch the kick at goal shall be allowed.

THE PAST SEASON, 1879-80.

The past season of Rugby Football in Ireland is one that may be looked upon with feelings of pleasure and satisfaction, not only from the fact that numerous new Clubs sprung into existence, but that the game itself has become more popular, both with the players and the public.

Almost every season opens with a flood of newspaper correspondence of generally a hostile nature to the votaries of the game, while the defenders of the noble sport, after repudiating emphatically the outrageous language of its abusers, cannot do more than uphold their pastime as a fair and legitimate sport, conducted on defined rules—some of which have for their object the reduction of the dangers of the game. And as a healthy, manly, outdoor amusement in which they have a perfect right, if they are so minded, as free men, to receive more kicks than halfpence, and to run what dangers to life and limb it pleases them in their favourite pursuit.

The season of 1879-80 was certainly very free from serious accidents. Naturally at the commencement of each year's play a few over zealous players come to grief, and are laid up for a short time; but taking the season all round, and comparing the number of matches played and the number of players engaged, football men can certainly claim as much immunity from danger as those that take part in any other manly sport. Irish players may certainly congratulate themselves that fine weather seconded their endeavours during the past year, and had not King Frost come on the scene for a few weeks, one unbroken season of football would have to be recorded.

Punctuality still remains a virtue unknown to football men, and often sorely tries the patience of many an anxious captain. Some stringent rule should be passed to ensure regularity.

The play last season was not much in advance of the previous year, but still some slight improvement was perceptible. In the "forwards" department of the game the most advancement was shown. Lacking neither pluck nor determination, the Irish forward is an equal match for his English or Scotch opponent. The quick, game, no flagging, always-on-the-ball sort of man is the one required for a forward team; and in this respect we may boast that we can put a very fair representative ten into the field. Our forward play in the late International Match, England *v.* Ireland, was simply A1 (see *Bell's Life* Report), although we were not so well together against Scotland in the subsequent match.

Our vulnerable point is behind the scrummage, and although we possess some very active, quick players, we are not able, when pitted singly, to hold our own against the cross-Channel representatives. Among the half-backs much improvement is manifest. Few men seldom indulge in what is known as the "gallery game"—the importance of playing the "passing game" having at length been instilled into their minds—while the importance of furnishing a run with a drop was very generally exemplified last season.

The amalgamation of all the Clubs under one Union has at length become *un fait accompli*; and it is hoped, by united and harmonious action, that Ireland, from a football point of view, will quickly rise to the level of the parent countries.

The sixth International Match between the representatives of the Rose and Shamrock was played at Lansdowne Road on Feb. 2nd, and any one who was present will be slow to forget the bold fight we made on that occasion.

In no previous contest did the Irish team show such determined pluck, and for nearly half the prescribed time had much the best of the friendly struggle. The splendid forward play of Forrest, Kelly, Scriven, and Cuppaidge is deserving of all praise, and the cheers that greeted the last-named, on securing a try for Ireland, seem to re-vibrate in our ears; but when sides changed over at half time our fortunes seemed to change, too, and the Englishmen, led on by Captain Stokes, whose drop-kicking was one of the features of the match, soon ran up a score which we failed to wipe off, and the verdict of our countrymen (and our countrywomen), when "No Side" was called, was placidly expressed in those few brief words: "Beaten, but not disgraced."

Just two weeks afterwards the Irish Fifteen, but not exactly the same set of men, journeyed to Glasgow to play the third International Match with Scotland. The Dublin contingent travelled by long sea, and had a pretty rough time of it.

With barely an hour for lunch, dressing and photographing, the team arrived upon the ground. It is needless to dwell upon the match. We were beaten in every department of the game; but certainly the recent travelling had something to say to it. It should, however, be mentioned that the Scotch public received us most cordially, while the team and officers of the Scottish Football Union vied with each other in attention to the visiting team, officers of the Irish Rugby Football Union, and visitors from Dublin and Belfast. On the Monday following, a Fifteen representing the

North of Ireland Football Club played the Edinburgh Academicals, and on the next day tried conclusions with the Glasgow Academicals. On both occasions the visitors had to succumb. The Interprovincial Matches last season proved, with one exception, a failure, owing to the prevailing frost. A team—indeed a very second-rate team—representing Leinster, visited Belfast, and at the Ormean ground, to general surprise, gained a victory over the Ulster Fifteen. That the visitors played well was generally admitted; while the home men, especially among the forwards, seemed to lack the usual dash and spirit of the North.

The now Annual Football Match played in Dublin, in aid of the Dublin Hospital Sunday Fund, between teams representing the United Hospitals and the County Dublin, has become firmly established; and it is to be hoped for the honor of Irish Football men that they will never let a year pass without organising a match in aid of this deserving charity. Thanks to the Committee of the Irish Champion Athletic Club, who kindly lent their ground for the occasion, and to Colonel Kent and Officers of the 77th Regiment (now in India) who gave the free service of their splendid band, the expenses were reduced to a minimum, and the sum of £34 14s. was available for the fund. In 1878 the amount handed over was £20 3s. 9d.

The Premier Club can hardly be congratulated on its display of Football last season, at least so far as the First Fifteen is concerned. Four matches played in one season is hardly a worthy return for such a team as the University. Certainly the match with the North of Ireland was postponed on account of frost, and was never arranged again. The Windsor Club failed to come up to town, while a match was proposed with Cambridge University, but the difficulties proved insurmountable.

Never did a better team do battle for old Trinity than that of last season, while the Second Fifteen, likewise, well sustained the traditions of Alma Mater. It is to be hoped that 1880-81 will see matches arranged with Oxford or Cambridge, Edinburgh and Glasgow Academicals, Manchester, Liverpool, and other foreign Clubs.

The Wanderers enjoyed a good season's play, as will be seen from the "Football Statistics." The season's tour was made to Belfast, Glasgow, and Edinburgh. At Belfast many of the team played for Leinster v. Ulster (Friday, Nov. 28, 1879), and the next day the Wanderers tried conclusions with the Windsor Club. The same evening the team left for Scotland, and had a most enjoyable moonlight trip up the Clyde, arriving at Edinburgh (Royal Hotel) about noon on Sunday. A severe frost prevailed, and, much to the regret of all, the match had to be postponed. The team left Edinburgh on Tuesday evening (Dec. 2nd) for Dublin, and although disappointed in the football way, managed to enjoy themselves to their evident satisfaction. The Second Fifteen had a most successful season, which reflects with much credit on the popular Captain. The Lansdowne Club stands high in the list of matches played, both teams winning more games than were lost. It is pleasing to note that this Club has become more independent of College aid, and that the Fifteen is not a Trinity team under another name. The energy displayed by the Hon. Sec. is the secret of its success. Kingstown Football Club requires a little brushing up, and should be able to play more than seven matches in the season. There are plenty of men, and good men, but unless the Committee exert themselves more the Club will not uphold its position in the Football world. The Phœnix Club could hardly have had a more unlucky season. It is not the fault of the officers of the Club, but the players, who on many occasions are very lax to put in an appearance. The Club visited Cork about Christmas time with a second-rate team. The North of Ireland Club enjoyed a good season, managing to play off thirty-two matches, with the small total of only five lost. The Belfast Clubs are, geographically speaking, in a better position to arrange matches with Scotch and North of England Clubs than Dublin or Cork, and, consequently, each year can boast of more foreign fixtures. The Windsor Club still musters a strong team, but last year disappointed Clubs on more than one occasion. Numerous letters and applications have failed in elucidating any of the particulars of last season's play. The same remarks apply to the Limerick Club, a circumstance much to be regretted.

Of the Clubs in the North, Armagh, Ulster Royal Academical Institution, North Down, and Dundalk seem to have made most progress. Travelling South, we find the Cork Club at the head of the poll of matches played, while it is pleasing to note the numerous minor Clubs that are gradually coming to the surface, and it is to be hoped next season will be better known in the Football world.

Football in the Queen's Colleges is certainly on the increase, and from reports to hand the coming season promises to be a busy one. Belfast and Cork have, certainly, more opportunities for playing matches than Galway, but the latter might easily make up the deficiency by arranging internal matches, such as, North *v.* South, Medical *v.* The Rest, A to M *v.* N. to Z, or the like. Queen's College, Belfast, won seven matches out of eight played, while Cork, likewise, only lost one out of six played.

Football in the Schools is what we like to see and hear of; and it is pleasing to note that the authorities of the several establishments throughout the country are only too anxious to foster and encourage it among the youthful aspirants to a green and gold cap. Kingstown School played last season no less than twenty matches with the small total of only six lost. Some years ago the First Fifteen was composed of about eleven "past" and four "present" men, but latterly the "Boys" were determined to stand on their merits, and always played a *bona fide* School team. Rathmines School was hardly up to old form last year, but managed to play a good number of matches. The Wesley College Club enjoyed a brilliant season of sixteen games, while Portarlington School played ten matches generally against visiting teams. The game was somewhat revived at St. Columba's College, while the Royal School, Armagh, completed a fair card of fixtures. Santry School is one of the most rising School Clubs, while it is pleasing to note the spread of the game to Knight's School (Co. Cork), and the Grammar School, Galway. Hospital Football is still popular, but the Medicals occasionally want a little stirring up. Once they take the field it is well enough, but there is a lack of inter-hospital matches during the season. For the past two years it has been urged, through the columns of the Press, the founding of an "Hospital Challenge Cup," and if it was once started, it would give a great impetus to the game. It is to be hoped that another year will not pass over without something being done.

The establishment of a "Challenge Cup" to be played for by Clubs throughout Ireland which are Members of the Irish Rugby Football Union has been strongly advocated by various Clubs. There ought to be no difficulty in bringing about such a desirable object, and the only obstacle at present in the way is the meeting of Clubs one with another; however, Football men may rely that the Committee of the Union will at all times bear in mind any suggestions offered, as their sole object is to encourage and foster the game of Rugby Football in Ireland.

THE RUGBY GAME.

Written by A. G. GUILLEMARD, Esq., President Rugby Football Union, for Alcock's "Football Annual," and by special permission of Mr. Alcock, is allowed to be inserted in Peter's "Irish Football Annual," 1880.

THE Rugby Football Union, founded nearly ten years ago, has not belied its title, inasmuch as it has succeeded in uniting within that period all the leading Clubs in the United Kingdom, and sundry outlying ones in the various Colonies and dependencies of our Empire, to play by its laws and uphold its interests in one body as the representative Society of Rugby football players. The following hints, as elaborating the Union Laws, may be useful to young players, whose first object should be thoroughly to understand the code, and to realise the spirit in which the game should be played. I have, therefore, tried to make them as palatable as possible by commencing with a short narrative of the leading features of the game as exemplified in practice.

The match to be played is between two Fifteens of rival Clubs, distinguished respectively by white and striped jerseys. The ground between the lines of goal should be about 120 yds. long by 70 wide, and should extend behind them to a distance of twenty yards or so, so as to allow plenty of space for a run-in, when the ball has to be touched down behind goal. From each goal a line should be cut in the turf to the edge of the ground: the ball when behind or on this line is *in goal*. The sides of the ground should also be marked out by similar lines at right angles to the goal-lines: these lines are called the *touch-lines*. Behind the *touch-line* and also behind the *goal-line* is *touch-in-goal*, on passing into which the ball is given up to the defending side to be started afresh. On each touch-line, at a distance of twenty-five yards from each goal-line, should be placed a conspicuous flag to mark the post whence the defending side should drop the ball out after having touched it down in their own goal, and also on each touch-line at a spot equi-distant from the two goals a conspicuous flag should mark the half-distance, in a line with which flags the ball is kicked off at the commencement of the game, at half-time, and also when a goal has been obtained. The goals are upright posts of indefinite height—from 15 to 16 ft. being perhaps the best—with a cross-bar 10 ft. from the ground joining them, over which the ball must be kicked in order to score a goal. The posts should be 18 ft. 6 in. apart, and are the better seen if—from the cross-bar upwards—they are painted white. Flags should never be fixed to goal-posts under any circumstances; there should be nothing besides the naked poles to interfere with the passage of the ball. Flag posts must never be placed along the goal-lines, but one should mark the spot where the goal-line and touch-line cut one another at each side of the ground, and others should be placed along the touch-lines at intervals of twenty yards, so that the players may be able to distinguish the limits of the field of play at a glance. These flag-posts should not be less than 6 ft. in height, or they will not be seen when players crowd round them, and a risk will be run of an awkward accident resulting from a player falling over them.

The following is the best disposition of the players in a fifteen-a-side match. Ten players are *forwards*, following up close on the ball and forming a scrummage round it when it is held and cannot be run with. Behind them two of the fastest and most active men on the side are placed to play *half-back*. They must be good at starting quickly and dodging, for it will be their duty to get away with the ball at top speed directly it makes its appearance from amongst the forest of legs in the scrummage. They should stand some five yards behind the scrummage, each watching one half of the semi-circle formed by the forwards of their side. Fifteen yards in rear of these half-backs, and at an equal distance from each of them, is placed a *three-quarters-back*, who should be a good drop with either foot, as he may often have a chance of dropping a goal, and is sure to get plenty of work both in attack and defence. To him the two half-backs will look to back them up and tackle any player who may pass them with the ball. Fifteen yards behind the three-quarters-back, each covering half of the breadth of the ground, are placed two *backs*, adepts at running, tackling, and drop-kicking, for they form the "forlorn hope" of the side, and have more responsibility upon their shoulders than the players at any of the other posts. There is no goal-keeper in a Rugby match, as the ball has to be kicked over—and not under—a fixed height, and his services would be useless; consequently every man on either side is in active play throughout the match.

Winning the toss gives choice of goals, or, if the winner has no choice, he may take kick-off, and leave his opponents to choose the goal they prefer. Kick-off must be a place-kick from the centre of the ground, the ball being kicked from the ground, where it rests in a small nick made by the heel, and the opposing side may not come within ten yards of it. If the ball pitch in touch, it must be brought back and kicked off again. Both sides being ready, the ball is kicked off high in the air to allow of the side getting as close to the backs as possible before one of them has caught it, and can take his drop or get well off round to the touch-line, and so away out of dangerous proximity to the goal. He is a little too quick for them though, and sends the ball flying back over their heads to one of their half-backs, who, before he can get into his stride, is tackled by three or four opponents at once, and brought to the ground with a run. The forwards of each side hurry up, and a scrummage is instantly formed, each ten facing their opponents' goal, packed round the ball, shoulder to shoulder, leg to leg, as tight as they can stand, the twenty thus forming a round compact mass with the ball in the middle.

Directly the holder of the ball has succeeded in forcing it down to the ground, he shouts "ball's down," and business may be commenced at once. Each ten, being bent on driving the ball through the ranks of their opponents, set to work to push, struggle, and kick, forcing, if possible, a passage through which the ball may emerge. Out it comes at last, kicked straight into the hands of an active half-back, who gets away round the scrummage and dodges the nearest half-back of his opponents before the forwards have extricated themselves from the crush. He is not destined, however, to make any further progress towards the enemy's quarters, for the three-quarters back is upon him, and, tackling him fairly round the waist, gives him no chance of escape or passing the ball, so that he is fain to cry "Have it down," without any further delay. The ball must be put down at once, and another scrummage is formed similar to the first, but the place is now nearer the line of touch, and the ball emerging at the side, is driven over the line, and touched down by one of the half-backs.

Upon the ball thus going into touch, the two sets of forwards form in lines facing each other, and stretching from the touch-line far out into the grounds, and the ball is thrown out from the spot where it crossed the line. But, instead of throwing the ball out, the player may bound it on the ground in the field of play and then run with it, or kick it, or pass it to one of his own side, or he may walk with it not less than five nor more than fifteen yards into the field of play and put it down. When the ball is thrown out, if the player who catches it can run with it, so much the better for his side, but as a rule the players are standing so close together that half-a-dozen pairs of arms are round the catcher immediately, and he is compelled to cry "Have it down." From this scrummage the ball is driven out in front of goal where a wily back is awaiting it, and has it under his arm in an instant; making the best of his opportunity and speed of foot, the forty yards that separate him from the enemy's goal-line are soon passed, and, having escaped the clutches of the nearest opposing back by an adroit dodge, he grounds the ball in triumph between the goal-posts. From such a run-in a goal should be almost a foregone conclusion, but the place-kicking has been decidedly indifferent of late years, and it is surprising that it is not more practised. Every week matches are left drawn, which would have been decided had there been a good-place kick amongst the two fifteens. It was in consequence of this that the present law—that a match may be won by a majority of tries—was brought in.

The method of taking the ball out for a try at goal after a run-in is as follows:—The captain of the side who gained the try deputes one of his men to bring the ball out of goal, and another to kick it. The former brings it up to the line of goal in a straight line from the spot where it was touched down, or, if touched down between the goal-posts, then from one of the posts, and makes a mark on the goal-line. From this mark he walks straight out with it at right-angles to the goal-line until he has reached a convenient spot for a place-kick. Here the kicker makes a small nick for the ball to rest in, and, on a level with this, the rest of the forwards form a line stretching away in front of the enemy's goal-line, behind which their opponents are arranged in like manner intently watching the holder of the ball. He, with one knee on the ground, holds it just off the grass, waiting for the kicker's sign before grounding it. Directly he places it in the mark, the opponents may charge and try to maul the kicker, or touch the ball on its way to goal, in which case no goal is scored, even though the ball go fairly over the cross-bar, and if any other player of the attacking side touch the ball after it has been taken into the placer's hands, their opponents may instantly charge and maul. If a goal is obtained, the sides change over to try their luck from a fresh position, when the side who lost the goal kick off from the middle of the ground as at the commencement of the match. If the try is a failure, the defenders may run with the ball out of goal if they can, but in the majority of cases they are so hemmed in by the attacking party that they are compelled to touch it down, in which case the opposing side retire, and one of the side who touched it down takes it out not further than the 25 yds. post and "drops" it. But if the ball when so "dropped" pitch in touch, and so out of the ground, it must be brought back, and the kick be taken again. In the case of a player who is running-in being tackled by one or more opponents outside goal, and carried over the line by the scrummage, only those who are touching the ball with their hands when it crosses the goal-line may remain in the maul, and when a player has once released his hold of the ball, he may not again enter the maul nor attempt to join in the play, under penalty of being dragged out by his opponents. On the other hand, if a player running-in is tackled inside the goal-line, only the player who first tackles him, or, if two or three tackle him *simultaneously*, they only may join in the maul.

If a try is obtained at a long distance from the goal-posts, so that a place-kick has little chance of being successful, a punt-out may be attempted. In this case a player, having brought the ball up to the line and made his mark, punts it out to his side spread out in front of goal to catch it. The catcher may then place it for one of his side to kick, or drop it himself, as he pleases. The defending side must be behind goal-line until the ball is punted out, and must not interfere with the punter, though they may stand at any point along the line.

Of all laws in the Rugby code, there are none that require to be more strictly observed than those relating to "off-side." Disregard of these fundamental laws will completely nullify all the science, and spoil all the spirit of the Rugby game. A player off-side is to consider himself as out of the game, and is not to touch the ball in any case whatever (either in or out of touch), or in any way obstruct any player, or interrupt the play until he is again *on-side*. Rule 22 in the Rugby Union code speaks plainly enough, and requires no explanation, and Rule 24 renders any comment on the way in which an off-side player is placed on-side quite unnecessary. Many clubs, however, show an utter disregard of Rule 25, by which off-side players are forbidden to *commence to run, or attempt to tackle or interrupt a player with the ball until he has run five yards*. With reference to the breaking of such a rule as this, the enforcement of a satisfactory penalty is well known to be impracticable; otherwise the transgression of the rules of off-side would demand some substantial redress which would fully meet the exigencies of the case. The Union Committee appeal to players to observe these Laws.

The practice of hacking, fondly considered by a few benighted individuals to be the chief feature of Rugby football, is utterly put a stop to by the Union code, and a player may go through a whole season without receiving a single hack, except from some clumsy or bad-tempered opponent. *Excès de zèle* might occasionally be pleaded as an excuse, but in reality in matches between clubs and schools, where the numbers are generally fifteen a-side, a subject for excuses should not be forthcoming, save under the most exceptional circumstances. A school captain would have little difficulty in bringing a refractory forward to order, if he were to make him stand in goal or play in slippers for the rest of the match. The practice of mauling, too, which was very prevalent round London some seasons ago, is now effectually kept in check by Rule 18, which necessitates the ball being put down directly, and play has become much faster in consequence.

Passing the ball back when a player is tackled is frequently a serviceable piece of play, and has conduced materially to many a victory. But players should at the same time bear in mind that a reckless throw back can never be good play, and a player who is ignorant of the principles of the game may thus throw away both ball and match together. To pass the ball back *into the hands* of one of your own side who has a chance of getting away with it is commendable enough, but if you cannot do that with safety, cry "Have it down" by all means, in preference to throwing it wildly back up in the air in the fond, but generally delusive, hope that it may fall into the clutch of a friend. Never sacrifice safety for effect. A man who plays "for the gallery" at football, is, as a rule, more to be dreaded by his own side than by his opponents.

It is to be regretted that "rouges" and other inexplicable terms still occasionally crop up in the accounts of Rugby Football published in the sporting papers. The term "rouge" has no existence either at Rugby or in the Union code. Why will a few clubs belonging to the Union persist in using it? *A touch-down* occurs when the defending side are compelled to touch the ball down in their own goal. When the attacking side touch the ball down in their opponents' goal, they gain a *try*. These definitions are simple enough, and if secretaries of clubs, following the Union rules, would remember them, their accounts of matches would be intelligible to others besides themselves. The term "quarter-backs," too, has of late been frequently used, especially by minor clubs, in place of "half-back." At Rugby, years ago, the word "quarter-back" was used as a term of reproach, applied to forwards, who, afraid to enter the scrummage themselves, sneak about at the heels of their more worthy fellows and utterly spoiled the play of their half-backs. There is no reason for changing the old name, especially when the substitute proposed is inapplicable.

The following brief hints on the requirements and duties of back, half-back, and forward players may prove of some slight service to many unacquainted with the working of the game; but to imagine that the Rugby rules can be learnt and put into practice by a mere perusal or knowledge of the laws of the code is to commit a great mistake, and this will be found to be the case by any one who plays the carrying game for the first time. And for this very reason it is a matter of no slight difficulty to put upon paper any hints on the practice of the Rugby game. To play well, a thorough knowledge of the working of these rules is indispensable, and when once the game, in all its branches, is understood from experience, common sense and perception will avail more than any written directions in bringing a player to an accurate understanding of what to do and how to do it.

A captain of a fifteen should select from his men two of the best at running, dodging and tackling, to act as half-backs. They must be the most active players on the side, always on the alert, for a moment's hesitation in an emergency has often lost a match. They must each choose their side (right or left) of the scrummage, behind which they must stand at a distance of about five yards, and they must keep their side throughout the game, or they will be continually trying to take the same ball, and so put each other out and do more harm than good. But they must not be content with watching for the appearance of the ball on their side of the scrummage only,

B

but must follow it up directly it is driven through by their forwards, and do their best to tackle their opponents' half-backs before they can pass it back or get off with it round to either side. Whenever the ball goes into touch, the half-back nearest the touch-line must stand up there just behind the ine of forwards, to prevent the progress of any opponent who takes advantage of a gap in the line in front of him to get through with the ball; the other half-back should go far out, at the very extremity of the line of forwards, and there be on the look-out for the ball, if thrown far out of touch. If a captain has three good half-backs in a fifteen, he will generally find it advisable to place one of them three-quarters-back, choosing the one best at dropping, and reducing his backs by one if his forwards want strength. It is a very common fault of half-backs to stand too near the scrummage; by so doing they have less time to pick up the ball, they lose sight of the movements of their opponents' half-backs, and very often their only chance left is to kick the ball against the backs of their own men in the scrummage, which is grossly bad play. Of all places in the game, that of half-back requires the greatest coolness and quickness, combined with the best judgment.

The three backs should play in a semi-circle, about five-and-twenty or thirty yards in rear of the half-backs, whom they have to back up and relieve of the ball when hard pressed by opponents. Directly the ball is driven past their half-backs, one of them who is nearest to it must rush in to meet it and pick it up and run with it if it is bounding or rolling along the ground, his two companions being ready to support him in case of his failing. If an opponent has got well off with the ball, and has passed the half-backs, one of the backs should drop to the rear, while the others rush in to tackle him, so that in case of his giving up the idea of trying to pass them, and taking his drop instead, there will still be a back in reserve to receive the ball when kicked over his companions' heads. When the play is in dangerous proximity to their own goal, the backs and half-backs should in no case keep the ball in front of goal if they can possibly get it away to the sides, though a back on the right side of goal should never run across the ground in front of goal to get away to the left. Thus, if a ball is in their half of the ground, they should always be anxious to carry it away to the sides, whence a drop-kick or run will not seriously imperil their goal; but when in the half defended by their opponents, every effort should contrariwise be made to bring the ball directly in front of the enemy's goal-posts. It is not so essential that backs should be fast at starting, as good runners when once well under weigh, as in nearly every case they will get a start of a few yards, their opponents driving the ball towards them. A back player should always *make sure of his drop without a chance of his being charged down;* let him run as far as he can, and pass as many players as he can, but as a general rule he should finish up his run with the longest drop he can take. A back or half-back running to the left cannot drop with his right foot, so those who are best at left-foot kicking should take the left side of the ground, but even a moderate back-player should be able to drop with both feet. The post of back is the most responsible of all, for he is the last hope of his side, and whereas the most grievous mistake of a forward or half-back may be retrieved by the instant co-operation of those around him, a back cannot hope to be rescued from his dilemma in a similar manner. A back must rely on himself alone, without trusting to the other backs, who have to keep their own places and not risk the safety of their goal by following the holder of the ball on the chance of getting it passed back to them. Round London good back-players are in a considerable minority as compared with half-backs, and nearly all the public school teams show better back play than the best of the clubs. The more confined limits of the field of play will to some extent account for this, for whereas on the Old Bigside at Rugby, a back getting the ball under favourable circumstances can bring all his speed into play, and has an excellent chance of running round the quickest of the opposing forwards, on most club grounds, before he has got properly into his stride, he finds the whole breadth of the ground guarded by an extended line, and, if he "plays the game," as in duty bound, he must take his drop. And so backs, as a rule, have a poor time of it, and are generally anxious to be metamorphosed into half-backs as speedily as possible. To make a good back three qualifications are absolutely necessary:—to be a safe drop with both feet, a sure tackler, and to have a thorough knowledge of the game.

Players generally, and backs and half-backs in particular, should always remember that it is infinitely better to be tackled than to run back, losing ground towards one's own goal in an attempt to elude an opponent. It is common enough to see a player get the ball out of touch and take it right across the ground to the opposite touch-line, losing ground all the way, owing to his being closely pressed by his opponents. He may run well and escape their hands till he runs into touch on the opposite side of the ground, only to find that the ball is ten yards nearer his own line of goal than it was when he started. He has done no good, but, on the contrary, a good deal of harm, and it would have been far better for him to have stopped and attempted to dodge his opponents, or to have taken his drop directly he found himself losing ground. Some players are, however, rather too much given to thinking that the longer they run the better, not considering in what direction they are going. And, lastly, a back must never think of taking a liberty, but must play the game strictly from kick-off to "No side." There is no goal-keeper in a Rugby match, the back being the last hope of the side—no one stands still with nothing to do, both backs and half-backs following up at their relative distances from the mass of forwards.

For forwards, good following up and playing together are the prime recommendations. Their duty is to work together in a body behind the ball, taking it through the ranks of their opponents in the scrummages by weight and skill combined, and following it up doggedly, not waiting for wind, but struggling on in spite of all obstacles to keep close to the ball. The highest praise that can be conferred on a Rugby forward, is conveyed in the words, few and simple, "He's always on the ball." Forwards should always remember how much the absence of even a single player is felt in a fifteen-a-side match, when it comes to a tough struggle in front of goal, and a captain finds his men not up to time after the punishing work in the last scrummage. There are exceptional cases when the forwards should not be so eager to drive the ball through a scrummage; for instance, when a side has taken the ball up into the heart of the enemy's quarters, and a scrummage is formed about twenty yards or so in front of the goal-posts, the forwards of the attacking side may sometimes not resist so vigorously the weight of their opponents, as the ball, if driven through, must go straight to one of their half-backs or backs, who may then have an easy chance of dropping a goal or running-in. On the ball going into touch close up to the opponents' goal line, the forwards should spread out well, their line stretching away as far as possible towards the centre of the ground, so that if one of their side gets the ball in touch, he may throw it well out, and thus bring the play in front of the enemy's goal. Of course, if one of the defending party touches the ball down he will throw it only a few yards out, so as not to imperil his quarters. In all cases it is necessary for each forward on either side to stand up to one of his opponents, as the ball will be always thrown to any one who, from having no opponents facing him, has a fair chance of getting away with it through the line. A forward on being tackled, if he find it impossible to get free at once or to pass the ball back to one of his own side, must cry "Have it down" at once, mauling, which was too prevalent in the majority of matches played round London, being forbidden. A scrummage should be formed as compactly as possible, every man pressing firmly on the man in front of him, bodies and legs close together, so as to form a firmly-packed mass to resist the weight of a like mass of opponents. Some players are given to putting their heads down in a scrummage so as to look after the ball the better, but it is a plan not to be commended, as it loosens the mass, a man with his head down taking up the space of two. The great point to be aimed at being to stop the progress of the ball towards one's own quarters, the first thing that a player should do, after having tackled an opponent carrying the ball, is to hold the ball. Holding the player alone is of no use, as he will forthwith pass or throw the ball back to another of his side, who will be off at top speed long before any one can get near him. There are few greater mistakes than that of making a fair catch in front of one's own goal, for the opposing side will come up to the mark with their backs and half-backs spread out behind them, so that even a good drop will fail to get the ball out of danger, whilst a shooter will result in a rush of the forwards carrying the ball straight before them over the goal-line.

A few last hints and I have done. Let forwards play thoroughly unselfishly, striving not for individual glory, but for the success of their side; let them think less of their hands and more of their feet, and learn what to do with the ball after getting it through a scrummage, not kicking it hard to one of the backs, but keeping it between their feet and dribbling it on with a well-concerted rush, each backing up the other—let half-backs think less of running in and more of dropping at goal—let backs remember their responsibility, never risking the sacrifice of safety for effect—and, finally, let place-kicking and dropping be more generally practised, and not only will more matches be decided, but there will be considerable improvement in Rugby Football.

FOOTBALL IN IRELAND.

By the PRESIDENT of the Irish Rugby Football Union.

SOON the re-appearance of winter shall have ushered in the commencement of the Sixth Football Season in Ireland. I say the *Sixth*, because for all practical purposes we may date the origin and progress of Irish Football from the winter of 1874-5, when, for the first time, an Irish Football Union was formed, and a challenge for an International contest sent to and accepted by the Committee of the Parent Rugby Union of England. In the Circular of December 24th, 1874, announcing the formation of an Irish Football Union, the senders of that challenge were, indeed, able to say that " the game has recently made rapid strides in this country." Previous progress had, however, been almost entirely confined to Dublin, Belfast, and their immediate neighbourhoods. In the South of Ireland, in our provincial towns and schools, the game of Rugby Football was even there, in the strict acceptance of the term, all but unknown. I am, I think, justified in considering that up to that time, despite the efforts of individual Clubs—notably of the D. U. F. C. and N. I. F. C.—the game, as a winter pastime, could scarcely have been called " racy of the soil." That the Committee of the I. F. U. knew how, if possible, to make it so, is shown by the following quotations from other paragraphs in the same Circular :—" With a view to make the game more popular in Ireland, it is proposed to establish an Annual International Match. . . . It is most desirable that Interprovincial Matches, and matches North *versus* South, such as are customary in England and Scotland, should be arranged, with a view both to improve the style of play in this country, and to facilitate the selection of the players on the Irish Twenty." These principles, thus clearly enunciated, have lain at the root of all subsequent growth in the popularity of the game.

In Ireland it might, perhaps, have been easily foreseen that a Football, any more than any other Union, could not long be expected to remain united. Almost simultaneously with the formation of the I. F. U. in Dublin, Belfast players, suspecting that their interests might not be safe in the hands of a Metropolitan Council, founded the North of Ireland Football Union. Seen in the light of subsequent events, this action of the Northern Clubs cannot but be regarded as having been both ill-advised and unfortunate. Its supposed necessity might possibly have been altogether averted had the respective leaders of Dublin and Belfast Football taken the precaution of consulting one another before founding either Union. At this time, however, both Unions seem to have been actuated by motives of sincerity, and to have preserved in their intercourse with one another the phrases of diplomatic courtesy, if not of absolute friendliness.

So long as Football in Ireland was mainly confined to Dublin and Belfast, this system of two distinct, rival, and more or less, discordant Unions, one representing Leinster and the other Ulster, wrought no particular injustice. The Irish XV. was annually selected, after the Interprovincial match, Leinster *v.* Ulster, had been played, by a combined Committee of the two Unions. The spread of the game to Munster soon introduced an obvious difficulty, capable of being settled only in one of two ways, either there should be a unification of existing " Unions," providing for a fair representation of Munster players on the new Committee of Management; or, a third Union should be formed of Southern Clubs, which might then obtain fair play in the selection of an Irish XV., by fighting a kind of triangular duel with its older rivals. The I. F. U., having been joined by the chief Munster Clubs, naturally took upon themselves the championship of their claims, advocating the adoption of the former of these expedients as being the most reasonable in itself, and the most likely to yield permanently satisfactory results.

In March, 1878, on the occasion of the Fourth International Match with England, the claim of Southern players to be represented on an Irish XV. was first practically recognised. In January, 1879, Ulster met and played Munster for the first time in Dublin, an event of importance in the history of Irish Football, as an acknowledgment on the part of the Northern Union, that henceforth Southern players might expect from them a candid consideration of their claims. Finally, on February 17th of the same year, immediately after the second Scotch International Match had been played in Belfast, a meeting of representatives from Leinster, Ulster, and Munster was held, in order to frame Rules for the guidance of a new Irish Rugby Football Union, built upon the amalgamation of existing Unions.

The main features of this new organization, as agreed on at that time, and finally ratified at the commencement of last season by general meetings of the I. F. and N. I. F. Unions, are as follows:—

(1). The formation of a single Union, having for its object the promotion of Rugby Football in Ireland.

(2). The establishment of Provincial Branches in connection with this Union, each Branch to manage the general interests of the Clubs belonging to the Union in their Province. There are, thus, three Branches—one each in Ulster, Leinster, and Munster. The affairs of each Branch are to be looked after by their own Committees, who will have in their hands the selection of their Provincial XV.'s, and the arrangement of Provincial Fixtures, &c.

(3). The Committee of the Union will consist of 18 members, including a President, two Vice-Presidents, an Hon. Sec., and an Hon. Treasurer. Each Branch to select six representatives on this Committee, which selects its own officers. It will meet annually in Dublin, after the Ulster *v.* Munster Match has been played there. Its duties to be confined to arranging International fixtures, and selecting the Irish XV. It will also form a court of appeal in case of a dispute arising between Clubs belonging to the Union, having power to remove from its roll the name of any Club which may be shown to them to have wilfully disregarded the Rules of the game. A special provision has been agreed on, by which Munster will only be represented by four delegates on this Committee, until they shall have either won or drawn a game with Leinster or Ulster. In the meantime the vacancies on the Committee are to remain unfilled.

(4). Leinster and Ulster are, as in former years, to continue to meet one another alternately in Belfast and Dublin.

General Rules for the management of the Branches were also agreed on, it being thought advisable to introduce some uniformity in their arrangement.

These Laws, which are to be found in detail elsewhere, were accepted and came into force for the first time last season. They were found to work smoothly, few unforseen difficulties cropping up to mar their intended action. Their details may indeed even yet require various modifications before they come to be regarded as a perfect code. They have, however, introduced an indestructible principle into Irish Football—a principle of genuine and friendly co-operation; they have united Irish players with a sense of a kindred love and a common endeavour; and they have opened up to southern Clubs special motives for increased exertion. All their beneficial results cannot be expected to be seen for a few years, but should the Provincial Committees of the coming season take a vigorous and hearty interest in their work, we may confidently look forward to the future as destined to unfold emphatic proofs of the value of a united union.

I have been led to make these remarks in order that our players may not imagine that the Irish Rugby Football Union was easily formed. It was the work, not of a day, but of years, during the whole of which time the manner, and even the advisability, of its foundation held the place of a "bone of contention" between its jealous predecessors. I have shown that we are partly indebted for its final achievement to the increasingly widespread popularity of the game. Probably we owe it still more to the fact that successive International defeats forcibly reminded us of the truth of that trite maxim, "United we stand, divided we fall."

I need scarcely dilate on the great advantages that must accrue to Irish Football, or, indeed, to Football generally, but in Ireland especially as the youngest in the sisterhood of Football-playing countries, through the means of these International contests. Having now in England, Ireland, and Scotland a common code of rules, we ought to study how, within certain limits, to preserve a common mode of interpreting them. Nothing can tend so effectually to preserve this uniformity as annual contests, where the chosen exponents of the game in their respective countries meet one another for the purpose of giving and taking lessons in the art of play, at the same time that they decide to which country the palm of honour should belong. The Rugby Code of Laws, were it not for these, would probably prove unable to maintain uniformity. Isolation would upset all the calculation of Law makers, and vicious modes of play might easily come to be adopted here or elsewhere.

We have now played nine International Matches, six being against England and three against Scotland. So many times we have suffered defeat. It may, indeed, be said that we are as far now from an international victory as ever. What if our boasted progress has nothing practical to show? This way of putting the case may and ought to double our exertions, but assuredly it ought not to discourage us. We have to bear in mind that progress has not been confined to Ireland, and that the style of play now is not what it was when we first played an International Match. We might even feel content if we could claim to have run parallel with the progress made elsewhere. A knowledge of the history of these matches would show that we have been able to effect even more than this. A becoming modesty lying, as it does, at the root of ultimate success, it may be well for Irish players clearly to recognise that only continued exertions, with no little sacrifice of personal convenience can, for some years to come place them on firm grounds of equality with their English or Scottish brethren. How soon that time will come depends on the strength of their own determination to make the necessary exertions.

I shall now briefly allude to some of the points, necessary factors in the progress of the game, which in Ireland seem to merit most attention. And first, then, as regards School Football. This essential element in Irish play is not yet fostered to the extent which, from every point of view, its importance deserves. We live in an age of concentration—

"When every hour
Must sweat its sixty minutes to the death."

Such an age is too apt to degenerate into one of "cram," to lack in solidity what it gains in intensity. Let our schoolmasters recognise that a lifelong brainwork cannot be built up on flimsy bones and flabby muscles; let them look for a sound mind only in a sound body, and let no disastrous attempts be made to treat either on the forcing principles of a hothouse. The animal wants of the growing boy demand attention, and they are to be wisely directed towards the enjoyment of invigorating sports, rather than let run riot in the pursuit of treacherous pleasures.

It would be well in schools, and indeed elsewhere, if players should come to appreciate more definitely that the Rugby game is one of skill—an art requiring both study and perseverance in its acquisition. It loses all its merits, and becomes a rough-and-tumble mudlark, if not played in strict accordance with the spirit of the rules. The too common notion, that it requires only strength and speed, is founded on an utterly false conception of the modern game. Some of our best players can scarcely boast of more than an average amount of these supposed necessities. Ready hands, steady feet, a quick eye and a cool head,—these are what the player wants, and what—it is not the least merit of the game—will come with its practice. Let therefore no big boy, vainglorious in his strength, seek to triumph through it alone over his weaker comrades. Time enough he may come to find himself more than matched in strength and baffled by skill.

All our School Clubs ought certainly to join the Union, which looks largely to them for support. Schoolboys have before now played on Inter-provincial and International Fifteens. If they join in sufficient numbers, the Union would, no doubt, more than repay them by inaugurating a Challenge Cup competition confined to schools. Perhaps this idea might best be carried out by each Branch of the Union holding a series of school contests in their respective provinces for a Cup presented by them. Such a competition already exists amongst Ulster schools. This would avoid the obvious difficulty of distant schools competing with one another in the final ties.

The leading Clubs should consider well the responsible position they hold in forwarding the interests of the game. Preserving only a healthy spirit of emulation, with the commencement of a new season's play let them cast aside all lower feelings of jealousy and enmity. They should use their influence on all occasions to insist on a rigidly fair style of play. Their Captains should see that not only do his XV. know the rules, but also that they practise them; and no player, however useful, should be allowed persistently to set at naught the spirit of the game. Much too frequently we have seen of late glaringly unfair play persisted in, undeterred on the player's own side by anything more than a half-approving rebuke. Freed of dishonesty, some men's play would be worthless; and it is imperatively necessary that the fact should not be concealed from them by their friends.

One custom, which of late has become more than ever prevalent, ought certainly to be discredited. I allude to the practice, largely indulged in by some well-known players, of constituting themselves for a season as freelances, at the service of whatever Club may offer the most inviting programme for a Saturday afternoon. While such a system persists, what chances have less known players of obtaining places on important matches, or what means have we of deciding the comparative merits of rival Clubs? I hope that this practice, which is inimical to progress, will not continue unchecked through the coming season. No professing first-rate Club should tolerate its chief members playing for another, with whose achievements its own will be compared at the season's close.

Much, indeed most, of the future of Irish football depends on the energetic administration of Committees of the Provincial Branches. In Ulster the love for the game is so firmly rooted, and its management is so confessedly energetic, that we need not look there for any symptoms of waning interest. An effort, made lately, to introduce into Belfast the Association Code of Rules, signally failed. Any renewed efforts at such an innovation will, I hope, meet with a like fate; not that the Association game is not a fine and skilful one, but because, even at present, we have too few players to let their attention be frittered away in various directions.

In Dublin a knowledge of the game has been steadily progressing among players, and what is of still better augury, the general public are becoming yearly more alive to its doings, and critical as to its niceties. For this we are largely indebted to the constant kindly interest of the Press. Still organization is imperfect, the Union work being piled on the too willing shoulders of an energetic few. Committee meetings, when summoned, are insufficiently and unpunctually attended, and the duties of administration are practically confided to the care of an oligarchy. Each Club, being represented on the Branch Committee, should elect only such representatives as are willing and able to attend its meetings, and watch their interests. In Munster football players suffer greatly from isolation, and the consequent difficulty in obtaining a sufficient number of matches to keep their interest in it awake. There are still, however, many fair-sized towns near enough to Cork and Limerick possessing as yet no Clubs, a defect which must be remedied before Munster can hope to strive on equal terms with Leinster or Ulster. Is the story mythical, or does that Professor still survive, who in the Queen's College of Cork has threatened vengeance on the luckless football player that comes beneath his jurisdiction? If the tale be true, would not the said Professor's threat form ample grounds for a question in Parliament by the hon. member for Cork city? Cork and Limerick must depend on the working and organizing capacities of their Local Committees if they are to succeed in popularizing the game in Munster, where it undoubtedly needs careful nursing. The Union having been framed largely so as to meet their views, it will be a discredit to them if the expectations of its founders be disappointed.

With regard to the general style of play during the last season, a few remarks on the improvements achieved and faults to be overcome may not here be considered as inappropriate or without use. There has been lately observable a marked yearly improvment in our forward play. It has become faster and more energetic; dribbling, passing back, and following up have become more generally understood, while our best forwards work together in a way unknown to those of old. These qualities have been so well learned from English and Scottish opponents, that last season the Irish XV. could fairly boast of a set of forwards unsurpassed in either country. Their concerted dribbling was one of the most notable features in the English match. Perhaps they have of late paid less than a due amount of attention to quick picking up and running with the ball, a feature in the game now more practised by our opponents, and one which, be it remembered, should make every yard run a clear gain. On the other hand, the faintest slip, of mind or foot, at the exhausting close of a splendid dribble may more than completely nullify its hard-won gain.

It is chiefly in back play that we are at present deficient, a curious fact when it is remembered that it was here we were strongest in the earlier International contests. Since then backs have improved in drop-kicking, but they have lost the art of running and grand power of tackling, which made their predecessors safe in defence as well as potent in attack. Compared with our International opponents, Irish backs want both pace and physique, though some of them do undoubtedly play the game, as an art, almost faultlessly. In this direction improvement is to be sought for in their more judicious selection by individual Clubs. Likely forwards might be selected and put in training, with a view to their one day filling effectively these very onerous and responsible places. Last year Ulster Clubs were particularly weak in this department of the game, which was not quite at such a low ebb in and around Dublin.

Tackling generally is a point in the game which has of late markedly deteriorated. Attempts are now all but universally made to tackle a runner either too high about the neck or too low by the feet. The fine old-fashioned grip around the hips is only occasionally seen in the play of those whose faces are dying away from the football field. Perhaps this may be accounted for by the lessened opportunities for practising it afforded now that a dribbling has to such a great extent supplanted a running game. Still I should in football regard an uncertain tackler much in the same light as in cricket an uncertain catch.

Never-ending appeals made to umpires in some matches as to whether the ball was thrown straight out of touch. and other obstructive tactics of this kind, were much too freely indulged in by losing sides last season. Umpires will best adhere to the spirit of the laws by deciding in such cases that all has been fair where honest intentions have not been followed by appreciable injustice.

On the subject of Umpires I may say that no feature of Irish play is so objectionable as the clamorously expressed dissent with which their decisions are too often greeted. Unfair decisions, frequent only in the heated imaginations of some players and their admirers, if made at all, may best be left to external opinion as their most fitting punishment. Such a course of conduct would better remind an umpire of his position than an undignified bandying of slightly-qualified Billingsgate.

Players should bear in mind that the rule which provides that the Captain alone of his side has the right of appeal to an Umpire. Otherwise the latter is neither compelled nor allowed to interfere. A Captain who abrogates his functions in this way to subordinates is unfit for his position.

The advice which I have here offered to the consideration of our players is necessarily stereotyped, and will be useless if it does not lead to habits of action on their part. They have much to be proud of, something to regret, much to learn and somewhat to unlearn. Above all let them be honest and earnest in their pursuit of the game. Then in the International contests of no distant future they will be able at all times to compel respect if not to ensure success.

"FOOTBALL IN MUNSTER."

By W. J. GOULDING, Captain of Munster.

THE past season has been a most disappointing one for the votaries of this manly pastime in the South of Ireland. Year by year the game has been making rapid strides in Munster, and new Clubs starting in the vicinity of Cork, but we regret we cannot say the same for Limerick; there Lawn Tennis has taken its place, owing to a lack of courage to sustain defeat, which has been their lot for the last few years, and with the exception of Messrs. Keon and Kennedy no energy has been displayed during the past season, and we fear next year it will be a game of the past within "the City of the Violated Treaty." They only entered the ring on two occasions in '79, first against Cork, to whom they had to succumb in the most feeble fashion, although ably assisted by Scriven, a "wearer of the green;" and, secondly, also on their own ground, against Queen's College, Cork, when a like fate awaited them. However, we have accounts very favourable from other parts of the South. In Tipperary the game, fostered by the Grammar School, has gained a footing, and we hear the recently formed Town Club will next season take its place on "the Union," and have already asked for early fixtures with Cork Clubs. In Waterford also, we believe, a Club has been established. In Cork the visit paid them by Leinster and by the two first-class Dublin Clubs (Trinity and Wanderers) in December, 1878, has brought forth good fruit, and this past season an immense amount of vitality has shown itself. Unbeaten at home, their energetic Captain, M'Mullen (late of Clifton College XV.) took them both to Limerick and the Metropolis where, unfortunately, a very strong team had to disport themselves on the ice instead of their native soil. This was likewise the fate of the Munster Team, we believe the strongest ever collected. A great deal of energy was displayed by the Southern Committee in taking over a team (unfortunately not a very strong one) to Wales where they received the most enthusiastic welcome, and played three matches, fully described in another page. The following are the names and positions of the picked XV. this season:—T. Harrison (Cork) (F. B.), Pierce and Leham (Cork) (H.B.), W. J. Goulding and S. Townsend (Cork) (Q. B.); forwards, Keon, Kelly, Kennedy, Griffiths (Limerick), M'Mullen, R. Townsend, Cummins, Burkett, Loane, and Carroll (Cork). Of this number Cummins and Burkett were elected on the International XV. In Cork there are at present about seven distinct Clubs, and the Cork Club have played on an average about three local matches a fortnight, while of foreigners they received visits from Midleton College, the 7th

Fusiliers, and the Phœnix, and over all gained easy victories; they also visited Limerick with a like result. Matches had been arranged with the Lansdowne in Cork, and with Portarlington School on their own ground, bu both fell through owing to the strangers lacking full teams. We think it i a great pity that secretaries should make fixtures if there is no chance o them coming off, and regret there is so great a want of courtesy shown to strange teams by wiring on the morning of a match to postpone it. The want of suitable grounds in the neighbourhood of Cork (such as one sees in other parts of Ireland) is a great drawback to the local Clubs, as the only place level enough to play is the Park, which certainly is a beautiful spot, but an idea of keeping spectators off the "Field of Play" dare not enter the head of the boldest.

The great fault in Munster is the goal-kicking. No one seems ever to think that this part of the game requires any practice, and consequently one hears frequently of a match being won by four or five tries, some of them got under the very post. We hope more attention will be paid to this next year, as while affairs remain *in statu quo* it would be futile to look for victory against a moderate foreign team. There has been a great improvement in passing of late and also in drop-kicking, but there still remains much room. Having received a place on "the Union" this past year has greatly inspirited Southern Clubs, and we hope that by taking every good tip and working with increased energy, we may see them next season on a par with the sister provinces.

IRISH RUGBY FOOTBALL UNION.

President—W. C. Neville.
Vice-Presidents—Richard Bell; W. J. Goulding.
Hon-Secretary—R. M. Peter, 24 Upper Merrion Street, Dublin.
Hon Treasurer—Edwin Hughes, 1 Lombard Street, Belfast.

Committee.
LEINSTER.—W. C. Neville, R. M. Peter, F. Kennedy, G. P. L. Nugent, G. Scriven, F. Schute.
ULSTER.—R. Bell, J. A. M'Donald, R. W. Hughes, W. T. Heron, E. Hughes, H. C. Kelly.
MUNSTER.—W. J. Goulding, W. Kelly, T. Harrison, J. J. Keon,
*———— *————

Hon. Secretaries of the Branches.
LEINSTER.—F. Kennedy, 25 Curzon Street, Dublin.
ULSTER.—W. T. Heron, Ballynafeigh, Belfast.
MUNSTER.—A. R. McMullin, 5 George's Quay, Cork.

Hon. Treasurers of the Branches.
LEINSTER—C. B. Croker, 5 Leinster Street.
ULSTER.—W. T. Heron, Ballynafeigh, Belfast.
MUNSTER.—A. R. McMullin, 5 George's Quay, Cork.

* By arrangement, Munster is only entitled to have Four representatives on the Committee until the "Munster Fifteen" either play a draw or win a match with the Leinster or Ulster.

RULES OF THE IRISH RUGBY FOOTBALL UNION.

I. That the name of the Union be "THE IRISH RUGBY FOOTBALL UNION."

II. That Branches in connexion with this Union be formed in Leinster, Ulster, and Munster, respectively, to manage the affairs of the Clubs in these provinces, belonging to the Union.

III. That the Committee of the Union consist of eighteen Members, six to be elected by each Province, on or before 1st November; that within a fortnight of their election they proceed to elect a President, two Vice-Presidents, an Hon. Secretary, and Hon. Treasurer out of their own body; and that in case of any Member of Committee retiring during his year of office, that branch of the Union which he represented proceed to fill up the vacancy so caused. That two Auditors for succeeding season be chosen at this Meeting.

IV. That the objects of the Union be to promote and foster the game of Rugby Football in Ireland, and so arrange interprovincial and international Matches.

V. That any Club willing to conform to the Rules of the Union be eligible for membership; but, before being admitted, such Clubs must be duly proposed and seconded by two Clubs belonging to the Union.

VI. That the annual subscription of each Club belonging to the Union be one pound, payable on or before 1st December; and that there be an entrance fee of one pound (Clubs at present belonging to either Union to be exempt from entrance fee); that the subscription and entrance fee for schools be one-half that for other Clubs—ten shillings each.

VII. That the Committee of the Branches consist of representatives from each of the Clubs in the province belonging to the Union, in the proportion of one representative for every twenty-five Members, or part of twenty-five over the half.

VIII. That the officers of the Union be elected by ballot; and that no one have a right to vote at any General Meeting of the Branches of the Union unless he be an Annual Subscriber of at least 2s. 6d. to the Branch of the Union to which he belongs.

XI. That the Hon. Sec. shall convene a Special General Meeting of representatives at any time on receiving a requisition to that effect, signed by the Captain or Secretaries of not less than two Clubs belonging to the Union.

X. That each Club be furnished with a copy of the Bye-laws and Laws of the Game, and be bound thereby; and in cases of wilful infringement of such laws by any Club, such Club be liable to expulsion from the Union at a General Meeting of Committee.

XI. That notice of any amendment or alteration in the Bye-laws of the Union, together with the names of the proposer and seconder of every such amendment and alteration, be given (in writing) to the Hon. Sec. three weeks at least before the General Meeting of Committee at which such amendment or alteration is intended to be proposed; and that such amendment or alteration be duly advertised fourteen days at least before such Meeting, and notice thereof sent to the Clubs belonging to the Union.

XII. That the Report and Statement of Accounts be printed, and sent to the Clubs belonging to the Union before the General Meeting of Committee.

XIII. That Leinster play Ulster and Munster, alternate years in Belfast and Cork, respectively.

XIV. That the Annual Meeting of Committee of the Union be held in Dublin after the interprovincial Matches.

XV. That the Union pay the travelling expenses (by railway and boat only) of representatives attending Committee Meeting who are not playing in the interprovincial Matches (as far as the funds are available).

By Order,

R. M. PETER,
Hon. Secretary, I.R.F.U.

LIST OF FOOTBALL CLUBS, WITH NAMES AND ADDRESSES OF HON. SECRETARIES.

ADELAIDE HOSPITAL.—J. L. Cuppaidge, 66 Morehampton Road.
ALBION.—R. H. Mayne, 11 College Square, East, Belfast.
ARMAGH.—E. J. Wolfe, Abbey Street, Armagh.
ARMAGH ROYAL SCHOOL.—R. W. W. Littledale, Royal School, Armagh.
BALLINASLOE.—H. A. Kennedy, Bank of Ireland, Ballinasloe.
BECTIVE COLLEGE.—Hon. Secretary, 15 Rutland Square, East.
BELMONT.—J. M'Ildowie, Belmont Park, Belfast.
BLACKROCK (Co. CORK).—Roger Burke, Shamrock Lodge, Douglas, County Cork.
BLACKROCK (CO. DUBLIN).—F. Orr, Brooklawn, Blackrock, Co. Dublin.
BRAY COLLEGE.—Hon. Secretary, B.C.F.C., Bray, Co. Wicklow.
CARRICKFERGUS.—J. G. Froggott, Bayview, Carrickfergus.
CATHOLIC UNIVERSITY.—Hon. Sec. C.U.F.C., St. Stephen's Green, Dublin.
CLANWILLIAM (CO. TIPPERARY).—F. S. Heuston, Ballykisteen, Tipperary.
CLONTARF.—G. G. Lemon, Yew Park, Clontarf.
CORK.—Wm. Peirce, jun., 11 Charlemont, Cork.
CORK BANKERS.—J. Menhear, Munster Bank, Cork.
CORRIG SCHOOL.—S. C. Dennis, Corrig School, Kingstown.
CUSACK'S ACADEMY.—M. Cusack, 37 Nelson Street, Dublin.
DALKEY COLLEGE.—The Warden, Dalkey College, Co. Dublin.
DROGHEDA.—E. H. M'Cormick, Bank of Ireland, Drogheda.
DUBLIN UNIVERSITY.—E. O'Farrell, 37 Trinity College.
DUNDALK.—G. Miller, Roden Place, Dundalk.
DUNDALK EDUCATIONAL INSTITUTION.—Hon. Secretary D.E.I.F.C., Dundalk.
DUNGANNON ROYAL SCHOOL.—R. F. Ringwood, Royal School, Dungannon.
EBLANA.—A. Sullivan, 19 Richmond Place, North Circular Road.
ENFIELD.—R. M. Kennedy, care of Messrs. J. Cunningham & Son, Waring Street, Belfast.

ENNIS COLLEGE.—L. Kidd, Ennis College, Co. Clare.
FOYLE COLLEGE (LONDONDERRY).—F.C.F.C., Londonderry.
GALWAY GRAMMAR SCHOOL.—R. Biggs, Grammar School, Galway.
HIBERNIAN.—W. Moore, R.H.M. School, Phœnix Park.
HIGH SCHOOL (DUBLIN).—Hon. Secretary H.S.F.C., Harcourt Street, Dublin.
KING'S HOSPITAL.—N. R. Haskins, King's Hospital, Oxmantown, Dublin.
KINGSTOWN.—A. Miller, 36 Corrig Avenue, Kingstown.
KINGSTOWN SCHOOL.—G. B. Pounden, K.S., York Road, Kingstown.
KNIGHT'S SCHOOL (CO. CORK).—Hobart Dorman, Patrick's Hill, Cork.
LANSDOWNE.—F. S. Searight, 78 Pembroke Road, Dublin.
LAURISTON.—James R. Magee, jun., Bedford Street, Belfast.
LEDWICH MEDICAL SCHOOL.—H. M'Gill, L.M. School, Dublin.
LONDONDERRY ACADEMICAL INSTITUTION.—A. L. Horner, Academical Institution, Londonderry.
LURGAN.—Andrew Geddis, Market Street, Lurgan.
LURGAN SCHOOL.—Hon. Secretary, L.S.F.C., Lurgan.
MEATH HOSPITAL.—A. Miller, 36 Corrig Avenue, Kingstown.
MERRION SQUARE ROVERS.—G. Vereker, 16 Merrion Square, S.
METHODIST COLLEGE, BELFAST.—A. M'Afee, Methodist College, Belfast.
MIDLETON COLLEGE (CO. CORK).—Hon. Sec. M.C.F.C., Midleton, Co. Cork.
MONAGHAN DIO. SCH.—Hon. Sec. F.C., Diocesan School, Monaghan.
MONKSTOWN.—H. K. Abbott, Victoria Lodge, Monkstown, Co. Dublin.
MOREHAMPTON.—A. J. Fleming, Bank of Ireland, Dublin.
MOUNT POTTINGER.—Donald MacArthur, Mount Pottinger, Belfast.
NEWTOWNARDS.—Adam Harbison, Model School, Newtownards.
NOMADS.—Hy. W. Nunn, 2 Trinity College, Dublin.
NORTH DOWN.—Wm. Heron, Comber, Down.
NORTH OF IRELAND.—Richard Bell, 4 Elmwood Terrace, Belfast.
NORTH WEXFORD.—Chas. Donaldson, Gorey, Co. Wexford.
ORDNANCE SURVEY.—P. Perdisatt, Ord. Survey Office, Phœnix Park.
PHŒNIX.—E. A. M'Carty, 28 Berkeley Road, Dublin.
PORTADOWN.—T. J. Collen, Portadown.
PORTARLINGTON SCHOOL.—W. S. Wybrants, Portarlington School, Queen's County.
PORTORA ROYAL SCHOOL.—H. Russell Joynt, Portora, Enniskillen.
QUEEN'S COLLEGE (BELFAST).—Augustine Henry, Queen's College, Belfast.
QUEEN'S COLLEGE (CORK).—Jas. H. Swanton, Sunmount, St. Luke's, Cork.
QUEEN'S COLLEGE (GALWAY).—Edw. A. Hackett, Queen's College, Galway.
QUEENSTOWN.—T. W. Scogings, Beach, Queenstown.
RANELAGH (ATHLONE).—Hon. Secretary, Ranelagh School, Athlone.
RATHMINES SCHOOL.—W. K. Johnston, Churchtown Park, Dundrum.
ROYAL ACADEMICAL INSTITUTION (BELFAST).—A. Alexander, R.A.I., Belfast.
SANTRY SCHOOL.—W. W. Smith, Santry School, Co. Dublin.
ST. COLUMBA'S COLLEGE.—T. S. Hillas, St. C. C., Rathfarnham, Co. Dublin.
ST. STANISLAUS COLLEGE.—Hon. Secretary, St. Stanislaus College.
STEEVENS' HOSPITAL.—Hon. Secretary, Steevens' Hospital, Dublin.
THE ABBEY (CO. TIP.)—Hon. Secretary Abbey F.C., Co. Tipperary.
ULSTER.—W. T. Heron, Ballynafeigh, Belfast.
UNITED HOSPITALS.—J. L. Cuppaidge, 66 Morehampton Road, Co. Dublin.
WANDERERS.—W. Kelly, Bank of Ireland, Dublin.

WESLEY COLLEGE.—Thomas R. Leonard, Wesley College, St. Stephen's Green, Dublin.
WINDSOR.—J. Pinion, 60 Apsley Place, Belfast.
YORK ROAD (BELFAST).—George Wood, Belfast and Northern Counties Railway, Belfast.

OTHER CLUBS (NAMES AND ADDRESS OF HON. SECRETARY NOT KNOWN).

ABERCORN.—
AYLESBURY.—
BELVIDERE.—
BULLDOGS (CORK).—
CARLISLE.—
LIMERICK.—
MAGEE COLLEGE.—
MILITARY ACADEMIES.—
ORMEAU (BELFAST).—
TULLAMORE.—
WEST END (DUBLIN).—

IRISH RUGBY FOOTBALL CLUBS, WITH NAMES OF OFFICERS AND REPORTS OF THE PAST SEASON.

ALBION FOOTBALL CLUB.

Club Ground—Rugby Road, Belfast.   *Colours*—Dark blue.
Captain—W. H. Mageean.
Hon. Secretary—R. H. Mayne, 11 College Square, East, Belfast.
Hon. Treasurer—M. H. Turnbull.
Committee—W. H. Arbuthnot, J. M'Lean, D. M'Caw, R. Mayne, M. Turnbull, W. Mageean, H. Hill.

The season 1879-80 cannot be said to have been a very successful one; neither indeed could it be termed unsuccessful. Considering that this is only the second season of the Albion F. C., and also taking into account that some of the members are rather inexperienced players—being what might be called "new hands" at football—it may be said that the Albion had a prosperous season on the whole. Great credit indeed is due to the Captain and Secretary, who during the entire season did their utmost, and put forth every availing effort in their power for the interest of the Club. Out of the nine matches played, as it will be seen, four were lost, four won, and one drawn. Of the four which ended unfavorably, two were against the North of Ireland (2nd XV.), one against Lurgan, and one against Carrickfergus. In the match against Carrickfergus, it is but fair to say that the Albion played two short, and several of their most reliable men were unavoidably unable to play. In all these matches the Albion acquitted themselves with very great credit, and we hope next season that we may be able to turn the tables on these rivals. Of the four which were won, one was against the Royal Academical Institution F.C., and also against the Methodist College F.C. Great praise indeed is due to the Albion for their victory over these teams, both of which competed for the "Schools Challenge Cup," so kindly presented by the North of Ireland Football Union. The Albion also scored against Ormeau and Belmont. The drawn match was with the Ulster F.C. (2nd XV.), against whom the Albion were unable to raise a good team. On the whole, reviewing the past season, the Albion have every reason to be satisfied with the progress made by their Club, and to congratulate themselves on their performances.

ARMAGH FOOTBALL CLUB.

Club Ground—The Mall, Armagh.   *Colours*—Scarlet and Black.
Captain—J. C. Wolfe.
Hon. Secretary—E. J. Wolfe, Abbey Street, Armagh.
Hon. Treasurer—C. Murphy.
Committee—W. J. Girvin, L. A. Pooler, H. Pentland, H. F. Lee, T. Gardner, R. Ellis.

This, the second season of the Club, has, all things considered, been very successful. The number of playing members is still small, which militates greatly against success in any foreign match. The only matches we lost were foreign ones, where, besides playing with very weak teams, we were also three or more short. Last season ('78-79) we played seven matches—won five, lost one, and one was drawn. This season, though a score of matches were on our card, only twelve were played. This was chiefly the fault of the weather. Of these twelve, six were won, two lost, three drawn, and one, viz., that with Dundalk, left unfinished, the Armagh Captain having to withdraw his men from the ground.

On October 22nd we opened our season by winning, with a weak team, the first of our annual matches with the Royal School, by a goal kicked by E. Wolfe off a try by J. Wolfe, and a try, E. Wolfe, to nil. November 1st brought a fairly strong 2nd XV. of the North of Ireland, with whom we played a most even draw. Only eleven could be mustered on November 8th to go to Dundalk, thus early giving a foretaste of the difficulties which were to beset all our foreign matches. Nov. 15th chronicled another victory for us, when Windsor 2nd XV. were defeated by a goal dropped by E. Wolfe to nil. We have now to record the first defeat of the season, when on Nov. 22nd Lurgan defeated us by a goal dropped by Larkin, and a disputed goal to a try by E. Wolfe; it is only fair to mention that in this match we were two men short. Nov. 29th we came in contact, for the first time, with a Metropolitan Club, when Dublin University sent down a representative 2nd to do battle with School and Club on two successive days. This was perhaps the hardest match of the season, as both sides were most evenly matched both forward and back, and the ground was in very bad condition; neither side scoring, the match was drawn. After this, for more than a month, the Mall was kept idle by the frost, and, after several disappointments, we were at length, on Jan. 28th, opposed by a team from Drogheda, whom we defeated by seven goals and six tries to nil. The goals were scored by Littledale (6), E. Wolfe (dropped). The tries were obtained as follows:—E. Wolfe (3), Pooler (2), J. Wolfe (2), King, Lee, Jones, L'Estrange (1 each). The following day was fixed for our match with Portadown, and only eleven turned up to go. Portadown, aided by a strong contingent from Lurgan, defeated us by a goal and a try to nil, and as they could not raise a team for the return, it was never played. Jan. 31st saw us in Belfast, playing a very strong 2nd of Ulster; we won by two tries (J. Wolfe and MacGeagh) to nil. On Feb. 7th we took our revenge upon Lurgan, when a magnificent match resulted in our favour by a try (Murphy) to nil. Feb. 11th was the day fixed for our return with the School, which we won by a try (Pentland) to nil; we played three men short.

We closed our season on March 13th by playing a XV. of the County against N.I.F.C. 1st XV. Armagh sent seven men, Lurgan six, Portadown two. The following was the team:—Back—Larkin (L). Half—E. Wolfe (A), Pooler (A). Quarter—Gorman (L), Pentland (A). Forwards—J. C. Wolfe (Captain) (A), Geddis (L), Collen (P), Adams (A), McGeown (L), O'Hanlon (P), Jones (A), Wetherall (L), Nolan (A), Greer (L).

Owing to short notice, some of the best county men were absent; it, however, resulted in a draw, neither side scoring.

As is the case with most County Clubs, we are badly off for backs; so much so, that we were obliged this season to dispense with a full back altogether, and play a third quarter instead.

Considering the whole season, we may give honourable mention to Pentland, Pooler, and Lee (quarter), the tackling of the first being above the average; and to Reilly, Robinson, Murphy, and Adams among the forwards, all of whom play a praiseworthy game. At the close of the season a concert was given in the Tontine by the members, and was, we are happy to state, a great success in every way.

The following are the cup-winners for '79 and '80:—
1878-79—W. J. Girvin, J. C. Wolfe, E. J. Wolfe.
1879-80—H. Pentland, H. Reilly, H. F. Lee.

ARMAGH ROYAL SCHOOL FOOTBALL CLUB.

Club Ground—The Mall, Armagh.   *Colours*—Marone and Navy Blue.
Captain—H. King.
Hon. Secretary—R. W. W. Littledale, Royal School, Armagh.
Hon. Treasurer—Rev. W. M. Morgan, LL.D.
Committee—Rev. W. M. Morgan, LL.D., Rev. W. F. Johnson, E. R. Johnson, L. A. Pooler, R. W. W. Littledale, J. D. FitzMaurice, R. S. Young, H. King, G. L'Estrange.

Our Football Season, 1879-80, was not, during the earlier part, very successful; but towards the close we managed to do very well, and keep up our name as a football-playing school. Our want of success during the first half of the season may be accounted for by the facts that our team was a new one and rather small, even for a school team, and we were in every instance pitted against town and county Clubs, and not against schools. Nevertheless, as the season advanced we began to get into better form, and succeeded in scoring some victories. We still hold the Schools Challenge Cup, presented by the Northern Football Union in 1876, to be competed for by the Schools in the Northern Union. We have won it in 1876, 1877, 1879, and 1880, thereby establishing our football reputation amongst the Northern Schools.

We began our season by playing the first of our two annual matches with the Armagh F.C. This Club mustered a strong team, and defeated us by a goal and a try to nil.

In spite of this inauspicious opening of the season, we shortly afterwards went with a fairly good courage to try conclusions with the Second Fifteen N.I.F.C. at Belfast. They were also strongly represented, and although our team all round played hard and pluckily, the superior weight of the home team told very much against the School, especially as the ground was in a very wet condition. The N.I.F.C. secured one goal and 3 tries to nil. Our next match was played against the D.U.F.C. 2nd XV. on the Mall. In this match their forwards, as far as size went, were superior to ours; nevertheless, our forwards made a very good stand against them, and managed to bring the ball through most of the scrummages, although with little effect, as the D.U.F.C. backs generally gained possession of the ball before advantage was taken of the situation. But a school team cannot hold out long against a heavier team which is in as good practice as themselves; and although our backs made some good runs and kicks, and several times relieved their goal, it was of no avail, and we were defeated by 2 goals and 2 tries to nil. After the frost, which commenced soon after this match was over, we played a match with R.S.A. Past and Present *v.* Lansdowne F.C. at Lansdowne Road. Although not very strongly represented, we managed to win by 3 goals and one try to nil. After the Christmas vacation, our first match was the return with the Armagh F.C., and after a closely contested match we were defeated by a try to nil. After several disappointments in fixtures, we hailed with joy the arrival of the N.I.F.C. 2nd XV. This was one of the best and pleasantest matches of the season. The School made a very good stand, and several times looked like winning. Shortly after the commencement of the match, King, by a good run, secured a try for the School close to the touch-line; but the try at goal was a failure. Later on in the game, one of the North quarter-backs, by a neat piece of play, dropped a goal; and, though two of the Armagh team made good shots at goal, we failed to add to our score, thus leaving the North winners by a dropped goal to a try. Next came our Cup tie matches. The first of these, R.S.A. *v.* Londonderry Academical Institution, was played on the Mall, after several postponements. The ground was very wet and dirty, which rendered both running and kicking a matter of great difficulty. After kick-off the ball was kept in Derry territory for some time, till their forwards, by a determined rush, forced it into the middle of the ground, where it remained some time. Nothing of importance was gained till towards the end of the match; Casement, by some neat dribbling, secured a try for Armagh. The kick at goal was missed, the ball going into touch close to the goal-line. From the throw-out L'Estrange ran in and secured a second try for Armagh, which King, by a splendid kick, converted into a goal. Nothing more of importance occurred till the end of the match, leaving us victors by a goal and a try to nil.

Our next tie was against the Methodist College, Belfast, who having beaten the Academical Institution, Belfast, played the final tie for the Cup with us. This match was also played on the Mall, and was hotly contested all through. Both sides gained a few trivial advantages throughout the match, but towards the end of the last 40, L'Estrange, by an exceedingly neat piece of play, hopping the ball out of touch, ran in, and secured the winning try for Armagh; but the kick at goal was missed. Soon after "No Side" was called, leaving us victors by a try to nil.

ROYAL SCHOOL, ARMAGH, F. C. FOOTBALL COMPETITION.

Drop-kick, won by R. W. W. Littledale, with an *average* distance of 52 *yards 2 feet*.

Place-kick, won by A. Hamilton Jones.

BALLINASLOE FOOTBALL CLUB.

Club Ground—Fair Green, Ballinasloe. *Colours*—Scarlet and Black.
Captain—A. J. Wilson.
Hon. Secretary—H. A. Kennedy, Bank of Ireland, Ballinasloe.
Hon. Treasurer—A. Benson.

No report furnished. Much praise is certainly due to the above-named gentlemen for their exertions to establish a Rugby Union Club in the West. Although at the first go off it may not seem to take, they should not be disheartened, and perhaps after a short time other Clubs may be started at some convenient distance, and so a friendly rivalry may spring up and lead to many pleasant and enjoyable matches.

Last season the Club played two matches, defeating the Ranelagh School, Athlone, but had to succumb to the Galway School Boys. Of the players, Benson, Cooper, Guinnessy, Doran, Sharpe, Wilson, and Kennedy showed best form.—[EDITOR.]

BLACKROCK (CO. DUBLIN) FOOTBALL CLUB.

Hon. Secretary—F. Orr, Brooklawn, Blackrock, Co. Dublin.

This once famous Club was not re-established last season, owing principally to the fact that most of the local men had joined other Clubs in and around Dublin.

There is no reason why the Club should not be organized next season. A good ground ought to be procurable, and no doubt a strong team could soon be mustered to do battle with many of the leading Clubs.—[EDITOR.]

CARRICKFERGUS FOOTBALL CLUB.

Club Ground—Luberlady, Carrickfergus. *Colours*—Crimson Jacket and Stockings, Blue Knickerbockers.
Captain—D. Blair Alexander.
Hon. Secretary—John G. Froggott, Bayview, Carrickfergus.
Hon. Treasurer—Robert Evans.
Committee—Thomas Vint, Henry Lynn, Henry M'Auley, George M'Combe.

This Club, which was only formed last November, and composed for the most part of members who had never before played Football, did not look forward to winning many honours in the field, and the measure of success which we met with has been most gratifying, and we hope and believe augurs well for the future prospects of our Club. We have played 16 matches, all except 3 against Clubs of considerable standing. Of the matches we won 7, had 1 drawn, and lost 8. We are fortunate in possessing some very fast men who, with a little more practice, will doubtless render a good account of themselves. Our ground has given every satisfaction, being well drained and of a very dry soil.

Arrangements are now being made with the Cricket Club for the erection of a pavilion, and the Committee look forward next season to putting the Club in every respect high upon the Football list.

CLANWILLIAM FOOTBALL CLUB.

Club Ground—Tipperary.   *Colours*—Blue, White Shamrock on breast.
Captain—W. Cooper Chadwick.
Hon. Secretary—Frederick S. Heuston, Ballykisteen, Tipperary.
Hon. Treasurer—Rev. Richard S. S. Ross-Lewin.
Committee—Waller O'Grady, William Eaton, H. B. H. Thompson, Thomas M. Griffiths.

This, the opening year of the Club, was one of continued success, partly owing to the efforts of the Committee, who wisely used all their influence to induce the players—many of whom were new to the game—to confine themselves for the early part of the season to practice. With that view some spirited practice matches were played, so that, when we did take the field, we found our team played very well together and succeeded in winning the first match, which tended greatly to our subsequent success.

Our first match was against a strong team from the garrison, which after a very well contested game was won by two tries to nil. In the return match the Club was again successful, winning by a goal and a try to nil; in this game some excellent play was shown.

After an interval of hard weather we next went to Limerick to play the County Club, but unfortunately had to go without some of our heaviest forwards, whose loss we badly felt, as our team was too light to make a stand against the Limerick forwards, who continually got away with the ball, producing a very fast game, which the splendid play of the Clanwilliam quarter and half backs turned into a success, our Club winning by one goal to nil.

A match with Waterford F.C. next arranged fell through, also matches arranged with The Abbey F.C., Limerick, also failed to bring up a team for a return match, which caused some disappointment.

To close the season a match was arranged for St. Patrick's Day with the 1/15th Regiment, which was played in the presence of a very large number of people, and proved the best fought game of the season. We forced our opponents to touch twice in defence to our once.

Our season thus closed without a single score being obtained against us.

Our Junior Club played some very good matches during the season, and we hope to have from them some good young players for next year's team.

The success of the Club was greatly owing to Chadwick, O'Grady, and Griffiths as forwards, who besides possessing great weight never spared like beginning early, and learning the ins and outs of the game, so that as you grow older and stronger your experience may increase in proportion. The first matches of the season '79-80 were played against the "Bulldogs," a local Club who won both games; but as some of the Cork Club played for the "Animals," it may account for their success. About the matches against the Queen's College much might be said in the way members of the Cork Club failed to put in an appearance, and this when a tough match was to be expected, was shabby in the extreme. A man should always try, when called on, to turn up for an important match, even at some slight inconvenience. Now, on both occasions against the College, Cork had not a fair representative team, and this must account for the wins, over which the Queen's men have so much exulted in. The Midleton College match was an easy walk over for Cork, for the ancient prowess of the Midletonians seems past and gone, but their juniors promise to turn out well, and some other time to make a better fight against Cork.

The match against the 7th Fusiliers was another easy win for Cork; for though the military turned out a much heavier team than their opponents, their want of training and practice completely lost them the match. The return was not played owing to the absence of some of the officers on leave. On St. Stephen's Day the Phœnix F.C. visited us from Dublin, and sustained a severe defeat by 1 try; but the travelling perhaps told against them, for after the first five minutes they had not a chance of success, although Cork only scored the one point.

The annual match, Limerick *v.* Cork, proved a decided win for the latter, the Limerick men displaying a great want of go, &c., and but for "a bit of Trinity I. XV." they got to help them, must have been walked off the field entirely. Two matches were played against the Cork Bankers, who proved very tough opponents, Cork only winning by 1 goal on one occasion, and 1 try on the other; both being scored in the last three minutes, and after a hard game. Old players know what that means. However, the Bankers deserve every praise for their plucky stand against the 1st of Cork.

The only failure of the season was, however unluckily, the most important fixtures, or series of matches, viz., The Dublin Trip, and this owing to a hard frost that set in, caused much disappointment in our football world, for Munster was never so well prepared for her annual contest with Leinster and Ulster. However, next year we hope the weather will prove more favourable; and when our opponents come South, we will try and render a good account of the members of the Cork F.C.

CORK BANKERS' FOOTBALL CLUB.

Club Ground—Cork Park. *Colours*—Blue.
Captain—Oliver Stokes.
Hon. Secretary—James Minhear, Munster Bank, Cork.
Hon. Treasurer—R. P. Murphy.
Committee—J. Maguire, W. W. Johnson, C. Haines, G. C. Harris, J. Fenton, R. P. Murphy, J. Cronin, J. Minhear, W. J. Sullivan, O. Stokes.

This Club, which was formed last October by the officials of the different banks in Cork, consists of about sixty members, forty of whom are bankers.

themselves; Mackenzie and MacCarthy, behind the scrummage, rendered equally good service, while the fact of no score being obtained speaks well for the back.

CLONTARF FOOTBALL CLUB.

Club Ground—Belvidere, Clontarf.   *Colours*—Red and Blue.
Captain—D. C. Maturin.   *Vice-Capt.*—J. Christian.
Hon. Secretary—G. G. Lemon, Yew Park, Clontarf.
Hon. Treasurer—P. J. Warren.
Committee—F. Millington, J. R. Trayer, W. Witz, Capt., Hon. Sec., and Treasurer, *ex-officio*.
Hon. Sec., 2nd XV.—R. L. Owens, Vernon Avenue, Clontarf.

THE 1ST XV.—The fourth season of the above Club has passed off with a loss of only one match, which, considering that it is still a young Club, and that it plays the best Clubs about Dublin, is rather a gratifying thought for its members. Like a good many other Clubs, most of its matches had to be put off on account of the frost which prevailed about the middle of the season, and which included the 2nd of the D.U.F.C. It is the full determination of all its present members to work up this Club next year, so as to make it one of the leading Clubs in Dublin, and also to play more matches from home. The finances for the year are in a healthful condition notwithstanding the great expenses which are incurred, but a great deal of which is paid by yearly subscriptions from non-players and gentlemen resident in the neighbourhood who take an interest in the Club.

THE 2ND XV.—The report of the 2nd XV. may be considered favourable. Of the twelve matches played, six were won; and, indeed, if certain players had turned up more regularly, the five defeats might have ended otherwise. During the season Warren, Maunsell, Sullivan, Quin, Butler, and Owens displayed good form.

CORK FOOTBALL CLUB.

Club Ground—Cork Park.   *Colours*—Black and Yellow.
Captain—A. R. M'Mullen.
Hon. Secretary—William Peirce, jun., 11 Charlemont Road.
Hon. Treasurer—Pierce A. Goold.
Committee—W. A. Cummins, T. Harrison, R. H. Townshend, S. Townshend.

The season '79-80 in the South may be looked on as having been a highly successful one, and vast improvement was made in the establishment on a firmer basis of our favourite winter sport. The Cork F.C. played a good number of matches with rather favourable results, but the great drawback met with was the want of opposition, there being no Club nearer than Limerick at all able to cope with Cork 1st XV. The consequence of this was, that our premier team seldom played together; and when a foreign match was played this told heavily, for it is the men who work well together win most matches. In the past season many new players turned out, and for beginners much good form was shown. Also junior members displayed an increasing knowledge of the game, and are sure to show up well for Cork on some future occasion; and this is as it should be, for there is nothing

The Club played matches with the Cork Club and the Queen's College, and although not being so fortunate as to score a victory, still was able to make a very good fight, and compelled their opponents to bring out all their strength.

No doubt but at the end of next season the Cork Bankers will be able to give a very favourable account of their matches, and with a little more practice will be able to put on the field a very good team.

CUSACK'S ACADEMY FOOTBALL CLUB.

Club Ground—Phœnix Park.   *Colours*—"Joseph's Coat."
Captain—W. R. Nally.
Hon. Secretary—M. Cusack (the Principal), 37 Nelson Street.
Hon. Treasurer—M. Cusack.
Committee—J. F. Fitzgerald, W. A. O'Connell, J. P. Curry, H. Ford, Captain, Sec., and Treasurer, *ex-officio*.

The season of 1879-80 being the first in which the above Club figured, may be said to have been highly successful, and more particularly so when we consider the very limited supply of materials from which the Club was formed. At the commencement of the season their position was thus:— There were four good "backs" and seven "forwards" attending lectures in the Academy, viz., Messrs. Nally, Fitzgerald, Roscingrave, and C. Ford; Cusack, H. Ford, W. O'Connell, Currey, Kelly, M'Grady, M'Cormack. In addition to this there was plenty of raw material in the shape of sturdy country fellows, who, with a little training and coaching, could be made into useful forwards. With these forces the "Gov." sallied out to the Park one evening, and sides having been picked, the C.A.F.C. entered on their first football match. This primary step having been taken, their progress seemed comparatively easy, when an unforseen misfortune for the Club cropped up as follows. The Civil Service Examinations came round, and no less than five of the football team passed, and of course were lost to the Club, so that the Committee were reluctantly obliged to recommend the election by ballot of four outsiders, on the strict understanding that they should engage not to play against the Academy during the season. Under these circumstances Messrs. J. M'Carthy, A. Spring, W. Moore, and T. Kearney were elected to supply the vacancies caused by W. A. O'Connell, who entered the R.I.C. as Sub-Inspector, and Messrs. M'Cormack, M'Grady, King, and Griffin, who obtained appointments in H.M. Customs. On the first Saturday in December the Academy played their first foreign match against the Belvidere at Clonturk House, and after a fierce fight the rival teams retired from a drawn battle. The Thursday succeeding saw them on the Catholic University ground at Sandymount, where after about five minutes' play, M'Carthy, quarter-back, ran in and gained the first try, and kicked a goal of it himself. The match eventually resulted in a victory for the Academy by 1 goal (M'Carthy) and 3 tries (Fitzgerald, Nally, and M'Carthy) to nil. On the next Saturday the return with Belvidere resulted in favour of the Academy by 2 tries gained by Bowles and Nally, and after being frozen out for a week they next played the Ordnance Survey, which was strengthened by some of the best players in the Phœnix F.C. The match was a remarkable one, inasmuch as that for fifty-five minutes out of the hour's play the Survey were closely penned round their own goal, when in the last two minutes, Dimond, P.F.C., got away in the dark, and gained the only try of the day for the home team. It is but fair, however, to say that Bowles got in twice, and M'Carthy once for the Academy; but the Umpire being unable to decide, the Academy, certain of victory, abandoned their claims. A veil should be drawn over the two matches against the Hibernian F.C., which were both lost by one try, each through the bad play of a certain back, who threw the ball wildly behind him into his own goal, possibly under the idea that he was passing it back. The matches against the Ephemerals and Butterflies proved hard-won victories for the Academy, for whom Messrs. Nally (1 goal and 1 try), M'Carthy (1 goal), and Cusack (1 try) were chiefly instrumental; and the return with the Survey was rather easily won by 1 goal—Yeabsley off Corrigan's try, and 2 tries, Moore and Bowles, to nil. Two matches against Kingstown School, of which the Academy won the return, and the match 1st XV. v. The Field, wound up the season.

We should perhaps mention that five of the Academy team went out to Santry School on Patrick's Day (a terribly wet day), and played a sort of a match there, but it was mutually agreed that it should not be counted. On the whole, as we have said before, the Academy have reason to be well satisfied with their first season; and under the leadership of such a sterling lover of the game as Mr. Cusack, they may reasonably expect to be even more successful next year.

DUBLIN UNIVERSITY FOOTBALL CLUB.

Club Ground—College Park.   *Colours*—Red and Black.
Captain—G. Scriven.
Hon. Secretary—E. O'Farrell, 37 Trinity College, Dublin.
Hon. Treasurer—R. J. Baker.
Committee—A. M. Archer, J. C. Bagot, J. L. Cuppaidge, C. Nolan, A. Whitestone, W. Wilson, M. H. Jellett, Captain 2nd XV., *ex-officio*.

The past season has been an unfortunate one for this Club in regard to its fixtures, but otherwise the condition of the Club has been very satisfactory. The number of members has considerably increased; and, owing to the energy of the Treasurer, we have been enabled to pay off a large portion of the debt left to us by our predecessors.

The 1st XV., with which we commenced the year, was, we believe, the best the Club ever had, and the 2nd XV. has proved that it is second to none in Ireland; but we feel sure that the Club will meet with the sympathy of football players when we mention that the 1st XV. was disappointed in nine fixtures, and the 2nd XV. in six. Our 1st XV. commenced the season by playing our old rivals the Wanderers, the match resulting in a victory for us by two goals to nothing. The play of the D.U.F.C. in this match warranted us in believing that we would have had a most successful year had our fixtures come off. The 1st XV. did not again take the field until January 17th, when we played Kingstown Club, winning by one goal to nothing.

The next match, on February 28th, was the return with the same Club, resulting in a victory for us by two goals to nothing.

The next and last was the return against the Wanderers. This match was played on March 13th, and, after a closely contested game, resulted in a draw, it being undeniable that our team showed the effect of having played so few matches during the season. The 1st XV. thus played four matches, winning three, the other being a draw, and nothing having been scored against the team during the year.

The 2nd XV. was a very strong team, and ought to contain the elements of a good 1st XV.; it was most successful during the year, though disappointed in many fixtures. It played twelve matches, winning ten and drawing two, and obtained the considerable number of twenty goals in the twelve matches. The D.U.F.C. had six men on the Irish Team, and contributed to the Leinster Team the five backs, two forwards, and two substitutes. In the competition for the Cups given by the Club for place-kicking and drop-kicking, that for the former was won by F. Bent, who scored eight out of a possible twelve, and that for the latter by M. Johnson, average 47·2 yds.; longest R.F., 56 yds.; L.F., 52 yds.

The caps for regular and superior play were given in the 1st XV. to A. M. Archer, C. Nolan, and M. Johnston, and in the 2nd XV. to F. Bent, J. Denning, H. C. O'Sullivan.

DUNDALK FOOTBALL CLUB.

Club Ground—Demesne.   *Colours*—Blue and Black.
Captain—J. Alfred Brabazon.
Hon. Secretary—George Miller, Roden Place, Dundalk.
Hon. Treasurer—Harry G. Freeman.
Committee—Robert Brown, J. C. Duffy, E. H. Macordle, J. R. B. Watson, J. Blackhouse.

"*Solvitur acris hiems*," or in English, the football season is over, and while the balmy breezes of spring play upon them, it falls to the lot of the football statisticians to perform their annual task—to review the past efforts of their Clubs and to look forward with hope to the future. It is with a willing pen I speak to the deeds of the Dundalk Football Club, for it has a bright record behind it. With a bad winter and a somewhat scattered membership against it, it has amply redeemed the pledges it gave last year. Playing only 1st XV's., and almost invariably those of leading Clubs, the D.F.C. record will contrast favourably with those of most Football Clubs. I notice with pleasure the great improvement in drop-kicking since the season 1878-79, but much more is needed in this direction. A little practice will do a great deal. Eleven matches in all were played during the season, and seven fell through, through frost and other more mundane causes. Of the eleven, four were won, four drawn, and three lost. Seven goals were scored for the Club and three against it. Fourteen tries for and eight against. These are the plain hard and dry facts, and now for the matches. The most interesting contests were those in Dublin and Belfast, and the home North of Ireland match. On the 15th of November, 1879, the D.F.C. met the "Wanderers" for the third time. Clyde Road was the venue, and both teams playing at their strongest, the result was a draw; true, the Wanderers claimed one try, but their own man, who was alleged to have gained it, expressed his decided opinion against it. The matches with the Drogheda Football Club are always pleasant meetings, and those played last season were no exception. D.F.C. went "all to pieces" on the 27th of December, when the Ulster Club sent down a rattling 1st XV., and walked over their twelve opponents. I am assured on reliable authority the season of the year had nothing to do with this crushing defeat; but, be this as it may, one Dundalk man at least was heard to exclaim after the match, "*O dura ilia Ulsterorum.*" Both teams will, no doubt, remember the weather in which the match took place, a state of climate which did not raise the spirits of the vanquished, and certainly damped those of the victors. N.I.F.C. *v.* D.F.C., played at Dundalk, showed the Club in their old form, a draw resulting after a good game. Two tries were gained by the home men, but were disallowed by the Northern Umpire—Dundalk being without one. The Lansdowne match also resulted in a draw, both Clubs playing their full strength. The matches with the Dundalk Educational Institution F.C. were pleasantly contested, and it was of no small advantage to the D.F.C. to have a local Club to contend with in matches oftener than the record shows. The season wound up with the visit of the Club to Belfast, where probably the best match of the season took place. To make up for the "draw" at Dundalk, N.I.F.C. put its best foot foremost. For the first fifty minutes of the game no advantage had been gained, but by a herculean effort Belfast then scored three successive tries, from which one goal was kicked. Among the matches knocked on the head by the hard winter was that arranged with the Windsor F.C. The return, however, was looked forward to, but Dundalk is numbered among the many whom that Club disappointed. Next year I hope to see the Dundalk Football Club extend its operation still further, if not from pole to pole, at all events to all get-at-able Clubs between Dublin and Belfast. Till then good-bye, and afterwards good luck.

[In thanking the Club for its interesting report, I can bear witness to the match with the Wanderers being "drawn," as the player who secured the questionable try admitted enough after the match to show it was not fairly gained. Respecting the umpire disallowing the tries in the first match with the N.I.F.C., I consider as Dundalk did not provide an umpire it should cheerfully acquiesce in the decision given, more especially coming from an ex-captain of the Irish Fifteen.—EDITOR.]

DUNGANNON ROYAL SCHOOL FOOTBALL CLUB.

Club Ground—Dungannon School.   *Colours*—Crimson and Brown.
Captain—F. F. Barlow.
Hon. Secretary—R. F. Ringwood, Royal School, Dungannon.
Hon. Treasurer—F. T. Trouton.
Committee—F. F. Barlow, R. F. Ringwood, F. T. Trouton, J. Shuter, W. H. Shuter.

Owing to the snow and frost we were unable to play any matches before Christmas. After Christmas we played Foyle College Football Club, whom, after a hard game, we beat by a goal, and a try versus a try. We then arranged a match with Armagh Royal School, which, owing to their not being able to come, was postponed. If weather permits, we hope to have more matches next season.

ENNIS COLLEGE FOOTBALL CLUB.

Club Ground—Drumcliffe.   *Colours*—Blue, with a Red Shamrock.
Captain—E. A. Gray.
Hon. Secretary—L. Kidd, Ennis College, Co. Clare.
Hon. Treasurer—R. H. Flynn, Esq.
Committee—R. H. Flynn, Irwin, Devenish, Humphries, Chute.

Last season, owing to the hard frost and a series of unfortunate contretemps, all our matches fell through. We practised regularly (three times a-week), and had hopes of turning out a very respectable team. We had fixtures on with Limerick F.C., Queen's College, Galway, Galway and Tipperary Grammar Schools, Midleton College and Ennis Town F.C.

GALWAY GRAMMAR SCHOOL FOOTBALL CLUB.

Colours—Blue and White.   *Captain*—H. S. M. Harpur.
Hon. Secretary—R. Biggs, Grammar School, Galway.
Hon. Treasurer—R. Biggs.
Committee—S. H. Bluett, W. T. Swan, J. E. H. Herrick, G. S. Fayle, H. S. M. Harpur.

The first match of this season was played against the Ballinasloe F.C., the time being four twenties. During the first twenty-two tries were obtained for the School by G. Fayle and S. H. Bluett respectively, which were converted into goals by H. Harpur. In the second twenty no advantage was gained by either side. In the third twenty the Ballinasloe F.C. obtained a goal, which was disputed. In the last twenty each side obtained a try, both being disputed, and, when time was called, the School was declared victorious by two goals, and a disputed try against a disputed goal and a disputed try. The next match was played against the Queen's College, Galway, and did not turn out so successful for the School, but, considering the great advantage the Queen's College team had over the School in weight, the result is not at all to be wondered at. The game was played in four twenties. During the first twenty the Queen's College obtained a touch from which they kicked a goal. Nothing else worthy of record happened in this match, except that in the last twenty the Queen's College got another try, which, however, they failed to convert into a goal. Thus the game finished, leaving victory to the Queen's College by one goal and one try to nil. The next match played was the return of the Queen's College match, and ended in another victory for the Queen's College team by one goal and two tries to nil. A match played against the Ranelagh School F.C., Athlone, was the next one played. This match proved most uninteresting, as it was almost all scrummaging, and when "No Side" was called, the game was declared a draw in favour of the Ranelagh F.C. The play of the Galway Grammar School team was very praiseworthy, their opponents being so much heavier in the scrummages.

The last match was played against a team of "Past" men. The game was played in four quarters, and, after a very pleasant match, the "Past" won by one goal to nil.

It now only remains to be remarked, that the play of this team was very good throughout the whole season, taking everything into consideration.

HIBERNIAN FOOTBALL CLUB.

Club Ground—Fifteen Acres, Phœnix Park.   *Colours*—Black and White.
Captain—M. Gavin.
Hon. Secretary—W. Moore, Hibernian School, Phœnix Park.
Hon. Treasurer—G. Yeabsley.
Committee—Gavin, Yeabsley, Guerrini, Moore, T. McKay, and Smith.

This Club was only formed in 1878 out of the remnant of the old Phœnix Club of 1874-5, and has, so far, been remarkably successful.

In the season of 1878-9 they played fifteen matches, of which four were lost, seven won, and four drawn.

During the last season they were equally successful (the 1st XV. at least), playing ten matches, of which one was lost, seven won, and two drawn.

Owing to want of men the 2nd XV. were not so fortunate, playing only two matches against Clontarf 2nd XV., in both of which they suffered defeat.

There appears to have been some mistake amongst other Clubs as to the nature of this Club; some taking it for granted that it was formed of pupils of the Hibernian School, and some ill-feeling was caused by the error. The name was, indeed, taken from the school, which is in the vicinity of the Club ground, and of the residences of most of the members; but Clubs intending to play may perhaps be glad to learn beforehand that it is not mere boys they have to deal with, but a team in all probability as strong and powerful as themselves.

[The H.F.C. is one of the Clubs comprised in the Irish Rugby Football Union.—EDITOR.]

KING'S HOSPITAL FOOTBALL CLUB.

Captain—E. Faris.   *Colours*—Blue.
Hon. Secretary—N. R. Haskins, King's Hospital, Oxmantown, Dublin.
Hon. Treasurer—E. Faris.
Committee—E. M'Alister, G. Keillor, J. Wiseheart, R. S. Montgomery, W. Cooper, J. Polson, F. Blakemore, and H. Smith.

The King's Hospital Club had a very successful season, only losing three matches out of nine played.

The First Fifteen scored an easy victory over the Mountjoy team, but in the succeeding match with Lansdowne Second Fifteen were defeated by one goal and three tries. On November 1st the Survey defeated the K.H. by one goal, and on the following Saturday the K.H. played a draw with the Hibernian F.C.

Playing against the Clontarf Second, the Club suffered a crushing defeat by 5 goals and 3 tries, and in the return match with the Survey, the Blue proved successful by 1 goal and 2 tries. The Second Fifteen played 3 matches, winning 2, losing 1. Next season the Club promises to do well, and hopes to play more matches and make many new friends.

KINGSTOWN FOOTBALL CLUB.

Club Ground—Adelaide Road, Glenageary. *Colours*—Black, Red, and White.
Captain—Richard Armstrong.
Hon. Secretary—Alfred Miller, 36 Corrig Avenue, Kingstown.
Hon. Treasurer—W. Ross.
Committee—Dickson, Newell, M'Blaine, Hickson, officers *ex-officio*.

The Hon. Secretary of this Club favoured me in July with a communication to the effect that he "was unable to write a report sufficiently flowing to appear in the Annual, not having a spare moment to think about football," and requesting that I would write my own opinion on the Club. In my opinion, the Secretary might have found time to favour me with some report after a lapse of three months, and I likewise regret that I have not time to make out reports for Clubs that are unmindful of their own interests.—[EDITOR.]

KINGSTOWN SCHOOL FOOTBALL CLUB.

Club Ground—York Road.
Colours—Blue Jersey and Stockings; White Knickerbockers; Skull and Cross-bones on Chest.
Captain—W. W. P. Fletcher.
Hon. Secretary—G. B. Pounden, Kingstown School.
Hon. Treasurer—W. H. Knapp.
Committee—W. Fletcher, R. M'F. King, J. R. Murray, G. J. Moriarty, and G. Williamson.

The 1st XV., at the beginning of the season 1879-80, was very weak, and, consequently, unsuccessful at first, losing two consecutive matches. This, however, did not discourage them, and being reinforced by several good men, they were victorious over the next two Clubs with which they tried conclusions; but playing the 2nd XV. Wanderers F.C., with a very weak team—one-third of which were 2nd XV. men—rather than disappoint them, they were again worsted.

The 2nd XV. were beaten in the first match of the season, but in all their subsequent matches their opponents invariably came out "second best." All the matches arranged for December had to be postponed on account of the frost.

After vacation the 1st XV. opened the second half of the season by trying their skill and strength with the 2nd XV. D.U.F.C., but were defeated by 1 try and 1 disputed goal. They next played Lansdowne 2nd XV. (won), Cusack's Academy (won), Rathmines School (won), 2nd XV. D.U.F.C. (return), lost, Lansdowne 2nd XV. (return) drawn, Cusack's Academy (return) drawn.

The 2nd XV. played three matches after vacation, all of which they won.

It will thus be observed that K.S.F.C. was far more successful at the close than at the commencement of the season, being defeated by no Club except "Trinity." This may be accounted for by the fact that several changes were made in both teams after vacation.

The 1st XV. always had a great disadvantage in the *weight* of its members—never during the whole season having a team opposed to it which had not much heavier "forwards." Nevertheless, they made up in spirit what they wanted in weight, and the backs always showed good form, especially in kicking. The 2nd XV. played with great spirit throughout the season, though it had not such odds against it as the 1st XV. On the whole, we think the K.S.F.C. had a busy and successful season.

[It is pleasing to see the "Death or Glory" boys coming to the front again, more especially as they now play all "Present" men. Some years ago the Club was very strong, as they played generally a Past or Present team in the proportion of 11 Past to 4 Present. It reflects better on a school always to play a Present team.—EDITOR.]

KNIGHT'S SCHOOL FOOTBALL CLUB.

Captain—R. W. Burkitt.
Hon. Secretary—H. Dorman, Patrick's Hill, Co. Cork.

The Knight's School F.C. only played two matches last season of any importance, both being against the Cork F.C. A number of the latter Club played for the "School," being "Past men," and in no small way tended to the victory of the "Boys."

LANSDOWNE FOOTBALL CLUB.

Club Ground—Lansdowne Road, Dublin. *Colours*—Red, Yellow, and Black.
Captain—E. H. Nunns.
Hon. Secretary—Fred. S. Searight, 24 Upper Merrion Street, Dublin.
Hon. Treasurer—H. Fingall Orr.
Committee—C. B. Croker, H. W. D. Dunlop, T. Moore, James Moore, E. H. Nunns, C. B. Owen.

The Lansdowne Football Club may fairly be congratulated on the success of the Club this season. It now holds a foremost position amongst the Clubs in Dublin, both regarding the number of members and the number of matches played. There are now fifty members in the Club, of which number twenty-four were new this year. The 1st XV. played fourteen matches, of which they won six, lost five, and three were drawn. The 2nd XV. played nineteen matches—won nine, lost eight, and two drawn. There was a decided improvement this year in the play of the members, they being a very light lot, and, with the exception of one or two matches, played well together. Owing to the frost and wet, twelve matches fell through—ten from the inability of the opposing Clubs to get up teams and various reasons, making in all fifty-six fixtures. At the commencement of the season the Club sustained a severe loss by the resignation of Mr. H. W. D. Dunlop, the popular Hon. Secretary, who had kept the Club on its legs since its formation.

The 1st XV. began the season by a series of victories, notably those over Clontarf, Nomads, and Wesley College. The tour to Limerick and Cork, fixed for the Christmas holidays, fell through, owing to the unsatisfactory state of the weather.

In the beginning of January the 1st and 2nd XV.'s met in friendly rivalry the respective 1st and 2nd XV.'s of the Wanderers F.C., and though not successful in either matches, the form shown by the L.F.C. was such as to prognosticate many successes in the future for the "red, yellow, and black." A very strong team travelled to Dundalk, and though they could not claim a victory, yet they compelled the home-team six times to touch-down in defence. In the match, Armagh Royal School (past and present), which was played on the 18th December, the Club was not all represented, playing six 1st XV. and five 2nd XV. men. Indeed the match should have been postponed, owing to the frost, as the ground was totally unfit for playing on. The 2nd XV., in the return match, amply avenged themselves on the Military Academies for their previous defeat. In the return match with the 2nd XV. of the Wanderers F.C. they made a far better fight than was expected, the W.F.C. failing to score till the last five minutes of play. The 1st XV. fixture with the Wanderers fell through, owing to casualties, and that with the Kingstown F.C. 1st XV. had to be put off in consequence of the match, Leinster v. Munster, being arranged to come off on the L.F.C. ground. The 2nd XV. fixture with the K.F.C. 2nd XV. had to be put off, owing to the Hon. Sec. of the latter Club fixing with the Wanderers 2nd XV. for the same date. As will be seen from the detailed account of matches played, three of the defeats which the Club sustained were inflicted by scratch teams. There is no satisfaction in playing scratch teams, and the sooner recognised Clubs discourage these scratch teams, by not playing them, the better.

If the L.F.C. make such progress next season, it will not be long before it finds itself at the "top of the tree." Possessing the best ground, and the most complete dressing arrangements of any Club in the vicinity of Dublin, the members are also entitled to "free admission to all sports held on the athletic ground at Lansdowne Road, from 1st October to 31st March; and as all the Interprovincial and International matches played in Dublin come off on this ground, the members of the L.F.C. certainly obtain great pecuniary advantages.

The Club closed its season by holding sports on the 22nd May, 1880, which were in all respects a great success. The drop-kicking was won by F. S. Searight, with an average distance of 49 yards, who also secured the prize for place-kicking, by scoring 6 goals out of a possible 7.

LAURISTON FOOTBALL CLUB, BELFAST.

Club Ground—Windsor Park, Belfast.   *Colours*—Dark Blue and White.
Captain—Henry Seaver, 32 Botanic Avenue, Belfast.
Hon. Secretary—James R. Magee, jun., Bedford Street, Belfast.
Hon. Treasurer—James R. Magee, jun.
Committee—Samuel Adams, James Brown, Arthur Herdman, Robert Ireland, and S. C. Hardy.

(The report of the season was not forwarded in time for publication).—[EDITOR].

LEDWICH MEDICAL SCHOOL FOOTBALL CLUB.

Captain—C. Burke Gaffney.
Hon. Secretary—H. M'Gill, Ledwich Medical School, Dublin.
Committee—Dr. T. Mason, V. Magrane, A. Courtenay, D. Browning, officers *ex officio*.

No replies received to communications sent.—[EDITOR.]

LONDONDERRY ACADEMICAL INSTITUTION FOOTBALL CLUB.

Club Ground—School Grounds.   *Colours*—Scarlet and White.
Captain—A. L. Horner.
Hon. Secretary—J. K. Blackwood, Academical Institution, Londonderry.
Hon. Treasurer—J. C. Dick (Resident Head Master).
Committee—A. L. Horner, J. K. Blackwood, J. H. MacLaughlin, W. A. Russell, J. Stewart.

The matches were fewer in number than usual, owing partly to the want of interest in games throughout the district, partly to the weather. If the Ulster Branch of the Northern Union could prevail on the railway companies to afford more facilities for schools meeting schools, the annual competition for their Challenge Cup would be much stronger. As things are, the Academical Institution was the only school in the North-west of Ireland that entered for it; and as they had to contend against great traditions, good play, and a strong team, the match *versus* Armagh Royal School went against them. However, notwithstanding defeat and the muddiness of the ground, the match was very pleasant. As this was their first trial for the "Cup," they hope to do better next time.

[The railway companies of Ireland generally do afford facilities to travelling football teams, such as return journey for single fare, provided ten tickets are purchased. The Irish Rugby Football Union will be happy to negotiate any such arrangement, if reminded, next season.—EDITOR.]

LURGAN FOOTBALL CLUB.

Club Ground—Lough Road View.   *Colours*—Yellow, Red, and Black.
Captain—James Gorman.
Hon. Secretary—Andrew Geddis, Market Street, Lurgan.
Hon. Treasurer—Andrew Geddis.
Committee—James Jackson, Patrick M'Geown, James Craig, Patrick Larkin, Thomas Harrison, William Russell.

Considering the low state of this Club during the season 1878-79, it may well be said that it has made great progress during the present one. It is now in a very flourishing condition, and although the number of working members is quite too few, being only twenty, yet those who are in it stuck to their colours and did their duty well, and the consequence is we have had a very successful season. The adage, "Nothing succeeds like success," has certainly been verified in this Club since its formation, or rather since the commencement of the year. The game had got into such popular favour that upwards of two thousand people would assemble to see a match. With one or two exceptions, matches were arranged with the best Clubs in Belfast and the neighbourhood, but it is to be regretted that a great many of these Clubs did not fulfil their arrangements, and thus prevented us from playing as many matches as we would otherwise have done. There was one thing which added in no small degree to the success of the Club, and that was the selection of the ground. A better position could not be had both for the comfort of the spectators and the convenience of the players. The field itself is not exactly what would be desired, being rather wet, but the committee believe this grievance could be easily remedied and at very little expense. Great thanks is due to Mr. Harkin for his kindness in giving the

Club the use of the field, and let us hope his kindness may yet be extended in allowing us to have it satisfactorily drained and levelled.

The matches played during the season only numbered 7, a great many having fallen through, and of those 7 we won 5, lost 1, and 1 was drawn.

Our first match was with our "County Rivals," Armagh F.C. It was a very exciting game throughout, and after two forties very hard play in which Larkin was conspicuous by dropping a goal, we were proclaimed the victors by one goal and one disputed goal to one try. Next came the match with the Albion F.C., but this did not prove so close a contest as the former as we won with a lot to spare, the visitors being quite too light for our team. On 26th December we travelled over to Banbridge to try conclusions there, and this, like the previous one, resulted in an easy victory for us, our Captain (Gorman) perhaps doing most service, adding four tries to our credit in quick succession. The match with Ulster 1st XV. was next on the list of fixtures, and it was expected that this would be a very tight struggle, but the visitors could only muster eleven men, and consequently we won rather easy. This was a most disagreeable match, being one continual scene of argument from beginning to end. The return match with Armagh F.C. now came to be decided, and as both Clubs had determined to put their strongest teams in the field, it was looked forward to with great interest. Unfortunately, however, our hopes as to raising our strongest team were not realized, having in the meantime lost the services of three of our best men; but this did not deprive the match of all its interest, as a most exciting and evenly contested game resulted, we being finally defeated by one try. The match with 2nd XV. N.I.F.C. was also very evenly contested, resulting in a draw, neither side having scored.

It has been a source of regret to the Committee that they were unable to get up even an average team to play in matches away from home, but I have no doubt from the interest taken in the Club this year our numbers will be greatly recruited in the coming season, and that this d'fficulty will to a great extent disappear.

Our last match was with Armagh Amateur F.C., but this was entirely deprived of its interest in being altogether one-sided. Our opponents were completely overmatched, for they never could manage to score nor even at any time to look dangerous. Harrison and Gorman as quarters played brilliantly, backing each other up and passing to an extent that drew repeated cheers from the spectators. The only thing now left for decision was the match between the County and 1st XV. N.I.F.C. This was a most desperate struggle, and although both teams again and again essayed to score, they were unable to gain the slightest advantage over each other, and it thus ended in a draw. Six of our Club were representatives of the County, viz., Gorman, Larkin, M'Geown, Geddis, Wetherall, and Brown. Of these M'Geown deserves special notice for his fine forward play, his dribbling being immensely superior. The team selected for the County did not at all represent the real strength of the County, as they wanted the services of Littledale and some others; but considering that the team was raised so hurriedly, they may well congratulate themselves on the result. This wound up a very successful season, but we hope to see next season still more successful. Let each member pull together and show the public it is yet the intention of the Lurgan F.C. to become classed among the first in Ireland.

MONKSTOWN FOOTBALL CLUB (CO. DUBLIN).

Colours—Not yet decided.   *Captain*—A. Findlater.
Hon. Secretary—H. K. Abbott, Victoria Lodge, Monkstown.
Hon. Treasurer—G. H. Acheson, 4 Longford Place, Monkstown.
Committee—H. Abbott, G. Acheson, A. Drought, P. Hodges, W. Murray.

As this is the first season in which it has been attempted to revive this Club, there were very few matches, and besides the Club were unable to procure a suitable ground. It is to be hoped that next year it will be more successful, and that some of the first rate players who reside in Monkstown may be induced to join it. The Club only played four matches this season, all of which were lost owing to its not being able to muster a full team on any occasion. Several other matches were arranged, but postponed for various reasons.

[There is no reason why the Monkstown Club should not yet flourish, and a fine should be inflicted on absent or late members who have promised to attend. In all the matches the Club played three or more men short.—EDITOR.]

MOREHAMPTON FOOTBALL CLUB.

Ground—Donnybrook.
Hon. Secretary—A. J. Fleming, Bank of Ireland, Dublin.
Captain—A. J. Fleming.

The Morehampton Club was formed in 1878, and enjoyed a very successful season. In 1879 the Club was just formed when the ground (adjoining the Hospital for Incurables) was taken for drainage purposes, and for some time the Club was without a field. When the works were completed the Captain found that nearly all his men had joined other Clubs, and consequently abandoned the Club for the season. It is to be hoped that in 1880-81 the Morehampton will again take the field, and if they can only do as well in the future as they have in the past, and secure the services of their popular Captain for another year's campaign, there is no reason why the M.F.C. should not be able to hold its place among the best of Dublin Clubs.—[EDITOR.]

MOUNT POTTINGER FOOTBALL CLUB.

Club Ground—Ormeau Park.   *Colours* {Navy Blue and White, hose and Jersey and blue knickers.
Captain—Wm. Johnstone.
Hon. Secretary—Donald MacArthur, Mount Pottinger, Belfast.
Hon. Treasurer—Wm. McCullough.
Committee—W. McBride, W. Johnstone, J. McVicker, R. Craig, — Nelson, W. McCullough, M. Cammack.

The report of the Mount Pottinger Football Club for the short part of the season which they played is not very long, but it is very creditable to a young team.

1. The first match we played was with the Ormeau F.C. We had the advantage of them both in strength and speed, and defeated them by two

goals and one try, with several disputed tries and numerous touches-down to nil.

2. Our next match was with the York Road F.C. We were defeated by one goal, which was obtained from a try about 15 minutes from the commencement of play. The game was evenly contested from this till call of "No Side," any advantage being in favour of York Road.

3. Our last match was with the Belmont F.C. The game, which was well contested throughout, resulted in our favour by one try.

We obtained three tries and the Belmont two.

NEWTOWNARDS FOOTBALL CLUB.

Club Ground—Newtownards. *Colours*—Blue and White stripes.
Captain—David J. Caughey.
Hon. Secretary—Adam Harbison, Model School, Newtownards.
Hon. Treasurer—David J. Caughey.
Committee—T. McVane, J. Gordon, W. R. Caughey, J. McBride, H. Brownlow, S. McCullough,
Captain, Hon. Secretary, and Hon. Treasurer *ex-officio*.

The Club played no matches this season.
[While thanking the Club for their good wishes for the success of the *Annual*, I sincerely hope Captain Caughey will bring his men to the front in 1880-81.—EDITOR.]

NOMADS FOOTBALL CLUB.

Colours—Black and White.
Captain—Robert Edward MacLean.
Hon. Secretary—Henry W. Nunn, 2 Trinity College, Dublin.
Hon. Treasurer—R. Nunn.
Committee—H. B. Morell, G. E. F. Molineux, B. D. Dickson.

The late season was one very badly calculated to show the merits of any team in the football field.

The frost, which commenced in January, and continued all through February, was the cause of the postponement of some fixtures, and the cancelling of many others.

In the few matches which the Nomads did play, they may be said to have been fairly successful; in fact, in the only match in which they were beaten, their defeat was owing to their having mustered a very weak team, which was further weakened by the loss of their full-back, who had to retire early in the game, owing to a rather severe injury.

At Drogheda the Nomads gained their first victory of the season, the Nomads losing the toss. The leather was started against a very strong wind. The match was very even until close on call of "half-time," when Atkinson dropped a neat goal. The next part of the game, with the wind in their favour, the Nomads showed their superiority getting two tries, off which, owing to the very wet state of the ground, no goal was kicked, and compelling the home team to touch-down innumerable times in self-defence.

At St. Columba the Nomads had things all their own way, winning by three goals and two tries.

At the Curragh, against the 38th Regiment, there was a most enjoyable match, in which the Nomads were victorious, Cronyn doing excellent service. His runs were magnificent; his play all through was nearly up to his old form.

In the next match against Lansdowne success again attended the team, though several of the Irish Fifteen were numbered in the ranks of their antagonists.

NORTH DOWN FOOTBALL CLUB.

Club Ground—Comber. *Colours*—Blue and Black.
Captain—John Andrews, jun.
Hon. Secretary—Wm. Heron, Comber.
Hon. Treasurer—Wm. Heron.
Committee—G. Turner, Wm. Graham, W. H. Drennan, Chas. Flynn, Edward Killen, W. Blackstock.

During the past season twelve matches were played by this Club, eight of which were lost and four won. As this is the first season the Club can be said to have existed, it is highly satisfactory that we are able to chronicle any victories, when it is borne in mind that our opponents were all, with one or two exceptions, old and tried Clubs. The matches during the season were very well contested with two exceptions, viz., the return with the 2nd XV. of the North of Ireland on 13th March, and the return with Carrickfergus on the 20th March. While we regret that such a crushing defeat was inflicted on the team while playing its two closing matches, after such previous successes, we may at the same time take consolation from the fact that on neither occasion was there anything like a representative team, and on each our Club played three or more men short.

On the 13th March eleven men responded to the call of the Secretary to do battle with one of the very best XV.'s the North of Ireland ever put into the field, and when we say that of these eleven had never played in a match before, and that the Ormeau grounds on the occasion presented something like the appearance of the river Lagan with the water removed, the only wonder is that a greater defeat was not inflicted. On the 20th March the Secretary was again unfortunate in getting up a team, and a severe defeat was again the inevitable result. When these circumstances are taken into consideration, we have no reason to be discouraged or dissatisfied; on the contrary, we may look back on the season's play with extreme satisfaction, and with better organization, more practice, and a perfect knowledge of the game, we may look forward to next season's work with pleasant anticipations. Before closing our report, we desire to thank the Messrs. Andrews for their kindness in allowing us, free of charge, the use of the field to practise on; and we also desire to thank our honorary members for their pecuniary support on behalf of the establishment of our Club.

NORTH OF IRELAND FOOTBALL CLUB.

Club Ground—Ormeau. *Colours*—Blue, Black, and Red.
Captain—R. B. Walkington. *Capt. 2nd XV.*—R. S. Smith.
Hon. Secretary—Richard Bell, 4 Elmwood Terrace, Belfast.
Hon. Treasurer—Richard Bell.
Committee—H. C. Kelly, W. Finlay, E. Hughes, J. R. Bristow, F. L. Heyn, Rev. R. H. Coote, H. Purdon.

Nineteen 1st XV. matches and twenty-nine 2nd XV. were arranged for the past season, making a total of forty-eight in all, being an increase of ten matches over the previous season. The 1st XV. played fourteen matches, seven of which they brought to a successful issue, four times they suffered defeat, and three matches were declared drawn. Of the five matches unplayed, three were put off on account of frost, and the remaining two owing to the inability of foreign Clubs to raise teams. The 1st XV. obtained nineteen tries, from which six goals were kicked, in addition to which two were dropped from the field of play—one by A. S. Matier, the other by R. B. Walkington. The tries were gained as follows :—J. F. Ross, 5 ; W. J. Heron, 3 ; J. Purdon, 2 ; E. Hughes, 2 ; W. Berkeley, J. S. Ferguson, A. H. Hartley, James Heron, W. Higgin, H. C. Kelly, and H. Purdon, 1 each.

The 2nd XV. played eighteen matches, of which they won fourteen, lost one, and three were drawn. They gained fifty-four tries, from which twenty-one goals were kicked, and five were dropped by Wheeler, Purdon, Finlay, and Hunter (two). The following gained tries :—Ross, 18 ; Smith (Capt.), 6 ; Morrison, 5 ; Hunter, R. M. Hartley, Gaussen, and Higgin, 3 each ; J. Purdon and Finlay, 2 each ; Ferrar, J. Irwin, H. Irwin, Houndsel, Campbell, Dalway, Shaw, Berkeley, and Williams, 1 each.

After indulging in a few preliminary Club matches, the 1st XV. entered on this season proper on 1st November, when, after a good match, they defeated Ulster F.C. by a goal and a try to nil. On the 22nd they met their old rivals, Windsor F.C., whom they defeated by a goal to a try. Windsor disputed the try from which the goal was kicked and retired, thus leaving the match in the hands of N.I.F.C.

Continued frost prevented the fixtures with Dublin University, Queen's College and Chester County being kept, and, after a four weeks' rest, the team again took the field against United County Down, the match ending in an easy win for the Club by three tries to nil. The first Saturday of the new year saw a very weak twelve in the field at Dundalk to represent the 1st XV. A good fight was made, and the twelve managed to score a draw.

Manchester visited Ormeau on the 10th, and just succeeded in winning by a try to nil. After this defeat three wins followed in succession. United County Down (twenty) were defeated by two goals and two tries to one goal; Queen's College by a goal and two tries to a goal and one try, and Ulster F.C. by two goals and a try to a try. N.I.F.C. next played at Edinburgh and Glasgow, on February 16 and 17, *v.* Academicals. Edinburgh Academicals won by two tries to one, and Glasgow by two goals and three tries to nil. Immediately on their return home N.I.F.C. again met Windsor, and a very hotly contested match resulted in a draw, each side having gained a try. Defeat was in store on the coming Saturday, when the College reversed the result of the previous match, winning by two tries to nil. At Lurgan the team played a drawn match with County Armagh, and on March 20th brought a successful season to an end, winning the Dundalk return match by a goal and two tries to nil.

A. H. Hartley (26 votes), and J. S. Ferguson and W. J. Heron (12 each), receive 1st XV. caps for good play during the season, and J. F. Ross (29 votes), and R. S. Smith (20 votes), the 2nd XV. caps.

NORTH WEXFORD FOOTBALL CLUB.

Club Ground—Gorey.   *Colours*—Red and Black.
President—Major-General J. C. Guise, C.B., V.C.
Captain—J. H. Brett.
Hon. Secretary—Charles Donaldson, Gorey, Co. Wexford.
Hon. Treasurer—James A. Scott.
Committee—W. H. Jones, Hon. G. Stopford, D. Harvey, P. C. Pounden.

This Club, the first of its kind in the county, was only founded in January, 1880, which accounts for the small number of matches played (2), and the want of success in both. However, the excellent material of which it is composed, and the enthusiasm with which the game was kept up this year, hold forth good prospect for next season, when we hope to see several Clubs established in the neighbourhood of Gorey.

[It is to be hoped that next season will see two or three Clubs in the County Wexford. The team that visited Dublin had some promising players, but, on the whole, will require a good amount of practice. The fifteen did not turn out well in the matter of uniform, hardly two being dressed alike. However, next season we will look for great improvements.—EDITOR.]

ORDNANCE SURVEY FOOTBALL CLUB.

Club Ground—Phœnix Park.   *Colours*—Red and White.
Captain—James Creegan.
Hon. Secretary—P. Perdisatt, Ordnance Survey Office, Phœnix Park, Dublin.
Hon. Treasurer—Thomas Farrell.
Committee—M. W. Gavin, C. Seabrooke, Thomas McKay.

The above Club played eleven matches, winning seven and losing four. Seven matches fell through, four owing to frost and wet weather, and three to opponents being unable to raise a team.

The play during the first half of the season was remarkably good, but, owing to the nature of the survey work, the Club cannot at all times depend on their men, who are invariably in the country when much needed for football.

There are always good men in connection with this Club, and in times past gave many a hard tussle to older Clubs.

The Ordnance Survey is noted for their prominence in athletic circles, and, in order to encourage sport of all descriptions, have on the premises a Gymnasium, and a Cricket, Football and Athletic Club, at present in good working order.

Encouraged by their success in the past, the Committee are determined to organise a strong, formidable team for the coming season.

PHŒNIX FOOTBALL CLUB.

Club Ground—Phœnix Park.   *Colours*—Scarlet and Amber.
Captain—D. M. Lehane.
Hon. Secretary—E. A. M'Carty, 28 Berkeley Road.
Hon. Treasurer—R. Clifton.
Committee—J. M'C. Rooke, H. G. Cook, and R. Bowles.

Founded in 1878-79, this young Club was distinguished as brilliantly successful in every respect in its first season, and has since continued to make ample progress. To have a long record of victories has not been its good fortune during the past season; but if we take as a test the amount of enjoyment afforded to its members in the noble game, the P.F.C. may be accounted amongst the best of the Metropolitan Clubs.

PORTADOWN FOOTBALL CLUB.

Club Ground—The Park.   *Colours*—Blue and White.
Captain—R. Donaldson.
Hon. Secretary—T. J. Collen, Portadown.
Hon. Treasurer—T. J. Collen.
Committee—R. M. Lindsay, S. Heron, T. A. Shellington, C. Stanley, F. O'Hanlon, W. J. Dawson.

This being the first season of the formation of the Club, has only resulted in the game being started properly in the town. Considering that most of the members never played before, or even had any knowledge of the rules, we have got on pretty fairly. We had several fixtures, but owing to the very unfavourable weather we were deprived of the pleasure of playing up to them, and, consequently, the interest that would have been taken in the game by the members has on these grounds been rather dull; but, notwithstanding all this, by the active way the Hon. Secretary acted with the members, and using all influence possible to show them the importance of as much practice as possible, the season has been as successful as could be desired. We hope next season to have a good Club, and able to compete with the leading Clubs of Ulster.

PORTARLINGTON SCHOOL FOOTBALL CLUB.

Club Ground—Portarlington.   *Colours*—Red and Black.
Captain—H. Tabuteau.
Hon. Secretary—W. S. Wybrants, Portarlington School.
Hon. Treasurer—W. S. Wybrants.
Committee—Hallaran, L'Estrange, Roake, Captain and Secretary *ex-officio*.

The football season of 1879-80 proved a most successful one for Portarlington School F.C.

Until Christmas the school was unusually victorious, and defeated every team with which it tried conclusions, except the Phœnix F.C. (which match resulted in a draw). On resuming play after the Christmas vacation the team found itself minus several of its old members, and took the field in so weak a condition that almost everyone predicted nothing but disaster for the "Scarlet and Black" in its opening campaign of 1880. However, though comparatively crippled, the P.S.F.C. once more resumed action, and, although defeated by the Steevens' Hospital (an unusually strong team), the Wanderers 2nd XV., and the D.U.F.C. 2nd XV. scored one more win in the return match against the Phœnix F.C.

On the whole we cannot regard the past season as anything but eminently satisfactory, and we sincerely congratulate Portarlington School on the excellent account which its XV. gave of itself and of the laurels which it won during its arduous campaign of 1879-80.

There is no team that ever goes to Portarlington but comes back with pleasant recollections of the kindness and hospitality of Dr. and Mrs. Wall.—[EDITOR.]

PORTORA ROYAL SCHOOL FOOTBALL CLUB.

Club Ground—Portora.   *Colours*—Gold and Black.
Captain—R. J. Mecredy.
Hon. Secretary—H. Russell Joynt, Portora, Enniskillen.
Hon. Treasurer—R. W. Studdert.

[The Hon. Secretary did not favour me with any report. From the diary it will be seen that the Club only played two matches, being successful in both. It is to be hoped that next season the Gold and Black will be seen oftener in the football field.—EDITOR.]

QUEENSTOWN FOOTBALL CLUB.

Club Ground—Ringmeen.   *Colours*—Red and White.
Captain—T. W. Scogings.
Hon Secretary—T. W. Scogings, Beach, Queenstown.
Hon. Treasurer—T. W. Scogings.

The Queenstown F.C. has been in former years very successful in all matches, and able, until the last two seasons, to send forth a team considered very formidable. Queenstown in 1877 and in former years defeated the famous "Cork F.C." in its full strength, also the "Midleton College F.C.," but during last year it fell away considerably, so much so that its principal players have become members of the "Cork F.C.," and have played in the chief matches during the past season.

QUEEN'S COLLEGE, BELFAST, FOOTBALL CLUB.

Club Ground—College.   *Colours*—Black and Blue.
Captain—J. W. Taylor; *Captain 2nd XV.*—C. Mulholland.
Hon. Secretary and Hon. Treasurer—Augustine Henry, Queen's College, Belfast.
Committee—S. J. Moore, W. Watt, C. Mulholland, R. W. Hughes.

The Committee regret to report that the number of 1st XV. matches was smaller than usual, but in what matches we played the men fairly held their own. The 2nd VX. had a series of interesting matches with the various Clubs in the neighbourhood, in which they were invariably successful. There was a fair amount of practice during the season, and in point of members the Club is in a better condition than it has been for some years.

QUEEN'S COLLEGE, CORK, FOOTBALL CLUB.

Club Ground—College Park.   *Colours*—Scarlet and Black.
Captain—Richard Hartland.
Hon. Secretary—James H. Swanton, Sunmount, St. Luke's, Cork.
Hon. Treasurer—George A. Rountree.
Committee—R. Thompson, E. Byrne, J. O'Callaghan, G. F. Marks, J. Clerke, W. Good, J. Long.   *Vice-Captain*—H. A. Haines.

The season 1879-80, which has just closed, has been the most successful on record in the annals of the Queen's College, Cork F.C., not one goal having been gained against us during the whole season. Notwithstanding that the wet weather, for which the South of Ireland is so noted, has greatly interfered in the way of practice matches, without which even the most celebrated Club must sooner or later become the reverse, yet there have been some which have been as interesting as the regular matches, and which have done much to keep up the interest in Football in the College. One complaint we have to make, and that is, that we are not represented on the Munster Team; but, however, we expect that as the love for the game increases within the College, and our popularity becomes greater, that we soon will have nothing to say on this point.

[There is nothing to prevent the Q.C.C. being represented in the Union. The Hon. Secretary should communicate with the Hon. Sec. of the I.R.F. Union on the subject.—EDITOR.]

QUEEN'S COLLEGE, GALWAY, FOOTBALL CLUB.

Club Ground—Queen's College.   *Colours*—Black and Yellow.
Captain—Thomas Smyth.
Hon. Secretary—Edward Augustus Hackett, Queen's College, Galway.
Hon. Treasurer—Bernard J. Joyce.
Committee—E. Ekine, John King, Robert Abernethy, David V. O'Connell, Captain, Hon. Secretary, and Hon. Treasurer *ex-officio*.

The chief difficulty this Club has to contend with is the scarcity of local Clubs. With the exception of the Grammar School, Galway, there is not a single Club within a radius of 50 miles; and even in the case of those the distance is often doubled on account of the indirectness of railway communication.

Some improvements were carried out on the ground during the season, which considerably enlarge the field.

During the season there were two inside and two outside matches. The former were Medical *versus* Arts, Engineering, and Law, and on the first occasion resulted in a victory for the Medical. The second was a better contest, and the result was a draw.

In both the matches against the Grammar School the College won easily.

RATHMINES SCHOOL FOOTBALL CLUB.

Club Ground—Richmond Hill.   *Colours*—Blue, White, and Blue.
Captain—T. Y. Chambers.
Hon. Secretary—W. K. Johnston, Churchtown Park, Dundrum.
Hon. Treasurer—F. K. Pounder.
Committee—T. Y. Chambers, W. K. Johnston, F. K. Pounder, C. Soady, G. Lewis, W. Moore, John Elliott, E. S. Barnard, H. Moore.

This season has not been so successful in the Football field for Rathmines School as last, owing principally to a number of the First Fifteen being unable to play, from sickness and other causes; however, some very good play has been shown by individual members of the Club, and we shall be sure to hear of them again.

The only School teams the 1st Fifteen played against were Santry School F.C. and Kingstown School F.C.; in the match with the latter Club, Rathmines had entirely the best of it.

The second match of the season was played at Lansdowne, against the Lansdowne 2nd Fifteen, who included seven members of their 1st Fifteen; the last match of the season was also against the same Club, and resulted in a draw in favour of the School.

Caps have been awarded to Chambers (*Captain*), Elliott, Moore, Lewis, and Soady for good play during the season.

ROYAL ACADEMICAL INSTITUTION FOOTBALL CLUB.

Club Ground—R. A. Institution.   *Colours*—Dark Blue.
Captain—C. T. Hagberg Wright.
Hon. Secretary—A. Alexander, R. A. Institution.
Hon. Treasurer—R. Nixon, Esq., M.A., Cantab.
Committee—C. Robb, F. Murray, A. De Wind, W. Harvey.

The Royal Academical Football Club closed its season early in March, which, although fairly successful, has, on the whole, been rather unsatisfactory, owing chiefly to the number of players who have been injured during the season. The Club possesses a very level but badly-drained ground, which has been the scene of many hotly-contested matches. The Institution competed for the School's Challenge Cup, which is presented by the Northern Branch of the Irish Football Union to the Schools of Ulster for annual competition. It is played in ties; the tie between the First and the Methodist College resulted in a victory for the latter—a victory which the R.A.I. may attribute to the indisposition of their Captain and several of their best players. The Institution played the Methodist College twice before, once obtaining the victory, and on the next occasion the match ended in a draw.

The return match against the N.I.F.C. was played under singularly adverse circumstances, the Institution mustering only ten players, while the North turned out in full strength; the ground was also no better than a "ploughed field," and, therefore, the superior weight of the N.I.F.C. had it all their own way. Exactly the same thing occurred in the match *versus* Lauriston, the First Team being almost entirely composed of 2nd Fifteen players. The severe frost prevented several of the return matches from being played, in which the Institution hoped to have retrieved some of their former defeats. Great improvement was made during the season by several of the players, especially by A. Alexander and W. L. Harvey. The finances of the Club have been in a most satisfactory state this year. The Club lost at the commencement of the season an efficient Captain (Douglas J. Calder), and several forwards.

SANTRY SCHOOL FOOTBALL CLUB.

Club Ground—Santry School.   *Colours*—Blue and Black.
Captain—G. W. Clarke.
Hon. Secretary—W. W. Smith, Santry School, Dublin.
Hon. Treasurer—S. Adair.
Committee—G. Clarke, Smith, Stanfield, Redmond, Finch, Parkinson, J. M'Quade, Woods.

The first meeting of the Santry School Football Club took place on Oct. 1st, in the School, at which officers were appointed, a Committee formed, and Rules drawn up. During the season much interest was taken by all the members of the School for the advancement of the Club. This interest, together with a better attendance at the practice matches, gave rise to more matches being played, and a greater average number of victories being obtained than in preceding years. Out of eight well-fought games, the School came off victors in five, only losing two. I may mention that in one of the matches lost by the School, a team of twelve present, with only three past, had to contend with a fifteen consisting of a high number of well-trained past men of the Wesley College. But even with this strong opposition, the School played the game very successfully.

Many matches which were arranged did not come off, owing chiefly to bad weather. I think I may safely say that Santry School will be able to send a strong team to the field next season, and will be at least as successful, if not more successful, than it has been this year. Play this season stopped on the 18th of March.

ST. COLUMBA'S COLLEGE FOOTBALL CLUB.

Club Ground—St. Columba's College.   *Colours*—White, Green, and Red.
Captain—W. F. Ogilvie.
Hon. Secretary—T. S. Hillas, St. Columba's College, Rathfarnham, Co. Dublin.
Hon. Treasurer—T. S. Hillas.
Committee—J. Alcock, C. Fred. Hyde, P. M. Skipworth, A. J. Orr, R. Orpen, Captain and Hon. Secretary *ex-officio*.

On the whole, in spite of drawbacks, we can say that the season has been a successful one. The weather has, indeed, been very unfavourable both from rain and frost. A source of regret is the bad condition and situation of our football ground. The College being situated on the slope of a mountain, it is next to an impossibility to obtain a piece of ground sufficiently large, and at the same time level enough for the game. Suffering from this, our ground becomes additionally heavy after rain, while the water accumulating in the lower parts, make the soil very sloppy and muddy.

Still, this might be rectified, and we have good hopes that it will be, before the commencement of next season. But the advantages are as numerous as the disadvantages; the neighbourhood is delightful, and the air fresh and enjoyable. The accommodation is very good, and everything supplied to the players that can reasonably be expected to make them comfortable and enjoy themselves while up here. This season there has been shown a decided increase in real interest for the game, compared to that shown in preceding years. This is partly on account of the great increase in the number of foreign matches played by the Club. If I remember correctly, we only played four, or at the most, six foreign football matches last season, and only two the season before that. This season we have played ten, and hope to keep up a good average in succeeding seasons. With regard to the team as a whole, much need not be said. They are, certainly, rather light, but make up for it by their unanimity. They all know their powers, and play well together. The forwards pack up closely, and keep steadily on the ball. The full-backs might, perhaps, be a trifle better, but they certainly cannot be accused of as being either wanting in will or in pluck. There must, of course, be always a certain amount of inequality between a school and a town Football Club, the latter having such a wide range from which it may select its members, while the former, even at the best of times, has but a comparatively limited one. This is the case with us.

[Although St. Columba's College may have a limited field from which to pick a Fifteen, it has an advantage in continually playing together, and by arranging matches with the Dublin Clubs, can materially tend to improve the style of play of its members. I think it right to state that the drive to Rathfarnham is most enjoyable, and the hospitality of the Reverend Warden proverbial.—EDITOR.]

ULSTER FOOTBALL CLUB.

Club Ground—Ulster C. C., Ormeau Road. *Colours*—Red and Black.
Captain—J. Henderson.
Hon. Secretary—W. T. Heron, Ballynafeigh, Belfast.
Hon Treasurer—Wm. Jackson.
Committee—Thomas Morgan, R. M. Kennedy, S. M'Cully, D. Hannay, R. W. Hughes, W. J. M'Gowan, J. Johnston.

The third season of the Ulster F. C., just concluded, can scarcely be said to have been so successful as was anticipated from the marked improvement shown during the year following the formation of the Club. This must be attributed partly to the loss of several of its most prominent members, and partly to the formidable rivals with which it has to compete in Belfast, the North of Ireland, Windsor, and Queen's College still proving too strong for the younger Club. The want of good back-play has also been a considerable detriment to success, as the forwards have invariably shown themselves capable of holding their own in the best company; and, indeed, any successes that the Club may have gained were mainly owing to their exertions. Thirty-four matches were arranged for the season, of which twenty-four were brought to an issue, and ten had to be abandoned, owing to frost and other causes. The 1st XV. played ten matches, six of which resulted in defeat, viz.:—N.I.F.C., Windsor F.C., Queen's College F.C.,

N.I.F.C. (R.), Windsor (R.), and Lurgan. It is but fair to state that in the latter match the U.F.C. was only represented by ten members, five of whom belonged to the 2nd Fifteen. Four matches resulted in victories:— Belmont F.C., Mountpottinger F.C., Dundalk F.C., and Belmont (R.) The Second Fifteen played fourteen matches, in seven of which they had to succumb to the opposing team, viz. :—Lauriston F.C., N.I.F.C. (2nd), Queen's College (2nd), Carrickfergus F.C., Armagh F.C., Lauriston (R.), and N.I.F.C. (R.) Four were brought to a successful issue—North Down F.C., Carrickfergus (R.), Portadown and North Down (R.), while three remained drawn—Institution, Ormeau, and Albion. During the season the Club obtained thirty-one tries, from which four goals were kicked, two by Heron, and one each by Henderson and Warden. A goal was also dropped from the field of play by R. Morrow. The tries were obtained by the following :—Heron, 4 ; Henderson and W. Watson, 3 each ; Jackson, Taylor, Johnston, J. Watson, Hunter, M'Cracken, and R. Murrow, 2 each ; Murray, Monteath, Thompson, Smith, Hastings, White, and Waddel, 1 each.

UNITED HOSPITALS FOOTBALL CLUB.

Captain—J. L. Cuppaidge.
Hon. Secretary—J. L. Cuppaidge, 66 Morehampton Road, Co. Dublin.

The season 1879-80 has not been marked by any signal success for the United Hospitals team ; but we hope that in a year or two, when the Club is better organized than it is at present, the sons of Æsculapius will do more than hold their own against the Clubs with which they compete. This is only the second year in which the above Club has been in existence, and although we do not advocate running to the Sassenachs for hints on every little subject, if it followed the example of the London Hospitals, and instituted a challenge cup to be competed for by all the Hospitals, we think it would be for the advantage of all players, by giving them more scope for matches, and a desire for becoming more proficient in the game. We hope that this suggestion will be taken up warmly by those who will have the management of the Club in the coming season.

The first match of the season took place on Nov. 8, '79, *versus* County Dublin, and resulted in favour of the County by one goal to nil. This match has now become annual ; the proceeds (from gate money) being given in aid of the Dublin Hospital Sunday Fund. In the presence of a large assembly of spectators, Cuppaidge kicked off for the Medicals, the ball being immediately returned by Bagot, the County Captain. Some heavy scrummaging now took place in neutral territory, but the County team proving the stronger, drove the ball behind the Medical goal-line, but were unable to touch it down. Kidd now dropped out, and the Doctors had a runaway rush up to their opponents' goal, where Whitestone dropped the ball as we thought over the cross-bar, but the umpire decided otherwise. Nothing of note occurred till after half-time, when A. Cronyn, after a splendid run in his old form, grounded the ball behind the Medical posts. The try was converted into a goal by Downing. The dribbling on the County side was worthy of mention.

The second match was played *versus* the Wanderers. In this the Medical

Captain preferring to kick off, played the first half of the match facing a bright sun, which greatly diminished his chance of success. During this time the Wanderers scored two tries, neither of which were converted into goals, and one goal dropped out of a scrummage. During the second half of the game, the Medicals putting all their energy together, gained a goal, which was also dropped out of a scrummage, but were unable to gain any further advantage.

The third match was a return *versus* the Wanderers, which resulted in a victory for the Medicals by one try to nil. The Hospital team losing the toss, were compelled to play facing a strong sun, but even that did not dispirit them, they fought hard, as they always have been known to do, so as to avert all chance of defeat. The play during this time was of the evenest description, neither sides gaining even a single point. In the second half-time the ball wandered after a series of assaults and repulses from one goal to the other, when, finally, Scriven making a rush, grounded the ball behind the Wanderers' goal-line. The kick at goal, however, proved a failure. Soon after the ball had again been set in motion, "No Side" was called, which ended the season for the Hospital team.

In addition to the above, several of the Hospitals were able to produce very good teams; and the following interesting matches were played:—

Adelaide *v.* City of Dublin. The latter scoring two goals, the former one.

Meath *v.* City of Dublin. The former winning by one try to nil.

The Meath also played the Wanderers, the latter winning by one goal and one try to nil.

WANDERERS FOOTBALL CLUB.

Club Ground—Lansdowne Road.
Colours—Blue, Black, and White Jersey and Stockings and Blue Knickerbockers.
Captain—F. Schute.
Hon. Secretary—Walter Kelly, Bank of Ireland, Dublin.
Hon. Treasurer—W. A. Wallis, 33 Bachelor's Walk, Dublin.
Committee—A. E. Darley, W. J. Goulding, G. Manders, F. W. Moore, R. M. Peter, H. F. Spunner.
Representatives on Irish Rugby Football Union—F. Kennedy, R. M. Peter, F. Schute.

The season 1879-80 of the Wanderers F.C. should remain a memorable one in their annals, the activity shown in starting the Dublin football season being fully maintained to its close. It will be remembered as a most successful season in the large number of "wins" the Club is credited with out of its list of engagements—probably the longest list, by the way, on the records of any Irish Club, not even omitting those of the spirited North of Ireland F.C., whose list of fixtures is always a very full one. The actual number of matches arranged for the 1st and 2nd XV.'s to those played were reduced by frost principally, and also other unavoidable causes, from 53 to 33; and a score of 24 wins and 3 draws to 6 losses shows considerably merit, especially when it is considered that the Wanderers play regularly two matches every Saturday, whether the services of their most reliable players are available or not. For the first time in their history, the W.F.C.

instituted the presenting of caps (two to each XV.) for merit shown in the previous season, and these were voted to

1st XV.—F. Schute, F. Kennedy. 2nd XV.—C. C. Byrne, H. Stoker.

The following members were this season elevated to the title of International players :—A. J. Forrest, F. Kennedy, and W. A. Wallis, all of whom did credit to the Club and Ireland by their consistent and conspicuously good play, either in the English or Scotch matches.

After playing for several years on the Clyde Road ground, the Wanderers were obliged to shift from their quarters after Christmas (owing to the field being required for tillage purposes), but the loss was quite counterbalanced by their obtaining a superior ground in the enclosure of the I.C.A.C. at Lansdowne Road; and they played the second half of the season side by side with the Lansdowne F.C. in complete harmony.

The season commenced on September 27th with a practice game (in which no fewer than 55 players took part), and foreign matches on October 10th. The next interesting fixtures were naturally those embraced in the Scotch tour, together with the Manchester match, and locally those with United Hospitals and Dublin University. With the tour may also be included the provincial match, Leinster *v.* Ulster, played on Friday, Nov. 28, '79, at Ormeau, as no fewer than ten Wanderers were included in the Leinster XV., and they won the match somewhat easily. On the following day the first match of their tour, that against the Windsor F.C. (Belfast), was only lost, after a most stubborn fight, by a try; and when it is considered that the previous Saturday the Windsor had made a draw with the N.I.F.C., and that on this tour the Wanderers were not obviously playing their usual, or by any means strongest team, they may fairly congratulate themselves on the result. They had bad luck as regards weather for the following matches, arranged with the famous Glasgow Academicals and Edinburgh Acads. Football Clubs in Scotland, the frost setting in with a fierceness, immediately on the team's arrival in Edinburgh, which put any playing out of the question, skating, on the contrary, being the order of the day. These Scotch Clubs promise a speedy return visit, and if we may indulge in the hope that they will visit us during the forthcoming season, and that the Wanderers will successfully prosecute their intended tour to the North of England, any disappointment the last year's Scotch tour raised will be speedily forgotten, and such "palmy" tours as that of '78-'79 to Cork and Limerick will stand out in bright relief. Against the Manchester F.C., at Lansdowne Road, on Jan. 12th, the game was lost by indifferent back-play, the "Sassenachs" agreeing they had a tough nut to crack forward; indeed, speaking generally, in their forward play consisted the main strength of the Wanderers last season.

The matches were respectively won and lost and drawn with United Hospitals and Dublin University, the last game especially with the 'Varsity causing a great deal of speculation and excitement in football circles throughout Ireland; it ended in a complete draw.

Drop-kicking and place-kicking competitions for cups wound up the season, A. J. Forrest securing the prize for the former, while E. G. Newell gained the latter, after a close struggle with D. F. Moore.

WESLEY COLLEGE FOOTBALL CLUB.

Club Ground—Donnybrook.   *Colours*—Blue, with Red Victoria Cross.
Captain—Louis M'Intosh.
Hon. Secretary—Thomas Robert Leonard, Wesley College, Dublin.
Hon. Treasurer—A. Andrews.
Committee—L. M'Intosh, A. Andrews, H. Fitzgerald, R. Fitzgerald, H. F. Kingston, W. A. Storey.

This Club played very few matches this season. Against Lansdowne 1st XV., at the opening of the season, they played in fine form, pressing their opponents very closely. Their "packing" here was really excellent, and was highly spoken of by the Lansdowne Captain. Santry and Portarlington Past were next defeated; but after this the Secretary began to experience great difficulty in getting the best men together, and so deemed it prudent to put off many important matches.

The 2nd XV. won both matches played, but the disbanding of the 1st necessitated their retiring. The Juniors, only, played through the whole season. They lost one match out of seven.

Though no public matches were played by the Senior Club for the last half of the season, practice was well kept up, and the material remaining over for next year was never more promising.

YORK ROAD, BELFAST, FOOTBALL CLUB.

Club Ground—Seapark.   *Colours*—Dark Blue.
Captain—John M'Dowell.
Hon. Secretary—George Wood, Belfast and Northern Counties Railway.
Hon. Treasurer—George Wood.
Committee—T. Hopkirk, H. Jackson, H. Stewart, A. Morton, H. Jamieson, and W. Thompson.

Started this season by a few in connection with the Northern Counties Railway, it soon had a roll-call of upwards of thirty members; and as they were nearly all new to the practical part of the game, it was deemed advisable not to enter into many matches, but confine ourselves principally to practice. The few matches, however, in which we did engage were satisfactory, as can be seen from our matches against Carrick, that although we did not win in either case, yet we reduced their majority of 2 goals and 1 try, in the first case, to 1 try in the second or return match, although they had a much stronger team in the latter than they had in the first.

We hope next season to engage in a large number of matches, and wish your *Annual* every success, as it will supply an admitted want.

ARMAGH ROYAL SCHOOL FOOTBALL CLUB.

Matches played, 8—lost, 5; won, 3; drawn, 0. Goals scored, 3; Tries, 4. Goals lost, 5; Tries, 7.

1879.
Oct. 25, at Armagh—v. Armagh F.C. Lost by 1 goal and 1 try to nil.
Nov. 12, at Belfast—v. N.I.F.C. 2nd XV. Lost by 1 goal and 3 tries to nil.
  „ 28, at Armagh—v. D.U.F.C. 2nd XV. Lost by 2 goals and 2 tries to nil.
Dec. 21, at Lansdowne Road—v. Lansdowne F.C. Won by 2 goals and 1 try to nil.

1880.
Feb. 11, at Armagh—v. Armagh F.C. (R). Lost by 1 try to nil.
  „ 28, at Armagh—v. N.I.F.C. 2nd XV. (R). Lost by 1 goal to 1 try.
Mar. 12, at Armagh—v. Londonderry Academical Institution. Won by 1 goal and 1 try to nil.
  „ 20, at Armagh—v. Methodist College, Belfast. Won by 1 try to nil.

CLANWILLIAM (TIPPERARY) FOOTBALL CLUB.

Matches played, 4—lost, 0; won, 3; drawn, 1. Goals scored, 2; Tries, 3. Goals lost, 0; Tries, 0.

1879.
Oct. 29, at Tipperary—v. 1/15th Regiment. Won 2 tries to nil.
Nov. 12, at Tipperary—v. 1/15th Regiment. Won 1 goal and 1 try to nil.

1880.
Jan. 7, at Limerick—v. Limerick F.C. Won 1 goal to nil.
Mar. 17, at Tipperary—v. 1/15th Regiment. Drawn; no score.

CLANWILLIAM JUNIOR FOOTBALL CLUB.

Matches played, 4—lost, 1; won, 2; drawn, 1. Goals scored, 0; Tries, 10. Goals lost, 0; Tries, 5.

1879.
Dec. 2, at Tipperary—v. Drummers 1/15th Regiment. Lost 3 tries to 2.

1880.
Feb. 14, at Tipperary—v. Drummers 1/15th Regiment. Won 2 tries to nil.
  „ 24, at The Abbey, Tipperary—v. Abbey Junior F.C. Won 5 tries to 1.
  „ 28, at The Abbey, Tipperary—v. Abbey Junior F.C. Drawn; 1 try each.

CLONTARF FOOTBALL CLUB.
1st XV.

Matches played, 13—lost, 6; won, 5; drawn, 2. Goals scored, 5; Tries, 15. Goals lost, 8; Tries, 9.

1879.
Oct. 4, at Clontarf—v. Kingstown F.C. Drawn.
  „ 18, at Phœnix Ground—v. Phœnix. Lost.
  „ 25, at Clontarf—v. West End F.C. Won.

DIARY OF MATCHES PLAYED DURING THE PAST SEASON.

ALBION FOOTBALL CLUB.

Matches played, 9—lost, 4; won, 4; drawn, 1. Goals scored, 5; Tries, 15. Goals lost, 4; Tries, 9.

1879.
Nov. 15, at College Square—v. R. A. Institution. Won by 2 tries; each side kicked a goal.
,, 22, at Belmont—v. Belmont 2nd XV. Won by 3 goals and 6 tries to nil.
,, 29, at Prospect—v. Ulster 2nd XV. Drawn; each side obtained a try.
Dec. at Lurgan—v. Lurgan. Lost by 4 tries.

1880.
Jan. 1, at Ormeau—v. North of Ireland 2nd XV. Lost by 1 goal and 1 try.
,, 17, at Rugby Road—v. Ormeau. Won by 1 goal and 5 tries.
,, 24, at Windsor Park—v. Methodist College. Won by 1 try.
Feb. 11, at Ormeau—v. North of Ireland 2nd XV. (R.) Lost by 1 goal and 3 tries.
,, 21, at Carrickfergus—v. Carrick. Lost by 1 goal.

ARMAGH FOOTBALL CLUB.

Matches played, 12—lost, 2; won, 6; drawn, 3; one unfinished. Goals scored, 9; Tries, 12. Goals lost, 3 (one disputed); Tries, 1.

1879.
Oct. 22, at The Mall—v. Armagh Royal School. Won by a goal and a try to nil.
Nov. 1, at The Mall—v. North of Ireland 2nd XV. Drawn.
,, 8, at Dundalk—v. Dundalk. Unfinished.
,, 15, at The Mall—v. Windsor 2nd XV. Won by a goal to nil.
,, 22, at Lurgan—v. Lurgan. Lost by 2 goals (one disputed) and a try to nil.
,, 29, at The Mall—v. Dublin University 2nd XV. Drawn.

1880.
Jan. 28, at The Mall—v. Drogheda. Won by 7 goals and 6 tries to nil.
,, 29, at Portadown—v. Portadown. Lost by a goal and a try to nil.
,, 31, at Belfast—v. Ulster F.C. 2nd XV. Won by 2 tries to nil.
Feb. 7, at The Mall—v. Lurgan. Won by a try to nil.
,, 11, at The Mall—v. Royal School. Won by a try to nil.
Mar. 13, at Lurgan—v. North of Ireland. Drawn.

Nov. 1, at Clyde Road—v. Wanderers F.C. Drawn.
,, 15, at Clontarf—v. M.A.F.C. Won.
,, 22, at Hospital Ground—v. Steevens' Hospital F.C. Won.
,, 29, at Lansdowne Road—v. Lansdowne. Lost.
1880.
Jan. 10, at Clontarf—v. Phœnix F.C. Won.
,, 31, at Clontarf—v. Ledwich Medical School. Lost.
Feb. 7, at Clontarf—v. Kingstown F.C. Lost.
,, 14, at Clontarf—v. Wanderers. Lost.
,, 21, at Clontarf—v. Santry School. Won.
Mar. 6, at Clontarf—v. Lansdowne F.C. Lost.

CLONTARF FOOTBALL CLUB.
2ND XV.

Matches played, 12—lost, 6; won, 5; drawn, 1. Goals scored, 9; Tries, 6. Goals lost, 14; Tries, 1.

1879.
Nov. 1, at Clontarf—v. Hibernian. Won by 1 try.
,, 8, at Clontarf—v. Santry School. Won by 2 goals.
,, 15, at Donnybrook—v. Wesley College. Lost by 2 goals.
,, 22, at Kingstown—v. Kingstown School. Lost by 4 goals.
,, 29, at Rathfarnham—v. St. Columba's College. Won by 1 try.
Dec. 6, at Clontarf—v. Phœnix. Prevented by frost.
,, 13, at Phœnix Park—v. Survey 1st XV. Agreed that it should not be called a match.
,, 20, at Clontarf—v. Kingstown. Lost by 5 goals.
,, 27, at Clontarf—v. Wanderers. Lost by 1 goal and 1 try.
1880.
Jan. 3, at Phœnix Park—v. Hibernian. Won by 1 goal.
,, 10, at Phœnix Park—v. Phœnix. Phœnix did not turn up.
,, 17, at Clontarf—v. Survey. Survey did not turn up.
,, 31, at Rathfarnham—v. St. Columba's College. Won by 1 goal.
Feb. 7, at Kingstown—v. Kingstown. Not played.
,, 14, at Lansdowne Road—v. Wanderers. Lost by 3 goals.
Mar. 13, at Clontarf—v. Lansdowne. Drawn.
,, 28, at Clontarf—v. King's Hospital. Won by 4 goals and 4 tries.

CORK FOOTBALL CLUB.

Matches played, 16—lost, 8; won, 8. Goals scored, 8; Tries, 26. Goals lost, 10; Tries, 17.

1879.
Oct. 25, at Cork Park—v. "Bulldogs." Lost by 1 goal and 2 tries.
,, 29, at Cork Park—v. "Bulldogs." Lost by 3 tries.
Nov. 14, at Cork Park—v. Queen's College. Won by 2 tries.
,, 17, at Cork Park—v. Goulding's Munster Team. Lost by 1 goal and 1 try.

Nov. 26, at Cork Park—v. Queen's College. Lost by 1 goal.
„ 29, at Cork Park—v. Midleton College. Won by 4 tries.
Dec. 18, at Cork Park—v. 7th Fusiliers. Won by 1 goal and 3 tries.
„ 26, at Cork Park—v. Phœnix F.C. Won by 1 try.
1880.
Jan. 6, at Limerick—v. Limerick F.C. Won by 1 goal and 4 tries.
„ 10, at Cork Park—v. Blackrock F.C. Lost by 1 goal.
Feb. 9, at Cork Park—v. Queen's College. Lost by 1 goal and 4 tries.
„ 25, at Cork Park—v. Cork Bankers. Won by 1 goal.
„ 27, at Cork Park—v. Blackrock F.C. Won by 2 goals.
Mar. 5, at Cork Park—v. Knight's School P. and P. Lost by 1 goal.
„ 10, at Cork Park—v. Cork Bankers. Won by 1 try.
„ 12, at Cork Park—v. Knight's School P. and P. Lost by 1 goal and 2 tries.

CUSACK'S ACADEMY FOOTBALL CLUB.

Matches played, 12—lost, 4; won, 6; drawn, 2. Goals scored, 5; Tries, 11. Goals lost, 4; Tries, 3.

1879.
Nov. 1, at Phœnix Park—v. The Field. Won by 2 tries to nil.
„ 8, at Belvidere Ground—v. Belvidere. Drawn.
„ 12, at Sandymount—v. Catholic University. Won by 1 goal and 3 tries to nil.
„ 15, at Phœnix Park—v. Hibernian. Lost by 1 goal to nil.
„ 20, at Clontarf—v. Belvidere. Won by 2 tries to nil.
„ 24, at Phœnix Park—v. Ephemerals. Won by 3 tries to nil.
„ 27, at Phœnix Park—v. Butterflies. Won by 2 goals to nil.
Dec. 6, at Phœnix Park—v. Ordnance Survey. Lost by 1 goal to nil.
1880.
Feb. 7, at Phœnix Park—v. Hibernian. Lost by 1 try to nil.
„ 21, at Kingstown—v. Kingstown School. Lost by 2 goals and 2 tries to nil.
„ 28, at Phœnix Park—v. Ordnance Survey. Won by 1 goal and 1 try to nil.
Mar. 20, at Phœnix Park—v. Kingstown School. Drawn; 1 goal each.

DUBLIN UNIVERSITY FOOTBALL CLUB.

1st XV.

Matches played, 4—won, 3; drawn, 1. Goals scored, 5.
1879.
Nov. 22, at College Park—v. Wanderers. Won by 2 goals to nil.
1880.
Jan. 17, at College Park—v. Kingstown. Won by 1 goal to nil.
Feb. 28, at College Park—v. Kingstown. Won by 2 goals to nil.
Mar. 13, at Lansdowne Road—v. Wanderers. Drawn.

DUBLIN UNIVERSITY FOOTBALL CLUB.
2ND XV.

Matches played, 12—won, 10; drawn, 2. Goals scored, 20; Tries, 18. Goals lost, 1; Tries, 1.

1879.
Nov. 22, at Clyde Road—v. Wanderers 2nd XV. Won by 1 goal and 1 try to nil.
  " 26, at College Park—v. Wesley College. Won by 3 goals and 2 tries to nil.
  " 28, at Armagh—v. Armagh Royal School. Won by 2 goals and 2 tries to nil.
  " 29, at Armagh—v. Armagh Town. Drawn.

1880.
Jan. 29, at Lansdowne Road—v. Lansdowne Road. Drawn.
Feb. 5, at Kingstown—v. Kingstown School. Won by 1 try and disputed goal.
  " 14, at Glenageary—v. Kingstown Club 2nd XV. Won by 2 goals and 1 try to 1 try.
  " 21, at College Park—v. Lansdowne Road. Won by 2 goals and 2 tries to nil.
  " 26, at Kingstown—v. Kingstown School. Won by 1 goal and 2 tries to nil.
  " 28, at Portarlington—v. Arlington House. Won by 3 goals and 3 tries to 1 goal.
Mar. 6, at College Park—v. Kingstown Club 2nd XV. Won by 1 goal to nil.
  " 13, at Lansdowne Road—v. Wanderers 2nd XV. Won by 5 goals and 4 tries to nil.

DUNDALK FOOTBALL CLUB.

Matches played, 11—lost, 3; won, 4; drawn, 4. Goals scored, 7; Tries, 14. Goals lost, 3; Tries, 8.

1879.
Nov. 1, at Dundalk—v. Dundalk Educational Institution F.C. Won by 4 goals and 2 tries to nil.
  " 8, at Dundalk—v. Armagh. Won by 5 tries (2 disputed) to nil.
  " 11, at Dundalk—v. Drogheda. Won by 2 tries to nil.
  " 15, at Dublin (Clyde Road)—v. Wanderers 1st XV. Drawn.
  " 22, at Dundalk—v. Kingstown 1st XV. Lost by 1 goal and 2 tries to nil.
Dec. 27, at Dundalk—v. Ulster 1st XV. Lost by 1 goal and 4 tries to nil.

1880.
Jan. 1, at Dundalk—v. North of Ireland 1st XV. Drawn.
  " 31, at Dundalk—v. Lansdowne 1st XV. Drawn.
Feb. 6, at Drogheda—v. Drogheda. Won by 3 goals and 5 tries to nil.
  " 20, at Dundalk—v. Dundalk Educational Institution. Drawn.
Mar. 20, at Belfast—v. North of Ireland 1st XV. Lost by 1 goal and 2 tries to nil.

DUNGANNON ROYAL SCHOOL FOOTBALL CLUB.

Matches played, 1—lost, 0 ; won, 1 ; drawn, 0. Goals scored, 1 ; Tries, 0.
Goals lost, 0 ; Tries, 1.

Mar. , at Dungannon—v. Foyle College. Won by 1 goal and 1 try to nil.

GALWAY GRAMMAR SCHOOL FOOTBALL CLUB.

Matches played, 5 ; lost, 3 ; won, 1 ; drawn, 1. Goals scored, 2 ; tries, 1.
Goals lost, 4 ; tries, 4.

1879.
Nov. 25, at Ballinasloe—v. Ballinasloe F.C. School won by 1 goal and 1 try.

1880.
Mar. 10, at School Ground—v. Queen's College, Galway. Queen's College won by 1 goal and 1 try.
,, 15, at School Ground—v. Queen's College, Galway. Queen's College won by 1 goal and 2 tries.
,, 17, at School Ground—v. Ranelagh, Athlone. A draw in favour of the Ranelagh F.C.
April 8, at School Ground—v. "Past." "Past" won by 1 goal.

HIBERNIAN FOOTBALL CLUB.
1st XV.

Matches played, 10—lost, 1 ; won, 7 ; drawn, 2. Goals scored, 5 ; Tries, 6.
Goals lost, 1 ; Tries, 2.

1879.
Oct. 25, at Fifteen Acres—v. Wanderer's 2nd XV. Lost by 1 goal and 2 tries to 1 try.
Nov. 8, at Fifteen Acres—v. King's Hospital. Drawn.
,, 15, at Fifteen Acres—v. Cusack's Academy. Won by 1 goal to nil.
,, 29, at Fifteen Acres—v. Steevens' Hospital. Won by 1 try to nil.

1880.
Jan. 17, at Nine Acres—v. Phœnix. Drawn.
,, 31, at Fifteen Acres—v. Surrey. Won by 2 tries to nil.
Feb. 7, at Fifteen Acres—v. Cusack's Academy. Won by 1 try to nil.
,, 14, at Fifteen Acres—v. Ledwich School of Medicine. Won by 1 goal and 1 try to nil.
Mar. 13, at Fifteen Acres—v. Eblana. Won by 1 goal to nil.
,, 27, at Fifteen Acres—v. Eblana. Won by 2 goals to nil.

2nd XV.
Nov. 1, at Clontarf—v. Clontarf. Lost by 1 try.
Jan. 3, at Fifteen Acres—v. Clontarf. Lost by 1 goal.

KING'S HOSPITAL FOOTBALL CLUB.
1st XV.

Matches played, 9—lost, 3 ; won, 5 ; drawn, 1. Goals scored, 8 ; Tries, 8.
Goals lost, 7 ; Tries, 9.

1879.
Oct. 4, at King's Hospital—v. Mountjoy. Won by 4 goals and 4 tries.
,, 18, at Lansdowne Road—v. Lansdowne 2nd XV. Lost by 1 goal and 3 tries.
Nov. 1, at Phœnix Park—v. Survey. Won by 1 goal.
,, 8, at Phœnix Park—v. Hibernian. Draw.

1880.
Feb. 14, at Phœnix Park—v. Survey (return). Won by 1 goal and 2 tries.
Mar. 28, at Clontarf—v. Clontarf 2nd XV. Lost by 5 goals and 3 tries.
1879.   2ND XV.
Oct. 25, at King's Hospital—v. Kingstown Sch. 2nd XV. Won by 1 goal
    and 2 tries to 1 goal.
Nov. 15, at King's Hospital—v. Kingstown 3rd XV. Won by 1 goal.
1880.
Jan.   at Kingstown—v. Kingstown Sch. 2nd XV. Lost by 3 tries.

KINGSTOWN FOOTBALL CLUB.
1ST XV.

Matches played, 7—lost, 3; won, 4; drawn, 0. Goals scored, 5; tries, 9.
    Goals lost, 4; Tries, 1.

    Kingstown—v. Phœnix. Won.
    Dundalk—v. Dundalk. Won.
    College Park—v. D.U.F.C. Lost.
    Glenageary—v. Wanderers. Lost.
    Clontarf—v. Clontarf. Won.
    College Park—v. D.U.F.C. Lost.
    Phœnix Park—v. Phœnix. Won.

2ND XV.

Matches played, 7—lost, 4; won, 3; drawn, 0. Goals scored, 5; tries, 8.
    Goals lost, 4; Tries, 3.

    Kingstown—v. Lansdowne 2nd XV. Won.
    Kingstown—v. Military Academies. Won.
    Kingstown—v. D.U.F.C. 2nd XV. Lost.
    Kingstown—v. Wanderers 2nd XV. Lost.
    Kingstown—v. Phœnix 2nd XV. Won.
    College Park—v. D.U.F.C. 2nd XV. Lost.
    Lansdowne Road—v. Wanderers 2nd XV. Lost.

KINGSTOWN SCHOOL FOOTBALL CLUB.

Matches played, 20—lost, 6; won, 12; drawn, 2. Goals scored, 26; Tries, 25.
1879.   Goals lost, 12; Tries, 13.
Oct. 25, at Santry—1st XV. v. Santry School 1st XV. Lost by 2 tries.
  ,, 25, at K.H. Ground—2nd XV. v. K. Hospital 2nd XV. Lost by 2
    goals 3 tries to 1 goal.
  ,, 10, at York Road—2nd XV. v. Corrig Sch. 2nd XV. Won by 6 goals
    5 tries to nil.
  ,, 28, at York Road—2nd XV. v. Santry 2nd XV. Won by 1 goal 4 tries
    (1 disputed) to nil.
Nov. 1, at Portarlington—1st XV. v. Portarlington School 1st XV. Lost
    4 goals 3 tries.
  ,, 4, at York Road—2nd XV. v. Wesley College 2nd XV. Won by 5
    goals 3 tries to nil.
  ,, 5, at York Road—1st XV. v. Merrion Rovers. Won by 1 goal 1 try
    to 1 try.
  ,, 11, at York Road—2nd XV. v. Rathmines School 2nd XV. Won by
    2 goals 1 try to nil.

Nov. 15, at York Road—1st XV. v. Wanderers' 2nd XV. Lost by 2 goals 1 try to nil.
 „   22, at York Road—1st XV. v. Clontarf 2nd XV. Won by 4 goals to nil.

1880.
Jan. 31, at York Road—2nd XV. v. King's Hospital 2nd XV. Won by 3 tries to nil.
Feb. 5, at York Road—1st XV. v. D.U.F.C. 2nd XV. Lost by 1 goal (off disputed try) and 1 try to nil.
Feb. 7, at York Road—1st XV. v. Lansdowne 2nd XV. Won by 2 tries to nil.
 „   11, at York Road—2nd XV. v. Williamstown F.C. Won by 1 goal to nil.
 „   18, at York Road—1st XV. v. Rathmines School 1st XV. Won by 1 try to nil.
 „   21, at York Road—1st XV. v. Cusack's Academy. Won by 2 goals 2 tries (1 disputed try) to nil.
 „   26, at York Road—1st XV. v. D.U.F.C. 2nd XV. Lost by 1 goal 2 tries to nil.
Mar. 3, at Lansdowne Road—1st XV. v. Lansdowne 2nd XV. Draw; 1 goal to 1 goal.
 „   8, at Rathmines—2nd XV. v. Rathmines School 2nd XV. Won by 2 goals 1 try to nil.
 „   20, at Phœnix Park—1st XV. v. Cusack's Academy. Draw; 1 goal to 1 goal.

KNIGHT'S SCHOOL FOOTBALL CLUB, CO. CORK.

Matches played, 2—lost, 0; won, 2; drawn, 0. Goals scored, 1; Tries, 2. Goals lost, 0; Tries, 1.

Cork Park—v. Cork F.C. Won by 1 goal and 1 try to 1 try.
Cork Park—v. Cork F.C. Won by 1 try.

LANSDOWNE FOOTBALL CLUB.

Matches played, 14—lost, 5; won, 6; drawn, 3. Goals scored, 5; Tries, 19 Goals lost, 10; Tries, 7.

1879.   1st XV.
Oct. 29, at Lansdowne Road—v. Nomads 1st XV. Won by 1 goal and tries to nil.
Nov. 15, at Lansdowne Road—v. Wesley College 1st XV. Won by 2 tries to a disputed try.
 „   22, at Phœnix Park—v. Phœnix 1st XV. Drawn.
 „   29, at Lansdowne Road—v. Clontarf 1st XV. Won by 1 goal and tries to nil.
Dec. 18, at Lansdowne Road—v. Armagh Royal School P. & P. XV. Lo by 2 goals and 1 try to nil.

1880.
Jan. 3, at Lansdowne Road—v. Wanderers 1st XV. Lost by 1 goal and tries to 1 goal.
 „   29, at Lansdowne Road—v. Dublin University 2nd XV. Drawn.
 „   31, at Dundalk—v. Dundalk 1st XV. Drawn.

Feb. 12, at Lansdowne Road—v. Steevens' Hospital XV. Won by 1 goal and 7 tries to nil.
,, 14, at Lansdowne Road—v. Phœnix 1st XV. (return). Won by 2 tries to nil.
,, 19, at Lansdowne Road—v. Nomads 1st XV. (return). Lost by 1 goal and 1 try to 1 try.
,, 21, at College Park—v. Dublin University 2nd XV. (return). Lost by 2 goals and 2 tries to nil.
Mar. 4, at Lansdowne Road—v. Armagh R. S. P. & P. XV. (return). Lost by 3 goals to nil.
,, 6, at Clontarf—v. Clontarf 1st XV. (return). Won by 1 goal and 2 tries to 1 goal.

2ND XV.

Matches played, 19—lost, 8; won, 9; drawn, 2. Goals scored, 14; Tries, 29. Goals lost, 15; Tries, 14.

1879.
Oct. 18, at Lansdowne Road—v. King's Hospital 1st XV. Won by 1 goal and 4 tries to nil.
Nov. 1, at Lansdowne Road—v. Rathmines School 1st XV. Won by 2 goals and 3 tries to nil.
,, 8, at Portarlington—v. Portarlington School 1st XV. Lost by 3 goals and 1 try to nil.
,, 15, at Kingstown—v. Kingstown 2nd XV. Lost by 1 goal and 3 tries to nil.
,, 19, at Lansdowne Road—v. Military Academies XV. Lost by 2 goals and 3 tries to a try.
,, 26, at Lansdowne Road—v. Merrion Rovers. Lost by 2 goals to nil.

1880.
Jan. 3, at Lansdowne Road—v. Wanderers 2nd XV. Lost by 3 goals and 3 tries to nil.
,, 7, at Lansdowne Road—v. Clontarf 2nd XV. Won by 1 try to nil.
,, 10, at Lansdowne Road—v. Monkstown XV. Won by 2 goals and 2 tries to nil.
Feb. 7, at Kingstown—v. Kingstown School 1st XV. Lost by 2 tries to nil.
,, 11, at Lansdowne Road—v. Military Academies XV. (return). Won by 1 goal and 2 tries to nil.
,, 18, at Rathfarnham—v. St. Columba College 1st XV. Lost by 2 tries to nil.
,, 21, at Gorey—v. North Wexford. Won by 1 goal and 7 tries to nil.
,, 28, at Lansdowne Road—v. Wanderers 2nd XV. (return). Lost by 2 goals to nil.
Mar. 3, at Lansdowne Road—v. Kingstown School 1st XV. (return). Drawn; each side obtained a goal.
,, 16, at Lansdowne Road—v. Monkstown XV. (return). Won by 2 goals and 4 tries to nil.
,, 20, at Lansdowne Road—v. North Wexford (return). Won by 3 goals and 3 tries to nil.
,, 24, at Lansdowne Road—v. Phœnix 2nd XV. Won by 2 tries to nil.
,, 27, at Lansdowne Road—v. Rathmines School 1st XV. (return). Drawn; each side obtained a goal.

LAURISTON FOOTBALL CLUB.

Matches played, 8—lost, 3 ; won, 5. Goals scored, 15 ; Tries, 13. Goals lost, 2 ; Tries, 6.

1879.
Nov. 15, at Windsor Park—v. Royal Academical Institution. Won by 5 goals and 6 tries to nil.
  „ 22, at Windsor Park—v. Carrickfergus. Won by 6 goals and 2 tries to nil.
Dec. 6, at Ormeau—v. North of Ireland 2nd XV. Won by 1 goal to nil.
  at Ulster Grounds—v. Ulster 2nd XV. Won by 2 goals and 2 tries to 1 try.
  at Belmont—v. Belmont. Lost by 1 goal to 1 try.

1880.
Feb. 14, at Windsor Park—v. Queen's College 2nd XV. Lost by 2 tries to nil.
  „ 18, at Comber—v. North Down. Lost by 1 goal and 1 try to 1 try.
  „ 28, at Ulster Ground—v. Ulster 2nd XV. (return). Won by 1 goal and 1 try to 2 tries.

LURGAN FOOTBALL CLUB.

Matches played, 7—lost, 1 ; won, 5 ; drawn, 1. Goals scored, 14 ; Tries, 14. Goals lost, 0 ; Tries, 2.

1879.
Nov. 22, at Lurgan—v. Armagh. Won by 1 goal, and a goal kicked under protest to 1 try.
  „ 29, at Lurgan—v. Albion. Won by 5 tries to nil.
Dec. 26, at Banbridge—v. Banbridge. Won by 3 goals and 2 tries to nil.

1880.
Jan. 17, at Lurgan—v. 1st XV. Ulster. Won by 3 goals, 1 disputed goal, and 1 try to nil.
Feb. 7, at Armagh—v. Armagh. Lost by 1 try to nil.
Feb. 25, at Belfast—v. N.I. 1st XV. Drawn.
Feb. 28, at Lurgan—v. Armagh. Won by 7 goals and 6 tries to nil.

LONDONDERRY ACADEMICAL INSTITUTION FOOTBALL CLUB.

Matches played, 6—lost, 2 ; won, 3 ; drawn, 1. Goals scored, 6 ; Tries, 4. Goals lost, 2 ; Tries, 4.

1879.
Oct. 18, at School Ground—Boarders v. Day Boys. Drawn.
Nov. 15, at Pennyburn—v. Gentlemen of North-west of Ireland. Won by 1 try to nil.
Dec. 5, at F.C. Ground—v. Gentlemen of North-west of Ireland (return). Lost by 2 tries to nil.

1880.
Feb. 21, at Magee College—v. Magee College. Won by 4 goals and 2 tries to 1 goal.
Mar. 12, at Armagh (Schools Challenge Cup)—v. Royal School. Lost by 1 goal and 1 try to nil.
Mar. 20, at School Ground—Boarders v. Day Boys. Boarders won by 2 goals and 1 try to 1 try.

MERRION SQUARE ROVERS' FOOTBALL CLUB.

Matches played, 4—lost, 2; won, 2; drawn, 0. Goals scored, 3; Tries, 3.
1879. Goals lost, 7; Tries, 8.

Nov. 5, at Kingstown—v. Kingstown School, 1st XV. Lost by 1 goal; each side secured a try.
Nov. 12, at Donnybrook—v. Wesley College. Won by one goal; 2 tries to a goal.
Nov. 22, at Clyde Road—v. Wanderers 2nd XV. Lost by 5 goals and 7 tries to nil.
Nov. 26, at Lansdowne Road—v. Lansdowne 2nd XV. Won by 2 goals to nil.

MONKSTOWN FOOTBALL CLUB (CO. DUBLIN).

Matches played, 4—lost, 4; won, 0; drawn, 0. Goals scored, 2; Tries, 0.
Goals lost, 8; Tries, 9.

Lansdowne Road—v. 2nd XV. Lansdowne F.C. Lost by 3 goals and 3 tries to nil.
Glenageary—v. Corrig Avenue. Lost by 1 goal and 4 tries to 1 goal.
Glenageary—v. Corrig Avenue. Lost by 2 goals to 1 goal.
Lansdowne Road—v. Lansdowne Road 2nd XV. Lost by 2 goals and 2 tries to nil.

MOUNTPOTTINGER FOOTBALL CLUB.

Matches played, 3—lost, 1; won, 2; drawn, 0. Goals scored 2; Tries, 4.
Goals lost, 1; Tries, 0.
1880.
Jan. 10, at Ormeau—v. Ormeau. Won by 2 goals and 1 try to nil.
Jan. 31, at Seapark—v. York Road. Lost by 1 goal to nil.
Mar. 20, at Belmont—v. Belmont. Won by 3 tries to 2 tries.

NOMADS FOOTBALL CLUB.

Matches played, 5—lost, 1; won, 4; drawn, 0. Goals scored, 9; Tries, 7.
1879. Goals lost, 3; Tries, 3.

Nov. 7, at Lansdowne Road—v. Lansdowne 1st XV. Lost by 1 goal and 2 tries to nil.
„ 14, at Drogheda—v. Drogheda 1st XV. Won by 1 goal and 2 tries to nil.
„ 27, at Rathfarnham—v. St. Columba's College. Won by 3 goals and 2 tries to 1 goal.
Dec. 11, at Curragh—v. 38th Regiment. Won by 3 goals and 2 tries to 1 goal.
1880.
Mar. 12, at Lansdowne Road—v. Lansdowne 1st XV. Won by 2 goals and 1 try to 1 try.

NORTH DOWN FOOTBALL CLUB.

Matches played, 12—lost, 8; won, 4; drawn, 0. Goals scored, 2; Tries, 20. Goals lost, 17; Tries, 15.

1879.
Oct. 25, at Comber—v. Windsor F.C. Lost by 2 tries to nil.
Nov. 1, at Comber—v. R.A. Institution. Won by 1 goal and 9 tries to nil.
„ 8, at Comber—v. Belmont. Lost by 1 goal to 1 try.
„ 22, at Comber—v. Ulster. Lost by 2 tries to 1 try.
„ 29, at Comber—v. N.I.F.C. 2nd XV. Lost by 2 goals and 1 try to nil.

1880.
Jan. 15, at Ballynafeigh Grounds—v. Ulster (R.) Lost by 1 goal and 3 tries to nil.
Feb. 7, at Comber—v. Carrickfergus. Won by 2 tries to nil.
„ 18, at Comber—v. Lauriston. Won by 1 goal and 1 try to 1 try.
„ 28, at Belmont—v. Belmont (R.) Lost by 1 goal and 3 tries to 4 tries.
Mar. 6, at Comber—v. York Road. Won by 2 tries to nil.
„ 13, at Ormeau, Belfast—v. N.I.F.C. 2nd XV. (R.) Lost by 8 goals and 3 tries to nil.
„ 20, at Carrickfergus—v. Carrickfergus (R.) Lost by 5 goals (one disputed), to nil.

NORTH OF IRELAND FOOTBALL CLUB.

1st XV.

Matches played, 14—lost, 4; won, 7; drawn, 3. Goals scored, 8; Tries, 13. Goals lost, 5; Tries, 10.

1879.
Nov. 1, at Belfast—v. Ulster. Won by a goal and a try to nil.
„ 22, at Belfast—v. Windsor. Won by a goal to a try (win disputed).
Dec. 27, at Belfast—v. United County Down. Won by 3 tries to nil.

1880.
Jan. 3, at Dundalk—v. Dundalk. Drawn; (N.I. played three men short).
„ 10, at Belfast—Manchester. Lost by a try to nil.
„ 17, at Belfast—Twenty of County Down. Won by 2 goals and 2 tries to 1 goal.
Jan. 31, at Belfast—v. Queen's College. Won by 1 goal and 2 tries to 1 goal and 1 try.
Feb. 7, at Belfast—v. Ulster. Won by 2 goals and a try to a try.
„ 16, at Edinburgh—v. Edinburgh Academicals. Lost by 2 tries to 1 try.
„ 17, at Glasgow—v. Glasgow Academicals. Lost by 2 goals and 3 tries to nil.
„ 21, at Belfast—v. Windsor. Drawn; 1 try each.
„ 28, at Belfast—v. Queen's College. Lost by 2 tries to nil.
Mar. 13, at Lurgan—v. County Armagh. Drawn.
„ 20, at Belfast—v. Dundalk. Won by a goal and 2 tries to nil.

2ND XV

Matches played, 18—lost, 1; won, 14; drawn, 3. Goals scored, 26; Tries, 34. Goals lost, 2; Tries, 4.

NORTH WEXFORD FOOTBALL CLUB.

Matches played, 2—lost, 2; won, 0; drawn 0. Goals scored, 0; Tries, 0. Goals lost, 4; Tries, 8.

1880.
Feb. 21, at Gorey—v. Lansdowne. Lost by 1 goal and 7 tries.
Mar. 20, at Lansdowne Road—v. Lansdowne. Lost by 3 goals and 1 try.

ORDNANCE SURVEY FOOTBALL CLUB.

Matches played, 11—lost 4; won 7; drawn, 0. Goals scored, 3; Tries, 8 Goals, lost, 4; Tries, 4.

1879.
Oct. 11, at Survey Ground—v. King's Hospital. One goal for King's Hospital.
Nov. 22, at Survey Ground—v. Military Academies. One try for Survey.
Dec. 6, at Survey Ground—v. Cusack's Academy. One goal for Survey.
 „ 13, at Survey Ground—v. Clontarf. One try for Survey.
 „ 20, at Drumcondra—v. Belvidere. One try for Survey.

1880.
Jan. 10, at Survey Ground—v. Belvidere (return). Three tries for Survey.
Jan. 31, at Hibernian Ground—v. Hibernians. One try for Hibernians.
Feb. 14, at Survey Ground—v. King's Hospital (return). One goal and 2 tries for King's Hospital.
Feb. 28, at Survey Ground—v. Cusack's Academy (return). One goal and 1 try for Academy.
Mar. 6, at Survey Ground—v. Eblana. One goal for Survey.
Mar. 20, at Survey Ground—v. Eblana (return). One goal and 2 tries for Survey.

PHŒNIX FOOTBALL CLUB.

1ST XV.

Matches played, 11—lost, 6; won, 1; drawn, 4. Goals scored, 3; Tries, 0. Goals lost, 7; Tries, 12.

Phœnix Park—v. Clontarf 1st XV. Upset by rain—drawn.
Phœnix Park—v. Lansdowne 1st XV. Drawn.
Phœnix Park—v. Steevens' Hospital. Drawn.
Cork—v. Cork. Lost by 1 try to nil.
Phœnix Park—v. Wanderers 1st XV. Lost by 2 goals.

Phœnix Park—v. Kingstown 1st XV.   Lost by 1 goal and a try.
Phœnix Park—v. Portarlington Past.   Won by 3 goals.
Lansdowne Road—v. Lansdowne 1st XV.   Lost by 2 tries.
Lansdowne Road—v. Wanderers 1st XV.   Lost by 4 goals and 7 tries (played four men short).
Clontarf—v. Clontarf.   Lost by a try.
Wesley College—v. Wesley College (Past and Present).   Drawn.

2ND XV.

Matches played, 10—lost, 6 ; won, 3 ; drawn, 1.

PORTADOWN FOOTBALL CLUB.

Matches played, 2—lost, 1 ; won, 1; drawn, 0.   Goals scored, 1 ; Tries, 1.   Goals lost, 0 ; Tries, 2.

1879.
Dec. 18, at Belfast—v. Ulster.   Lost by 2 tries to nil.
1880.
Jan. 29, at Portadown—v. Armagh.   Won by 1 goal and 1 try to nil.

PORTARLINGTON SCHOOL FOOTBALL CLUB.

Matches played, 10—lost, 3 ; won, 6 ; drawn, 1. Goals scored, 17 ; Tries, 8.   Goals lost, 8 ; Tries, 8.

1879.
Oct. 26, at Portarlington—v. Phœnix 2nd XV.   Drawn ; 1 try to 1 try.
Nov. 8, at Portarlington—v. Lansdowne 2nd XV.   Won by 3 goals and 1 try to nil.
Dec. 15, at Portarlington—v. Santry School.   Won by 3 goals to nil.
Nov. 1, at Portarlington—v. Kingstown School.   Won by 3 goals and 3 tries to nil.
 ,, 18, at Portarlington—v. Past XV.   Won by 3 goals and 1 try to 1 goal.
1880.
Feb. 18, at Portarlington—v. Steevens' Hospital.   Lost by 1 goal and 3 tries to nil.
Mar. 6, at Portarlington—v. Wanderers 2nd XV.   Lost by 2 goals to 1 goal.
 ,, 13, at Portarlington—v. University 2nd XV.   Lost by 3 goals and 3 tries to 1 goal.
 ,, 20, at Portarlington—v. Phœnix 2nd XV. (return).   Won by 2 goals and 1 try to 1 goal.
Nov. 25, at Curragh Camp—v. 38th Regiment.   Won by 1 goal and 1 try to 1 try.

PORTORA ROYAL SCHOOL FOOTBALL CLUB.

Matches played, 2—lost, 0 ; won, 2 ; drawn, 0.   Goals scored, 2 ; Tries, 2.   Goals lost, 1 ; Tries, 1.

1879.
Oct. 25, at Londonderry—v. Foyle College.   Won by 1 goal to 1 try.
Nov. 29, at Portora—v. Foyle College.   Won by 1 goal 2 tries to 1 goal.

QUEEN'S COLLEGE, BELFAST, FOOTBALL CLUB.

Matches played, 8—lost, 1; won, 7; drawn, 0. Goals scored, 8; Tries, 15. Goals lost, 1; Tries, 7.

1879.
Nov. 8, at Windsor—v. Windsor 2nd XV. Won by 2 goals and 1 try to nil.
„ 15, at Ulster Grounds—v. Ulster 2nd XV. Won by 1 goal to 1 try.

1880.
Jan. 17, at R.A.F. Grounds—v. Royal Academical Institution. Won by 4 tries to 2 tries.
„ 31, at Ormeau—v. N.I.F.C. 1st XV. Lost by 1 goal and 2 tries to 1 goal and 1 try.
Feb. 7, at Methodist College—v. Methodist College 2nd XV. Won by 3 goals and 4 tries to 2 tries.
„ 14, at Lauriston—v. Lauriston 2nd XV. Won by 2 tries to nil.
„ 28, at Ormeau—v. N.I.F.C. 1st XV. Won by 2 tries to nil.
Mar. 6, at Ulster Grounds—v. Ulster 2nd XV. Won by 1 goal and 1 try to nil.

QUEEN'S COLLEGE, CORK, FOOTBALL CLUB.

Matches played, 6—lost, 0; won, 5; drawn, 1. Goals scored, 6; Tries, 13. Goals lost, 0; Tries, 3.

1879.
Dec. 3, at Cork Park—v. Cork. Won by 1 goal to 1 try.

1880.
Jan. 15, at Limerick—v. Limerick. Drawn.
„ 26, at Queenstown—v. Queenstown. Won by 2 goals and 4 tries to 1 try.
Feb. 3, at Cork Park—v. Cork Bankers. Won by 1 goal and 4 tries to nil.
„ 12, at Cork Park—v. Cork. Won by 1 goal and 4 tries to nil.
Mar. 24, at Cork Park—v. Cork Bankers. Won by 1 goal and 1 try to 1 try.

QUEENSTOWN FOOTBALL CLUB.

Matches played, 1—lost, 1; won, 0; drawn, 0. Goals scored, 0; Tries, 1. Goals lost, 2; Tries, 3.

1880.
Feb. 24, at Queenstown—v. Queen's College, Cork. Lost by 2 goals and 3 tries to 1 try.

RATHMINES SCHOOL FOOTBALL CLUB.

Matches played, 10—lost, 6; won, 2; drawn, 2. Goals scored, 2; Tries, 2. Goals lost, 7; Tries, 8.

1879.
Oct. 25, at R. S. Ground—v. Military Academies. Lost by 1 goal.

Nov. 1, at Lansdowne Road—v. Lansdowne 2nd XV. Lost by 2 goals and 3 tries.
1880.
Feb. 14, at R. S. Ground—v. Wanderers 2nd XV. Lost by 1 goal and a try.
,, at R. S. Ground—v. Abercorn Club 1st XV. Won by 1 goal and a try.
Mar. 14, at R. S. Ground—v. Santry School 1st XV. Drawn.
,, at R. S. Ground—v. Abercorn Club 1st XV. Won by 1 try to nil.
,, at R. S. Ground—v. Kingstown School 1st XV. Lost by 1 try to nil.
,, at R. S. Ground—v. Kingstown School 2nd XV. Lost by a goal and a try.
,, at R. S. Ground—v. Kingstown School 2nd XV. Lost by 2 goals and a try.
Mar. 27, at Lansdowne Road—v. Lansdowne 2nd XV. Drawn; each side secured a goal.

ROYAL ACADEMICAL INSTITUTION FOOTBALL CLUB, BELFAST.

Matches played, 11—lost, 7; won, 1; drawn, 3. Goals scored, 1; Tries, 5. Goals lost, 9; Tries, 27.

1879.
Oct. 11, at R.A.I. Ground—v. Albion. Lost by 1 goal 2 tries to 1 goal.
,, 18, at R.A.I. Ground—v. Ulster 2nd XV. Drawn; 1 try each.
Nov. 7, at Comber—v. North Down. Lost by 1 goal and 5 tries.
,, 8, at Ormeau Road—v. N.I.F.C. 2nd XV. Lost by 1 goal and 2 tries to 1 try
,, 15, at Wellington Park—v. Lauriston. Lost by 5 goals and 6 tries.
,, 22, at R.A.I. Ground—v. Methodist College. Won by 1 try.
,, 29, at R.A.I. Ground—v. Windsor 2nd XV. Drawn; Windsor claimed a try.
1880.
Jan. 17, at Wellington Park—v. Queen's College 2nd XV. Lost by 4 tries to 2 tries.
,, 29, at Ormeau Road—v. Methodist College. Drawn.
Feb. 7, at Ormeau Road—v. N.I.F.C. 2nd XV. Lost by 1 goal and 5 tries.
Mar. 4, at Ormeau Road—v. Methodist College. Lost by 2 tries.

SANTRY SCHOOL FOOTBALL CLUB.

Matches played 8—lost, 2; won, 5; drawn, 1. Goals scored, 2; Tries, 6. Goals lost, 4; Tries, 4.

1879.
Oct. 25, at Santry—v. Kingstown School. Won by 2 tries to nil.
Nov. 1, at Donnybrook—v. Wesley College (Past and Present). Lost by 1 goal and 2 tries.
,, 15, at Rathmines—v. Rathmines School. Drawn.
,, 22, at Santry—v. Wanderers 2nd XV. Won by 2 tries to nil.
,, 27, at Santry—v. Drogheda 1st XV. Won by 1 try to nil.

F

Nov. 29, at Portarlington—v. Portarlington School. Lost by 3 goals to nil.
1880.
Feb. 28, at Clontarf—v. Clontarf 1st XV. Won by 1 goal to 2 tries.
Mar. 17, at Santry—v. Cusack's Academy. Won by 1 goal and 1 try to nil.

ST. COLUMBA'S COLLEGE FOOTBALL CLUB.

Matches played, 10—lost, 6 ; won, 3 ; drawn, 1. Goals scored, 3 ; Tries, 6. Goals lost, 7 ; Tries, 13.

1879.
Nov. 6, at St. Columba's College—v. Mr. Dickson's XV. Lost by 2 goals and 3 tries to nil.
„ 12, at St. Columba's College—v. "Nomads XV." Lost by 2 goals and 2 tries to 1 goal.
„ 18, at St. Columba's College—v. Mr. Maunsell's XV. Lost by 2 goals and 1 try to 2 tries.
„ 26, at St. Columba's College—v. Mr. Oliver's XV. Won by 1 goal and 1 try to 1 try.
„ 29, at St. Columba's College—v. 2nd XV. Clontarf F.C. Lost by 1 try to nil.
1880.
Jan. 31, at St. Columba's College—v. 2nd XV. Clontarf. Drawn.
Feb. 7, at St. Columba's College—v. Mr. Johnstone's XV. Put off.
„ 14, at St. Columba's College—v. 3rd XV. Kingstown F.C. Won by 1 goal and 1 try to 1 try.
„ 18, at St. Columba's College—v. 2nd XV. Lansdowne F.C. Won by 2 tries to nil.
„ 21, at St. Columba's College—v. Mr. Maunsell's XV. (return). Lost by 1 goal and 1 try to nil.
„ 25, at St. Columba's College—v. Mr. Sidley's XV. Lost by 3 tries to nil.
Mar. 6, at St. Columba's College—v. 2nd XV. Wanderers F.C. Put off.

ULSTER FOOTBALL CLUB.

Matches played, 24—lost, 13 ; won, 8 ; drawn, 3. Goals scored, 5 ; Tries, 27. Goals lost, 13 ; Tries, 23.

1879.   1st XV.

Oct. 29, at Ulster Ground—v. Belmont. Won 1 goal 2 tries to nil.
Nov. 1, at Ormeau—v. N.I.F.C. Lost 1 goal 1 try to nil.
„ 8, at Ulster Ground—v. Windsor. Lost 1 goal 1 try to nil.
Dec. 25, at Ulster—v. Mountpottinger. Won 1 goal to 1 try.
„ 27, at Dundalk—v. Dundalk. Won 1 goal 6 tries to nil.
1880.
Jan. 3, at Belmont—v. Belmont. Won 1 try to nil.
„ 17, at Lurgan—v. Lurgan. Lost 1 goal 1 try to nil.
Feb. 7, at Ormeau—v. N.I.F.C. Lost 2 goals 1 try to 1 try.
„ 14, at Ulster Ground—v. Windsor. Lost 1 goal 2 tries to nil.
Mar. 6, at Ulster Ground—v. Queen's College. Lost 1 goal 1 try to nil.

2ND XV.

Oct. 18, at Institution Ground—v. R.A. Institution. Drawn; 1 try each.
Nov. 5, at Ulster Ground—v. Carrickfergus. Lost 1 goal 2 tries to 1 goal.
,, 15, at Ulster Ground—v. Queen's College (2nd). Lost 1 goal to 1 try.
,, 19, at Ormeau—v. N.I.F.C. (2nd). Lost 2 ties to 1 try.
,, 22, at Comber—v. North Down. Won 2 tries to 1 try.
,, 29, at Ulster Ground—v. Lauriston. Lost 2 goals 2 ties to 1 try.
Dec. 17, at Ulster Ground—v. Portadown. Won 3 tries to 1 nil.
,, 20, at Ulster Ground—v. Albion. Drawn; 1 try each.
,, 26, at Carrickfergus—v. Carrickfergus. Won 1 try to nil.
Jan. 17, at Carrickfergus—v. North Down. Won 1 goal 3 tries to nil.
,, 31, at Ulster Ground—v. Armagh. Lost 2 tries to nil.
Feb. 12, at Ulster Ground—v. Ormeau. Drawn; 1 try each.
,, 28, at Ulster Ground—v. Lauriston. Lost 1 goal 1 try to 2 tries.
Mar. 10, at Ormeau—v. N.I.F.C. Lost 1 goal 2 tries to nil.

UNITED HOSPITALS' FOOTBALL CLUB.

Matches played, 3—lost, 2; won, 1; drawn, 0. Goals scored, 1; Tries, 1. Goals lost, 3; Tries, 2.

1879.
Nov. 8, at Lansdowne Road—v. County Dublin. Lost by 1 goal to nil.
1880.
Jan. 31, at Lansdowne Road—v. Wanderers. Lost by 2 tries; each side securing a goal.
Mar. 20, at Lansdowne Road—v. Wanderers. Won by 1 try to nil.

WANDERERS FOOTBALL CLUB.
1ST XV.

Matches played, 18—lost, 4; won, 11; drawn, 3. Goals scored, 15; Tries, 20. Goals lost, 5; Tries, 3.

1879.
Oct. 10, at Clyde Road—v. Queen's College XV. Won by 1 goal to nil.
,, 11, at Clyde Road—v. Pembroke Rowing Club. Won by 2 goals and 2 tries.
,, 18, at Clyde Road—v. Rest of Club. Won by 1 goal and 1 try.
,, 25, at Clyde Road—v. Meath Hospital. Won by 1 goal and 1 try.
Nov. 1, at Clyde Road—v. Clontarf. Drawn.
,, 15, at Clyde Road—v. Dundalk. Won by 1 try.
,, 22, at College Park—v. Dublin University. Lost by 2 goals.
,, 29, at Belfast—v. Windsor. Lost by 1 try.
Dec. 13, at Phœnix Park—v. Phœnix. Won by 2 goals.
1880.
Jan. 3, at Lansdowne Road—v. Lansdowne. Won by 1 goal and 3 tries to 1 goal.
,, 10, at Kingstown—v. Kingstown. Won by 1 try.
,, 12, at Lansdowne Road—v. Manchester. Lost by 1 goal and 1 try.
,, 31, at Lansdowne Road—v. United Hospitals. Won by 1 goal and 2 tries to 1 goal.

Feb. 14, at Clontarf—v. Clontarf. Won by 1 goal and 2 tries.
  „ 21, at Lansdowne Road—v. Phœnix. Won by 5 goals and 7 tries.
Mar. 10, at Lansdowne Road—v. Armagh (Past). Drawn.
  ,, 13, at Lansdowne Road—v. Dublin University. Drawn.
  ,, 20, at Lansdowne Road—v. United Hospitals. Lost by 1 try.

2ND XV.

Matches played, 15—lost, 2; won, 13; drawn, 0. Goals, scored, 26; Tries, 23. Goals lost, 8; Tries, 6.
1879.
Oct. 25, at Phœnix Park—v. Hibernian. Won by 1 goal and 2 tries to 1 try.
Nov. 8, at Clyde Road—v. Merrion Square Rovers. Won by 2 goals and and 5 tries to nil.
  „ 15, at Kingstown—v. Kingstown School. Won by 2 goals and 2 tries to nil.
Nov. 22, at Clyde Road—v. Dublin University 2nd XV. Lost by 1 goal and 1 try to nil.
Dec. 13, at Donnybrook—v. Wesley College. Won by 1 goal to nil.
  „ 27, at Clontarf—v. Clontarf 2nd XV. Won by 1 goal and 1 try to nil.
1880.
Jan. 3, at Lansdowne Road—v. Lansdowne 2nd XV. Won by 3 goals and 3 tries to nil.
  „ 17, at Kingstown—v. Kingstown 2nd XV. Won by 1 goal and 1 try to 1 goal.
Feb. 7, at Rathmines—v. Rathmines School. Won by 2 goals and 3 tries to nil.
  „ 14, at Lansdowne Road—v. Clontarf 2nd XV. Won by 3 goals and 2 tries to nil.
  „ 21st, at Phœnix Park—v. Phœnix 2nd XV. Won by 5 goals and 4 tries to nil.
  „ 28, at Lansdowne Road—v. Lansdowne 2nd XV. Won by 2 goals to nil.
Mar. 6, at Portarlington—v. Portarlington School. Won by 2 goals to 1 goal.
  „ 9, at Lansdowne Road—v. Kingstown 2nd XV. Won by 1 goal to nil.
  „ 13, at Lansdowne Road—v. D.U.F.C. 2nd XV. Lost by 5 goals and 4 tries to nil.

WESLEY COLLEGE FOOTBALL CLUB.

Matches played, 16—lost, 5; won, 9; drawn, 2. Goals scored, 17; Tries, 13.
1879.   Goals lost, 7; Tries, 8.
Nov. 1, at Donnybrook—v. Santry School. Won by 1 goal and 2 tries to nil.
Nov. 12, at Donnybrook—v. Merrion Rovers. Lost by 1 goal and 2 tries to 1 goal.
  „ 15, at Lansdowne Road—v. Lansdowne 1st XV. Lost by 2 tries to nil.

Nov. 19, at Donnybrook—v. Aylesbury. Drawn; 2 goals, 1 try each.
 „ 22, at Donnybrook—v. Portarlington Past. Won by 2 goals.
 „ 26, at College Park—v. Dublin University 2nd XV. Lost by 3 goals and 2 tries to nil.
Dec. 13, at Donnybrook—v. Wanderers 2nd XV. Lost by 1 try to nil.

2ND XV.

Nov. 15, at Donnybrook—v. Clontarf 2nd XV. Won by 2 goals and 1 try to nil.
 „ 29, at Donnybrook—v. Phœnix 2nd XV. Won by 1 goal to nil.

JUNIORS.

Oct. 28, at Donnybrook—v. Carlisle. Drawn.
Nov. 31, at Donnybrook—v. Abercorn. Won by 2 goals to nil.
1880.
Feb. 23, at Donnybrook—v. Abercorn (return). Won by 1 goal and 2 tries to nil.
Mar. 6, at Donnybrook—v. Clontarf 3rd XV. Won by 4 goals to nil.
 „ 13, at Santry—v. Santry 3rd XV. Lost by 1 goal to 1 try.
 „ 16, at Donnybrook—v. Santry 3rd XV. Won by 1 goal and 2 tries to nil.
 „ 27, at Clontarf—v. Clontarf 3rd XV. Won by 4 tries to nil.

"YORK ROAD" BELFAST FOOTBALL CLUB.

Matches played, 4—lost, 3; won, 1; drawn, 0. Goals scored, 2; Tries, 0. Goals lost, 3; Tries, 4.

1879.
Nov. 15, at Carrick—v. Carrickfergus. Lost by 2 goals and 1 try.
1880.
Jan. 31, at Seapark—v. Mountpottinger. Won by 1 goal to nil.
Feb. 21, at Seapark—v. Carrickfergus. Lost by 1 goal and 1 try to 1 goal.
Mar. 6, at Comber—v. North Down. Lost by 2 tries to nil.

FOOTBALL STATISTICS, 1879-80.
(RUGBY UNION RULES.)

Name of Club.	Matches. Playd.	Won.	Lost.	Drn.	Goals. Won.	Lost.	Tries. Won.	Lost.
Albion	9	4	4	1	5	4	15	9
Armagh	12	6	3	3	9	3	12	1
Armagh Royal School	8	3	5	0	3	5	4	7
Carrickfergus	16	7	8	1	—	—	—	—
Clanwilliam 1st XV	4	3	0	1	2	0	3	0
Do. 2nd XV.	4	2	1	1	0	0	10	5
Clontarf 1st XV.	13	5	6	2	5	8	15	9
Do. 2nd XV.	12	5	6	1	9	14	6	1
Cork	16	8	8	0	8	10	26	17
Cusack's Academy	12	6	4	2	5	4	11	3
Dublin University 1st XV.	4	3	0	1	5	0	0	0
Do. 2nd XV.	12	10	0	2	20	1	18	1
Dundalk	11	4	3	4	7	3	14	8
Dungannon Royal School	1	1	0	0	1	0	1	0
Galway Grammar School	5	1	3	1	2	4	1	4
Hibernian 1st XV.	10	7	1	2	5	1	6	2
Do. 2nd XV.	2	0	2	0	0	1	0	1
King's Hospital	9	5	3	1	8	7	8	9
Kingstown 1st XV.	7	4	3	0	5	4	9	1
Do. 2nd XV.	7	3	4	0	5	4	8	3
Kingstown School	20	12	6	2	26	12	25	13
Knight's School	2	2	0	0	1	0	2	1
Lansdowne 1st XV.	14	6	5	3	5	10	19	7
Do. 2nd XV.	19	9	8	2	14	15	29	14
Lauriston	8	5	3	0	15	2	13	6
Lurgan	7	5	1	1	14	0	14	2
Londonderry Acad. Inst.	6	3	2	1	6	2	4	4
Merrion Square Rovers	4	2	2	0	3	7	3	8
Monkstown	4	0	4	0	2	8	0	9
Mountpottinger	3	2	1	0	2	1	4	0
Nomads	5	4	1	0	9	3	7	3
North Down	12	4	8	0	2	17	20	15
North of Ireland 1st XV.	14	7	4	3	8	5	13	10
Do. 2nd XV.	18	14	1	3	26	2	34	4
North Wexford	2	0	2	0	0	4	0	8
Ordnance Survey	11	7	4	0	3	4	8	4
Phœnix 1st XV.	11	1	6	4	3	7	0	12
Do. 2nd XV.	10	3	6	1	—	—	—	—
Portadown	2	1	1	0	1	0	1	2

FOOTBALL STATISTICS—*Continued*.

Name of Club.	Matches. Playd	Won.	Lost.	Drn.	Goals. Won.	Lost.	Tries. Won.	Lost.
Portarlington School	10	6	3	1	17	8	8	8
Portora Royal School	2	2	0	0	2	1	2	1
Queen's College, Belfast	8	7	1	0	8	1	15	7
Queen's College, Cork	6	5	0	1	6	0	13	3
Queenstown	1	0	1	0	0	2	1	3
Rathmines School	10	2	6	2	2	7	2	8
Royal Acad. Institution	11	1	7	3	1	9	5	27
Santry School	8	5	2	1	2	4	6	4
St. Columba's College	10	3	6	1	3	7	6	13
Ulster	24	8	13	3	5	13	27	23
United Hospitals	3	1	2	0	1	3	1	2
Wanderers 1st XV.	18	11	4	3	15	5	20	3
Do. 2nd XV.	15	13	2	0	26	8	23	6
Wesley College	16	9	5	2	17	7	13	8
York Road, Belfast	4	1	3	0	2	3	0	4

THE MUNSTER TOUR TO WALES.

"*In vino veritas.*"

"A chield's amang you takin' notes,
And faith he'll print them."—BURNS.

THIS is the first Irish inter-provincial team that has had the courage to cross the Channel to measure its strength with its Sassenach brethren, and though the result was two to one against them, much credit is due to them for the plucky way they played; having by no means a good team, for at the last moment some of the best players disappointed, as is usually the case. The originator of this tour was Mr. W. J. Goulding, who acted as Captain, &c., to whom much credit is due for the energetic manner in which the arrangements were carried through.

It was proposed, before crossing, that the Munster team should play twenty of the Cork Football Club, and the match was arranged to take place in the Cork Park at 1 o'clock; and after a well-contested and spirited game, resulted in a win for the Munster team by two goals and two tries to spare.

The Munster team, composed as follows, played their first match for the purpose of getting together in the Cork Park against the best XX. the Club could muster.

T. Harrison (full-back), W. Girvan and T. Scoggins (half-backs), W. J. Goulding (captain), and W. Pierce (quarter-back); G. R. Meyer, F. Guy, A. R. M'Mullen, W. Cummins, H. Morrell, G. Manders, F. Lewis, W. Kelly, and F. Purdon (forwards); F. Kennedy joining them in Wales. The match resulted in an easy win for the XIV., Goulding dropping a goal. Morrell secured two tries, one of which Harrison converted into a goal, and one try secured by Purdon to nil.

The Dublin contingent displayed a little of the ancient customs of Spanish serenading while strolling through the town before the commencement of the game, Kinch especially making himself conspicuous by doing Zachariah from the boughs of a Cork Sycamore tree.

The team left Cork by steamer for Milford at half-past 4, and were cheered lustily by a throng of the Cork inhabitants who had crowded down to see their departure. The steamer having at last got out of harbour, the team, one and all, set about making themselves comfortable. As a preventative against sickness, Mr. Girvan, in his usual liberal and hospitable manner, prevailed upon the unwilling team to accompany him into the saloon, where he caused brandy and soda to be served round at his expense. This display of good feeling at once set the company in good humour, Charlie, a chance shipmate, and the Dublin Boxer swearing eternal friendship. Harrison, we are sorry to say, grew bilious from the effects of a heavy supper (sea sickness, we are authorised to state, had nothing to do with it), and was the first to show the example of getting berthed; he was soon followed by most of the others, leaving only three or four to pace the deck in solitary silence smoking the pipe of peace; while over the monotonous sounds of the engine were frequently heard the imprecations of Charlie Corbett, or the solemn whispering of the Policeman and Kinch, who up to this time "had stuck to their desks and never went to sea," and whose fears of a watery grave led them to suggest the advisability of making a collection by way of doing something religious. The last to retire to rest were the Boxer and Curley Morrell, and as only one berth could be got for the two, notice of ejectment was served upon the pugnacious Charlie, who did not seem disposed to give up his holding, although in the end the law took its course, and the discomfited warrior had to remove, "bag and baggage."

The team landed at Milford, and proceeded direct to Newport. On the way the Captain received a telegram from the Mayor, inviting the visitors to a banquet, which invitation we need hardly say was accepted. Seldom had such a scene been witnessed at the Newport Railway Station, as the very fact that the visitors on this occasion were coming from a great distance tended to heighten the regard which Football matches generally demand. About two thousand people had gathered at the station, who cheered lustily as the team issued forth. The Volunteer Band, which had come out for the occasion, led the way to the hotel in great style, though the man with the big drum was afterwards heard to remark that the strangers had forgot to stand them a liquor for their trouble.

The match was announced to take place at 3 o'clock. About half an hour before the match the Secretary of the Newport team had a four-in-hand at the hotel to convey the players to the ground. It was rather an amusing sight to see the anxiety displayed by the old women to grasp the hand of any of the team, and we may mention in confidence that the Captain had to give an old lady his arm as far as the drag. When the team got fairly settled, after a fight for the front seats, some of the mothers held up their children to receive a blessing from the friends from the Old Country. After considerable delay they got fairly started, and were cheered lustily all the way to the ground. Every available spot was crowded to excess. We have rarely seen a ground better laid out for the game, it being as smooth as a billiard table, and railed off in such a manner that the spectators could in no way interfere with the play.

The Munster Captain having won the toss, shouting "Harp for Ould Ireland," took the pavilion goal, and Phillips kicked off; the Welchman following up hard, compelled Harrison to touch down. After drop out, some hard scrummaging took place, and finally Phillips got in, and a goal resulted for Newport, which was immediately followed by two tries, both kicks going wide. The Munster men then played better together, and the ball was kept in the centre till half time. Goulding started the "Gilbert" and Munster splendidly, led by Cummins, Kennedy and M'Mullen forward, and, by useful spurts of Goulding and Pierce, gradually worked towards the Newport goal line; Morrell passing the ball well to Harrison, the latter by a fine and well-timed drop scored a goal. After kick-off some fumbling among the Munster backs, coupled with wild passing, gave the ball to Newman, who, by a lucky drop, secured another goal for Newport. From this to the end the game was kept in Newport territory; but nothing more resulting, Newport were left victors by two goals and two tries to one goal. We think this decisive victory was mainly due to the sea passage and two nights travelling of the Irishmen, who, at the commencement of the match, were left standing. We must also state that the Newport XV. have always played together exactly the same for three years, and their passing and following up was a treat to see. The running and dropping of Goss was the feature of the match.

The game being over, the team resumed their seats on the drag, and, giving a real Irish cheer for the ladies, thousands of whom had graced the ground with their presence, they all returned to the hotel, and, after some confusion in changing their football garments for the more civilized garb of every-day life, proceeded to the King's Head Hotel, where they had been so kindly invited to a banquet—the Mayor presiding. No team could have received more hospitality, or so much enjoyed an evening as did the Munster, the following gentlemen making themselves conspicuous in the musical line:—Morrell, Maunders, Kennedy, and Girvan sung "The Wearin' o' the Green," which was encored twice. Everything was done to make it a success, both by the entertainers and the entertained. The toast of the evening was proposed by the Mayor, and appropriately responded to by Mr. Goulding, and Mr. Kennedy responded, as only he could, to the toast of the ladies. There was some difficulty in getting the team out of the hotel, several members having got confused among the passages; this necessitated the Captain becoming whipper-in, but he, too, succumbed to the intricacies of the place. On arriving at their own hotel, a Scotchman living there, who had proved himself obstreperous in an earlier part of the evening, was summarily dealt with, poor Sandy being taken per force from his warm bed, carried down three flights of stairs, and laid on the bare flags, to the utter disgust of poor Scottie. Some of the team, it appears, got themselves into disrepute by mistaking strangers' rooms for their own, and were ignominiously expelled, the alarm-bell ringing furiously. This unfortunate accident having alarmed the household and incensed the host, the night's revellings were put a stop to. In the morning the team were waited on by the Corporation, who showed them round the town, and would not allow them to depart without crowning their hospitality in a stirrup-cup. The team started in good heart, but rather in bad form, by the 11 o'clock train to try conclusions with the United South of Wales at Swansea. On the way down much persuasive power was wasted on Guy to induce him to part with his beard, but without success. He seemed to think, like the Israelites of old, that a shaven face was a disgrace unto him, and seemed to have a hazy idea that, like Sampson of old, his strength was in his hair. Kinch, meantime, was at his old tricks, and the unwary passenger who was fool enough to lay his money on the ace of spades generally left it in Kinch's hat, when he bade him good morning at the next station. With such innocent pastimes they spent the journey between Newport and Swansea, where they arrived about twelve o'clock.

After this defeat by Newport, Munster journeyed to Swansea, and played the picked XV. of South Wales, and a splendidly close match resulted, thus showing the previous day's form was at fault. The game was played in two thirty-fives, and nothing resulted until a few minutes before call of time, when Munster, losing the services of Girvan (nervously injured), Saunders of Cardiff (who played splendidly throughout) secured a disputed try off which a goal was kicked, the ball being placed under the direction of the umpire, who showed a lamentable ignorance of the rules throughout the whole match, and proving a most timely and energetic adviser to the Welchmen on all occasions.

In the evening the team were too hospitably entertained by the Swansea Football Club, in the Mackworth Arms, under the auspices of the Mayor and distinguished members of the Corporation. The amount of punch consumed was noticeable by the great "exuberance of verbosity" of some of the members. After the dinner the Irishmen sallied forth to enjoy the pure air, and then commenced a scene which will long be remembered in Swansea. On arriving at the door Mr. Harrison, having been disabled, left them; four policemen having been introduced to the Dublin Policeman, had to be reminded of the custom of taking off their hats on such occasions. This reminder was given by our friend, Frank Purdon. Strange to say, our Irish boys were seen shortly afterwards practising the 100 yards.

A carriage meeting the procession, and passing over the bodies of Meyer and Morrell, was capsized, the occupant being ejected into the arms of the Policeman. The team, shortly after this display, retired to the Arms of the hospitable proprietor, where a scene of wild confusion occurred. The proprietor, being ignorant of the system of Irish wakes, which was held on discovering our dearly beloved friend, Tom Harrison, apparently dead to the joys and sorrows of the evening, objected to his being laid out on the dinner-table in the costume of Lazarus, upon which Mr. Harrison's friend, the Boxer, cut up exceedingly rough, and, only for the persuasion of the Captain, would have left the Arms with his football toggery tucked up under his arm.

We may state, in spite of all contradiction, that the number of chairs broken did not exceed sixty, and that brandy and milk were not much asked after.

The next day Munster played the Meath Club in a high gale of wind, occasionally varied by a snow-storm. Here they secured the services of Saunders, who, with Goulding, Pierce, and Morrell, kept up a running fire on the home goal, Morrell in the end dropping a fine goal, and thus securing a victory for his side. Here, again, we regret to have to question the decision of the umpires, it being our impression that each of the above-named secured a try, as also Meyer, who, apparently improved instead of deteriorated by his numerous escapades, displayed grand form, and proved himself a terror to his opponents and the admired of the beholders, by his superhuman powers of collaring and throwing his men.

We are happy to state that matches are arranged for 1880 between the same hospitable loving team and their Welsh brethren.

May we be there to see.

REPORTS OF MATCHES.

ENGLAND *V.* IRELAND.

Played at Lansdowne Road, Co. Dublin, Monday, February 2nd, 1880.

(From *Bell's Life*, London, February 7th, 1880.)

AFTER being photographed, and some preliminary punt-about, the rival teams faced one another. Looking at them, the Englishmen seemed to have the advantage in point of size, but the Irishmen were a very evenly-weighted lot of men, and appeared thick set, fast, and strong, as they afterwards proved. There were some alterations from the teams originally chosen, Twynam, Vernon, Ellis, and Schofield taking the places of Taylor, Budd, Burton, and E. T. Gurdon, who were unable to play on the English side, and Cummins, Burkett, and Finlay being replaced by Hughes, Purdon, and Kennedy. Kelly, winning the toss for Ireland, chose the western goal for the first half time, having the wind and sun at his back Stokes kicked off at about 3 o'clock, and the ball going high, fell into the hands of Walkington, who, finding the English forwards close upon him, made his mark, and dropped into touch at his leisure. The English forwards began with some dash, and, aided by a short run from Twynam, carried the ball towards the Irish goal, but Bagot, by a useful punt, returned it to the centre. Hunt then getting hold of it from a long throw in from touch, made a neat run, but was finally tackled by Heron. The Irish forwards, by some good forward play, pressed their opponents back, but Twynam, by a useful run, and Jackson, by a long punt, regained the lost ground, and Markendale was to the fore with a pretty dribble. Walkington came to the rescue, and, with a long drop, sent the ball into touch near the centre. Still the Englishmen for a time maintained the attack, Vernon and Gurdon doing a lot of work for them forward, while Hunt and Stokes were in good form behind. At last the Irish forwards pulled themselves together, and, headed by Kelly, Forrest, and Scriven, rushed the ball into the English half of the ground, and, bearing down all opposition, sent it into touch near the English twenty-five yards flag. Here the Englishmen rallied, and the long punting of

Jackson for a time relieved his side. Again, however, the Irish forwards asserted their superiority, and Whitestone had a chance of dropping a goal, but, leaving it till too late, was finely charged down by Rowley, who made the best of his way to the centre. Soon, however, Whitestone had another drop, which sent the ball behind the English line, and Fry touched down in self defence Stokes re-started the ball, sending it to Twynam, who made some twenty yards; Ellis and Markendale then dribbled the ball in fine style towards the Irish goal, but, just as they seemed bound to secure a try, Woodhead, by an injudicious kick, sent the ball behind into Walkington's hands, who touched it down. A magnificent rush by the Irish forwards then carried the ball from one end of the ground to the other, Fry stopping them near the English twenty-five yards flag, and neatly dropping it back to the centre. Taylor next came forward with a strong run, but was stopped by Hunt; the Irish forwards, however, were not to be denied, and Forrest, dribbling magnificently, took the ball into touch, close to the English line. Here a long throw in from touch fell to Kelly, and the ball bounding from him to Cuppaidge, the last-named got over the line and grounded the ball near the English goal, amid deafening cheers from the spectators, this being the first try ever gained by the Irish in an international match. The place kick was entrusted to Walkington, who for some unaccountable reason missed the goal, and England again touched down. Vernon then made a good run, but the Irishmen, working splendidly together, literally swept the Englishmen back, and Forrest ultimately crossed the goal line and claimed a try. This, however, was disallowed on the ground of off side. Gurdon, Rowley, and Neame then worked the ball away, and half time found the ball near the centre, though still in the English half.

On change of ends England had the aid of the wind. Kelly re-started the ball, and his forwards, following up quickly, were down on Twynam before he could return it. Rowley and Gurdon, working hard for England, loosened the scrummage up, and Woodhead made an unopposed run to the centre. The long dropping of the English backs now began to tell, and, in spite of the splendid efforts of their opponents, gradually drove the Irish back. Jackson made a neat run, but Walkington tackled him, and they both fell over together; here Neame and Markendale found the ball dead on the ground, so dribbled it on, and the last named touched it down in the Irish goal near the touch line. An objection was raised to the try on the plea that the ball had been picked up, but this not being the case, Kelly at once gave in. The place kick by Hunt was a good one, but the ball went just outside the post. Walkington dropped out, and Jackson, by a beautiful kick, almost secured a goal, the ball passing only about a yard to the right. Ireland again touched down. Following up the kick out Taylor charged Hunt down before he could do anything, and the Irish forwards, coming again dribbled the ball on towards the English lines. Hornby dropped it almost out of danger, where Bagot caught it, and made his mark, and Walkington, by a fine place, sent it rather near the English posts; but Hornby again punted it away out of danger. A long drop by Stokes sent the ball into touch near the Irish twenty-five yards flag, and the English forwards, playing hard, carried the ball over the line, and Ellis and Gurdon tackled Walkington simultaneously. Ellis retired from the maul, and Walkington succeeded in touching down, Gurdon not quite understanding that he had to prevent it. The kick out was returned into touch, and Ellis, getting hold of the ball, made a fine run to within three yards of the Irish posts, and again getting hold of it after a short scrummage, grounded it most distinctly on the Irish goal line. The English umpire declared it to be a try, and the Irish umpire and the referee had not seen it. Some of the Irish team and many of the spectators (who were now crowding behind the Irish goal line) asserted that the ball had touched the ground before reaching the line. But the English captain, having seen the whole thing most plainly, refused to listen to the spectators, and Kelly backing him up, declared that he was satisfied with the umpire's decision. Stokes kicked an easy goal for England. Walkington kicked off, and the game recommenced in the English quarters; but a fine run by Gurdon and some pretty passing between him and Stokes took the ball past half-way. Bagot then distinguished himself by a very good run, finishing up with a punt into touch. Rowley then made a strong run, and after some passing with Twynam, ran in and secured a try, but as he started when offside, the ball was brought all the way back. The next feature was a long drop at goal by Stokes, the ball going just outside the post and causing Walkington to touch down. The rest of the game was stubbornly contested in the Irish half, but no further points had been scored when no-side put an end to one of the best matches ever played. Though defeated by a goal and a try to a try, Ireland may be congratulated on the vast improvement her players have made since last year. Her forwards carried all before them, being splendidly together, and dribbling with great skill, and altogether unselfishly. At times they played somewhat offside, but on the whole there was nothing to find fault with. Behind, too, there was a marked improvement, the tackling and picking up the ball being much better than in former years; but still most of them have to learn to drop more. The English forwards were not at all together, and in this respect were no match for their opponents, who came through them just as they liked. Individually, most of them played well, especially Gurdon, Ellis, and Rowley. The English backs had a very difficult game to play owing to the rushes of the Irish forwards, so that none of them showed up very prominently. Jackson did a lot of useful work, and Fry did what he had to do well. For Ireland, Kelly set his men a splendid example, and to him the pleasantness of the match was to a great extent due. Forrest was conspicuous amongst the forwards, his dribbling being irresistible. Scriven, Cuppaidge, and Taylor were also all there. Behind, Walkington's kicking and tackling were invaluable to his side, and Heron played a good defensive game. The English Fifteen were subsequently entertained at dinner at the Shelbourne Hotel.

(*From the Irish Times, February* 3, 1880.)

THE sixth International match has been played and won, and, as on former occasions, the Rose asserted its superiority over the Shamrock. Before detailing the play, it becomes necessary to say a few words on the formation of the Irish XV. After nearly three years arranging details, the formation of the Irish Rugby Football Union became an accomplished fact. The main features are these—A committee of 16 from the three provinces comprise the Union, and the external affairs of each province are managed by a separate committee, styled the branch of the Union. This proved the first occasion that the Union met for the purpose of electing the Irish XV., and certainly they are entitled to much credit for the impartial and unfavoured manner they decided on their representatives.

The weather held up splendidly, and the ground was in capital order. Early on Monday the Union committee had to map out the entire field of play, as everything was wrong—the goal-posts were too far apart, the distance between the touch-lines was short, and the lines were not parallel. The Dublin University Athletic Club very kindly lent their ropes for the occasion, and they proved a great advantage to both the players and the public. A number of stewards were appointed to keep the ground, but, as usual, with few exceptions, they proved more in the way than the general public. The number of ladies present far surpassed any previous occasion, and, judging from their anxiety, they took a lively interest in the game, two ladies in particular almost occupying the position of full-back—perhaps Hornby and Fry can explain this. The general arrangements were carried out under the directions of Messrs. Neville (President I.R.F. Union), C. F. Martin (Hon. Sec. I.C.A.C.), and R. M. Peter (Hon. Sec. I.R.F. Union), and gave every satisfaction. Previous to the match both teams were photographed by Messrs. Mansfield, of Grafton Street, and shortly before 3 o'clock the teams were in readiness to play. It was agreed to play for two periods of forty minutes each, and Ireland having won the toss, elected to defend the pavillion goal. L. Stokes (captain) kicked off, and Walkington gained a "free," returning the ball into touch. After some loose scrummaging the Englishmen worked the ball near the Irish goal, but the good play of Johnston brought it down the field. Twynam got away, but chucked to Hunt, and after Jackson made a short run, finally passing to Twynam, the leather went into touch at the Irish 25 yards post. Forrest and M'Donald now came to the rescue, and hostilities were resumed in neutral territory. Vernon got the ball, but passed to Hunt, who made a good run, and for some time the ball was up and down the field between the Irish 25 yards post and the centre flag. After much scrummaging a cheer announced that the Irish had invaded the English territory, and with Forrest, Scriven and Miller in the van, the Irish forwards carried all before them to the English 25 yards post. The excitement was now intense, and the ball was chucked back to Whitestone for a drop, but he was charged down. However, the Irish kept the ball close to their opponents goal, and eventually the Englishmen touched down in self-defence. Stokes kicked off by a slow dribbling kick, and Twynam took up the running, but not going far, the ball was scrummaged in English territory, where it was kept for some time, until Vernon made a splendid run to near the Irish 25 yards. Bagot punted back, but Fry returned the ball to the half-way post. The Irish forwards now came with a rush, and carried the ball to within five yards of the English goal-line. The scrummaging grew desperate, and eventually Cuppaidge cleverly grounded the ball behind the English goal-line. The try—a very easy place—was badly missed by Walkington. Stokes started the leather, to which Whitestone replied, and, aided by a good run of Stokes, the visitors slowly worked the ball close to the Irish goal, and compelled Ireland to touch down in self-defence. For some time the home team kept the ball near the goal-line, and "half-time" was called.

The sides having changed over and lemonized, Kelly (captain) kicked off to Hunt, who was cleverly charged down by Heron. Ireland again looked dangerous, but Woodhead made a telling run until collared by Walkington. After some scrummaging Jackson gained a free, which was placed for Stokes, who made a splendid attempt at goal, but Walkington punted back into touch. After much scrummaging near the Irish goal, Mackendale secured a try, but Hunt failed at goal—by no means an easy kick. Ireland touched down and kicked out; the ball was returned, and Ireland touched down for the second time. Walkington again kicked off, and Stokes booked a "free." Bagot made a capital run in reply, and Twynam next got away, and soon after Ireland again touched down in self-defence. After kick-off the ball was worked near the Irish goal, and Ellis secured a try (which was disputed, on the ground that the ball was not put down on or over the goal-line, but the umpire decided *contra*, an opinion in which we concur). The try at goal was entrusted to Stokes, and, of course, it proved a "moral." During the remainder of the match some capital forward was shown by Gurdon, Kilner, Vernon, and Neame. Stokes made some splendid drops at goal, and Hornby did some good runs. Ireland several times rallied splendidly, but never could get within ten yards of the English goal. Heron collared splendidly, Johnston worked hard, Bagot played well, and Whitestone did good service, while the forwards worked with a will, and deserve special mention; and when "no side" was called the victory rested with the English by one goal to nil, each side having secured a try.

SIDES.
ENGLAND.
Full-backs—T. Fry, Queen's House; A. Hornby, Manchester.
Half-backs—L. Stokes (captain), Blackheath; R. Hunt, Manchester.
Quarter-backs—A. H. Jackson, Blackheath; H. T. Twynam, Richmond.
Forwards—S. Ellis, Queen's House; C. Gurdon, Richmond; B. Kilner, Wakefield, Trinity; E. T. Mackendale, Manchester Rangers; S. Neame, Old Cheltonians; H. C. Rowley, Manchester; J. Schofield, Manchester; G. F. Vernon, Blackheath; C. Woodhead, Huddersfield.
Umpire—J. M'LAREN.

IRELAND.
Full-back—R. B. Walkington, N.I.F.C.
Half-backs—J. L. Bagot, Dublin University; A. Whitestone, Dublin University.
Quarter-backs—M. Johnston, Dublin University; J. Heron, N.I.F.C.
Forwards—J. L. Cuppaidge, Dublin; H. Purdon, N.I.F.C.; A. J. Forrest, Wanderers; R. W. Hughes, Queen's College, Belfast; H. C. Kelly, N.I.F.C.; F. Kennedy, Wanderers; J. M'Donald, Windsor; A. Miller, Kingstown; G. Scriven, Dublin; A. Taylor, Ulster.
Umpire—W. C. NEVILLE.
Referee—G. P. L. NUGENT.

RESULT OF PAST MATCHES.
1875—February 19, London. English won by 2 goals and 1 try.
1875—December 13, Dublin. English won by 1 goal and 1 try.
1877—February 5, London. English won by 2 goals and 1 try.
1878—March 11, Dublin. English won by 2 goals and 1 try.
1879—March 24, London. English won by 3 goals and 2 tries.
1880—February 2, Dublin. English won by 1 goal and a try to a try.

SCOTLAND v. IRELAND.

PLAYED AT GLASGOW, FEBRUARY 14, 1880.

(From the North British Daily Mail.)

THE third international football match between the representative teams of Scotland and Ireland, under Rugby rules, came off on the West of Scotland ground, Hamilton Crescent, Partick, on Saturday afternoon. The weather was of the most favourable description. This, combined with the prospect of seeing one of the strongest teams which Ireland has yet turned out, as evidenced by the close fight with England about a fortnight previous, drew out between two or three thousand spectators, including a number of ladies, a large contingent of whom journeyed from Edinburgh. A hearty cheer greeted the Irish team when they made their appearance in the field. The Scotchmen were similarly received when they appeared. The play was disappointing on the whole, the Scotchmen having it too much their own way. The match was by no means uninteresting; however, as the brilliant play of the quarters, and the rare combined play, dribbling, and chucking of the Scotchmen forward, made the contest thoroughly enjoyable to spectators, who were liberal in their applause. One or two changes were made on the Irish team, but the Scotch one turned out as originally chosen.

Mr. Kelly won the toss for Ireland, and chose to fight up the hill during the first half of two forties, the Scotchmen having the disadvantage of a strong sun in their faces. At twenty minutes past three the Scotch captain set the ball in motion, and it was well returned by Bagot. Finlay next got the ball, and returned the complement, Bagot's return drop going to Masters, who dropped it judiciously into touch, close to the Irish 25. From the throw in, the first maul was formed, and, as usual, the tussle was closely scanned, the Scotchmen ultimately carrying it amid cheers. Petrie, Ainslie, and Grahame were well up, and a minute after Ireland had to touch behind in self-defence. The kick out from the 25 sent the ball to Cross, that player returning it to Cuppaidge, who had a useful run for Ireland. Masters now got well back into Irish territory, and when tackled, chucked, but it was cleverly caught by one of the Irish forwards, who carried the fight well into Scotch territory. The Scottish forwards now got the ball in tow, and, led by Dr. Irvine, they came dribbling down the hill amid great cheering, Petrie, Grahame, Ainslie, Brewis, and M'Cowen in turn showing well in front. After some give and take play between the forwards in Irish ground, Sorley-Brown got the ball, and amid great excitement the Gala lad went off like a deer, tended by his colleague quarter, to whom he chucked just in the nick of time, Masters taking the ball to within a dozen yards of the coveted line before he was brought to bay. The Irish forwards fought brilliantly at this time, and drove the Scotchmen up the hill to the centre flag, where a stand was made, ere the Scottish forwards again resumed the offensive. The raid was well followed up by a run of Sorley-Brown's, which landed the ball well up to the Irish goal posts, and Walkington missing his drop was tackled within six yards of the posts, and forced to have the ball "down." The Irishmen drove their opponents off, but one of their forwards kicking too hard, sent the ball to Finlay, and enabled the celebrated Scottish half-back to take a drop, which sent the ball right between the Irish posts, amid ringing cheers, just ten minutes from the start. The kick-off from the centre sent the ball over the Scottish lines, but Malcolm Cross refused to touch behind, and pluckily ran the ball into play, dropping neatly into touch beyond the 25 and centre flags. The Irish forwards went up to the 25, and out of a loose scrummage Bagot secured the ball and had a great run ere he was splendidly tackled by Masters, an unlooked-for bit of play that earned the Institution quarter a hearty round of cheering. Masters immediately after secured the ball and fairly astonished the Irishmen by running right through them, and when tackled, chucked to Ainslie, who got behind. The ball, however, was said to have been taken offside before Masters got it, and after some discussion the Scottish captain agreed to a "hack off." Dashing forward play, led by Kelly, Scriven, and Wallace, brought the fight to the centre flags, where Masters got the ball, and ran it well down to the Irish 25, when Irvine, Ainslie, and Grahame became conspicuous. Lively forward play at the Irish 25 ultimately compelled Ireland a second time to touch behind, through too hard kicking on the part of one of the Scottish forwards. After the kick out from the 25, Finlay secured the ball, and by one of his long drops compelled Ireland a third time to touch behind. A capital kick out sent the ball, which Cross missed, over the Scottish lines, but Maclagan refused to touch behind, but ran the ball into play. A grand run of Sorley-Brown's carried the fight to the Irish 25. Masters next had a run, and chucked prettily to Finlay, who a second time dropped a splendid goal, the ball going over about a foot inside the post amid cheering. A long discussion ensued, and as the umpires were not sufficiently near to see, the Irish captain contended that the referee who gave it a goal had no say in the matter—a point which it was agreed to refer to the Rugby Union of England. Pending the decision, a hack off was agreed to. Masters and Sorley-Brown next had runs before Kelly got the ball, the stalwart Irish captain carrying it bravely up the brae to the centre flags ere he was collared. Brewis came away with a good run, which Masters followed up by taking the ball to within six yards of the Irish goal line. Here some of the prettiest chucking probably ever seen in Scotland occurred among the Scottish forwards, Stewart, Petrie, Grahame, Ainslie, and Brewis taking part ere the ball was sent to Masters, who ran right round all the opposing quarters, halfs, and back, when he grounded the ball right between the posts—a brilliant bit of play, which was deservedly cheered, for some time amid cries of "Well played." Malcolm Cross had the easy place and earned another goal for Scotland. Half time was called immediately after, before anything particularly noteworthy occurred, and ends were changed.

With the hill in their favour, the followers of the green were confident the strangers, with their weight, would now score. This looked extremely probable, as the Irish forwards went off with great dash at the outset, Cross being the first to stay their progress by dropping the ball to the Irish 25. Sorley-Brown now had a useful run when he chucked to Finlay, whose drop caused Ireland again to touch behind, while runs of Masters and Sorley-Browne a minute or two after, necessitated more touches behind. Fine dribbling on the part of M'Cowan, Brown, Grahame, Tait, and Brewis enabled the Scotchmen again to occupy Irish ground, Dr. Irvine finishing with a grand run close up to the Irish lines. Heron gave his team timely relief, and soon after Bagot got a fair catch, but the difficult kick was not successful, Cross not even touching behind. The Irishmen made a great effort to get in, but the ball got into touch within a dozen yards of the Scottish line. Irvine, M'Cowan, Ewart, and Brewis came splendidly away after the throw in, Ewart finishing up by a run behind. Cross had the place, but failed to make it a goal. After the kick off. Forrest had one of the best runs of the day for Ireland. Masters neutralised this fine effort by an equally good run, during which he dodged right through his opponents. Soon after the same player got the ball, when he chucked to Grahame, who in turn chucked to Finlay, whose run was spoiled by a grand bit of tackling on the part of Heron, who brought his opponent down into touch. The Irishmen were now sorely pressed by the Scottish forwards within their 25, Masters getting within six yards when in chucked to Sorley-Brown, whose eagerness lost him the ball within a few feet of the goal line. Grahame, Brown, Petrie again broke away with some pretty dribbling, Cronyn, Hughes, Purdon, Johnston, and Heron showing splendid defence at this time. Brewis next made for the goal, but he was nicely tackled, but Sorley-Brown got the ball and ran behind. The ball was, however, ruled offside before Brewis got it, and was brought back. Heron next had a magnificent run for Ireland, his great speed taking him right past his opponents till he came to Finlay, who nursed him beautifully, and finished by bringing him down in touch. Masters, Cross, and Ewart next had runs, which ended in Ewart getting right behind. Cross again had the place, but kicked rather low, and thus enabled one of the Irishmen to touch the ball with his finger, and though it went over the bar it went for nothing. The Irish backs were kept pretty busy, Whitestone and Walkington in particular during the remainder of the time till no side was called, leaving Scotland victors by three goals (one disputed) and two tries to nothing.

For Ireland, Kelly, Cuppaidge, Miller, Scriven, and Cronyn, in the second half, among others, did good service, Heron and Bagot being most conspicuous behind the scrimmage. The feature of the day's play, however, was that of the Sottish quarters, to whose brilliant, combined, and unselfish play in chucking the victory was in a great measure due. Cross tackled as effectively as of yore. Finlay came off with his dropping, while Maclagan had a sinecure as back. Ainslie and Ewart shone in the exceptionally brilliant forward play, while Dr. Irvine early settled any misgivings as to his place in the team by playing with all the old dash and endurance which characterised his play while the popular Captain of the Edinburgh Academicals. Dr. Neville, President of the Irish Rugby Union, umpired for Ireland; Mr. H. W. Little, Vice-President of the Scottish Football Union, for Scotland; while Mr. A. Buchanan, President of the Scottish Union, acted as Referee. Teams:—

IRELAND.

Back—R. B. Walkington (North of Ireland.)

Half-Backs.

J. L. Bagot (Dublin University.)   A. L. Whitestone (Dublin University.)

Quarter-Backs.

M. Johnston (Dublin University.)   J. Heron (North of Ireland.)

Forwards.

J. L. Cuppaidge (Dublin University.)	A. J. Forrest (Dublin Wanderers.)
G. Scriven, do.	W. Wallis, do.
H. C. Kelly (North of Ireland), *Capt.*	A. Miller (Kingstown.)
A. B. Cronyn (Dublin University.)	A. Taylor (Ulster.)
H. Purdon (North of Ireland.)	R. W. Hughes (Windsor.)

SCOTLAND.

Back—W. E. Maclagan (Edinburgh Academicals.)

Half-Backs.

M. Cross (Glasgow Academicals.)   N. Finlay (Edinburgh Academicals.)

Quarter-Backs.

W. Hay-Masters (Edinburgh Instit.)   W. Sorley-Brown (Edin. Instit.)

Forwards.

Dr. R. W. Irvine (Edinburgh Academicals), *Captain*.	J. B. Brown (Glasgow Academs.)
	A. G. Petrie (Royal High School.)
J. H. S. Grahame (Edinburgh Academicals.)	N. Brewis (Edinburgh Instit.)
	R. Ainslie do.
J. Tait (Edinburgh Academicals.)	D. M'Cowan (West of Scotland.)
E. N. Ewart (Glasgow Academicals.)	C. R. Stewart do.

In the evening the Irish team were entertained at dinner in the Queen's Hotel by the Scottish Football Union. Mr. R. Buchanan (Royal High School), the President, occupied the chair; Messrs. Little (West of Scotland), and John Brewis (Royal High School), acting as croupiers; and among others present, in addition to the players, were Dr. Neville and Mr. R. M. Peter, President and Hon. Secretary, respectively, of the Irish Union; Rev. Mr. Coote (Dublin University), Messrs. A. R. Stewart (Wanderers), Exham (Dublin Wanderers), S. Stubbs, R. Howe (Dublin), R. Macnair (Edinburgh Academicals); W. Cross (Glasgow Academicals), H. B. Anderson (West of Scotland), Cunningham (Edinburgh Institution), &c. After an excellent dinner, and the usual loyal toasts, Mr. Buchanan, in complimentary terms, proposed the "Irish Fifteen," to which Mr. Kelly replied, and concluded by giving "The Scottish Fifteen," for which Dr. Irvine responded. Mr. H. W. Little gave "The Irish Football Union," for which Dr. Neville replied, while "The Scottish Football Union," given by Mr. Walkington, was coupled with Mr. J. Brewis, the courteous Hon. Secretary of the Union. Other toasts and a number of songs followed.

LIST OF IRISH FOOTBALL PLAYERS, WITH NAME OF CLUB, AND REMARKS ON STYLE OF PLAY, &c.

Abernethy, W. (Queen's College, Galway)—A good forward.

Acheson, G. H. (Monkstown, Co. Dublin)—Good forward, and can play back.

Adams, H. W. (Wanderers)—An energetic forward; did not play much last season.

Adams, Samuel (Lauriston)—A splendid half-back, possessing great speed and dodging powers.

Adams, W. (Armagh)—A fine, heavy forward; follows up and tackles well; a little wild at times.

Alexander, A. (Roy. Acad. Inst., Belfast)—A good forward; has greatly improved.

Allen, T. C. (Lon. Acad. Inst.)—A plucky forward; very fond of a run (?)

Allen, W. H. (Wanderers)—A good quarter-back; sure collar; might drop more.

Allen, W. S. (Wanderers)—A hard-working forward. Played for Leinster v. Ulster, 1875, and Ireland v. England, 1875.

Amber, J. S. (Wanderers)—A capital, hard-working forward.

Andrews, A. (Wesley College)—A useful forward; lots of pluck; always on the ball.

Andrews, E. A. (Wanderers)—A promising forward; good dribbler.

Andrews, J. (North Down)—A hard-working forward; almost always on the ball.

Andrews, jun., J. (North of Ireland)—A most promising, hard-working forward.

Andrews, J. (Queen's College, Galway)—Splendid forward; very active and quick, and works hard.

Apjohn, G. (Dublin University)—A very powerful, but somewhat awkward forward.

Arbuthnot, W. (Lauriston)—A good half-back; drops well; good collar; somewhat slow.

Arbuthnot, W. H. (Albion)—A smart player as quarter-back; picks up well; sure tackler.

Archer, A. M. (Dublin University and United Hospitals)—A hard-working fast forward; good dribbler.

Armitage, L. (Cork)—A fair forward.

Armstrong, R. (Kingstown)—A valuable man where weight is required; a very fine drop and place-kick.

Askin, J. C. (Armagh Royal School)—A hard-working, active forward.

Askin, T. (Phœnix)—A most reliable forward; follows up well and dribbles neatly.

Atkinson, J. R. (Dublin University and Nomads)—A neat runner and good drop, and makes an excellent quarter-back.

Austin, A. (Galway Grammar School)—An active, plucky forward, always following up hard.

Axford, N. (Queen's College, Galway)—A good light forward.

Backhouse, H. (Dundalk)—An energetic forward.

Backhouse, J. (Dundalk)—A very plucky and hard-working forward.

Bagot, J. C. (Dublin University and Lansdowne)—Considered about the best half-back in Ireland; splendid drop and punt; very fast and sure collar. Played for Ireland 1879-80 v. England and Scotland.

Bailey, W. (North of Ireland, Queen's College, Belfast)—Hard-working forward; plays well up throughout the game.

Baker, R. E. (Cork Bankers)—Splendid quarter-back; picks up quickly, and smart runner.

Baker, R. J. (Dublin University and United Hospitals)—An energetic forward; plays well in the loose.

Barlow, F. F. (Dungannon Royal School)—Captain; always on the ball; reliable collar.

Barnard, E. S. (Rathmines School)—A good, hard-working, plucky forward.

Bate, L. (Wesley College)—A good quarter-back; runs well; good drop at goal.

Baxter, F. (Clanwilliam)—A splendid long-drop and good place-kick; runs strongly, but not enough; a reliable half.

Beatty, D. C. (Kingstown School)—A most energetic forward and good tackler; can play quarter-back if necessary.

Bell, Richard (North of Ireland)—Captain of the Irish Twenty, 1875; Vice-President Irish Rugby Football Union.

Begant, J., Rev. (St. Columba's College)—Makes a good full-back, although some time out of practice; collars well.

Bennett, James (North Down)—A useful player, especially in the scrummages.

Bent, G. (Dublin University and Nomads)—A very fast quarter-back of great promise. Winner of D.U.F.C. Cup for place-kicking, 1880.

Biggs, R. (Galway Grammar School)—A quick runner and safe tackler.

Black, H. B. (Wanderers)—A strong forward, but lacks energy.

Black, J. (Albion)—A hard-working forward; will improve; lacks pace.

Blackader, J. (Dundalk)—A good forward; works hard; is always on the ball.

Blackader, R. (Dundalk)—A good forward for his weight.

Blackemore, F. C. (King's Hospital)—A good half-back; can drop well with either foot; good tackler and runner.

Blackwood, J. K. (Lon. Acad. Inst.)—A safe back; drops well, and sure place-kick.

Blair, J. (Lauriston)—A fast forward.

Blood, F. W. (Wanderers)—A good man behind the scrummage.

Bluett, S. (Galway Grammar School)—A fast and active quarter-back.

Bolton, — (Dundalk)—A splendid forward; works hard.

Bolton, J. (Dublin University)—A strong forward.

Boswell, W. (Wanderers)—A hard-working quarter and good drop; has pace.

Bowles, R. (Phœnix)—A hard-working, heavy forward. Played for Leinster v. Ulster and Munster, 1878-79.

Boyd, John (Ordnance Survey)—A good full-back; sure tackler.
Boyd, T. (Cork Bankers)—Good quarter or half-back.
Brabazon, J. Alfred (Dundalk)—Captain; a very plucky and hard-working forward.
Bradshaw, A. (Merrion Square Rovers)—A good hard-working forward.
Bradshaw, J. (Lansdowne)—Heavy, energetic forward.
Bradshaw, R. (Clontarf)—An energetic forward.
Brady, T. (Kingstown)—A very powerful forward and fast runner, and likely to improve with his knowledge of the game.
Bratten, — (Dundalk)—A very plucky and hard-working quarter-back.
Brett, C. P. (Wanderers)—Will make a good player.
Brett, J. H. (North Wexford)—Captain; a materially useful back; good runner and kicker.
Brett, W. J. (Wanderers)—A promising forward, with more practice.
Bristow, J. R. (North of Ireland)—A first-rate forward; inclined to play on the outside of the scrummage; uses his feet well.
Brown, Ed'e S. H. (Wanderers)—A splendid half-back; most reliable; excellent drop with either foot; lacks pace.
Brown, F. (Wesley College)—A sure, steady full-back; never "loses his head;" a youth of great promise.
Brown, Robert (Lurgan)—A good, hard-working forward.
Brown, S. (Hibernian)—A fair forward; keeps well on the ball.
Browne, Gerald W. (Lansdowne and Kingstown)—Good "quarter" or "half;" is a fast runner and good tackler.
Browning, D. (Wanderers)—A very strong, hard-working forward; good dribbler and place-kick.
Buckley, T. (Queen's College, Galway)—A light and very active forward, and very sharp and quick.
Bunbury, K. (Galway Grammar School)—A fast forward.
Burkett, H. (Cork)—Splendid forward; dribbles well, and works hard in the scrummage.
Butler, J. (St. Columba's College)—A steady forward.
Butler, W. C. (Clontarf)—A good quarter, with great speed.
Butley, J. (Cork Bankers)—Hard-working forward; plays well on the ball.
Byrne, C. C. (Wanderers)—A reliable full-back; good drop and sure collar.
Byrne, E. (Cork)—A solid forward; plays hard.
Buchanan, A. M. (Cliftonville Association and Banbridge Academy)—Splendid goal-keeper; old member of Queen's Park F.C., Glasgow; almost up to Scottish International form; being resident some distance from Belfast, was only occasionally able to play for Cliftonville.
Bullick, W. E. (Cliftonville Association)—Very fair back or half-back; good kick, but rather shaky when pressed.

Callaghan, J. (Wanderers)—A good forward, with much dash.
Campbell, T. V. (Lon. Acad. Inst.)—Very fond of a run; plays well on the ball.
Campbell, R. (Knock)—A fast wing forward.
Canavan, E (North Wexford)—Active on his feet; good dodger; useful back.
Cannon, T. C. T. (Lansdowne)—Hard-working and plucky forward.
Card, D. (Banbridge Academy)—A promising young forward.
Card, W. (Banbridge Academy)—A forward, good dribbler, but rather slow.

Carey, Thomas S. (Lansdowne and Clontarf)—A really first-rate forward works hard in the scrummage, and can run fast when the opportunity arises.
Carroll, J. (Cork and Cork Bankers)—A good heavy forward; always on the ball.
Carroll, J. (Santry School)—A heavy forward; plays with spirit, using his weight well.
Casement, R. (Armagh Royal School)—Best forward in the team, always on the ball, and follows up well.
Cassidi, F. (Kingstown)—A good light forward; does splendid work in the loose scrummages.
Chadwick, W. Cooper (Clanwilliam)—Captain; a heavy, active forward always in good wind; plays well on the ball, with pluck and dash.
Chambers, J. (Rathmines School)—A good forward; follows up hard.
Chambers, T. Y. (Lansdowne and Rathmines School)—An excellent forward always on the ball
Chapman, J. (Banbridge Academy)—A reliable back and very sure kick.
Christian, George D. (Lansdowne and Clontarf)—First-rate "half," sure tackler, fast runner, and good " drop."
Christian, J. A. H. (Lansdowne and Wanderers, Clontarf)—Determined forward; can play half-back; is a good collar.
Clarendon, Fredk. V. Nassau (Lansdowne)—Heavy forward; can play a fair back game as well.
Clarke, E. (Santry School)—An energetic forward; plays a very fair half back.
Clarke, G. (Santry School)—An active and strong full-back, collars well and a first-rate drop; occasionally plays a good half-back.
Clarke, George (Queen's College, Belfast)—Light but useful forward.
Clarke, Walter (Lansdowne)—A very strong forward; plays a most determined game.
Clayton, F. S. (Lansdowne)—Plays a very good forward game; is very fast when the scrummage breaks up.
Clifton, R. (Phœnix)—A resolute and plucky forward; can also play well behind the scrummage.
Collen, T. J. (Armagh)—A good useful forward; is improving fast.
Collen, T. J. (Portadown)—Very useful either half-back or forward; tackles well.
Colles, A. (Armagh Royal School)—A steady, light-weight forward.
Collier, G. (Dundalk)—A fast and plucky half-back.
Collis, W. S. (Wanderers)—A good forward.
Concannon, H. J. (Phœnix)—A good and energetic forward; works to the last.
Cook, H. C. (Phœnix)—A good player in any position; always on the ball; tackles and dribbles well.
Cooke, C. (Phœnix)—An active forward, and useful in the loose scrummages.
Cooke, H. J. (Banbridge Academy)—Back; a strong kick, and makes good use of his weight.
Cooper, W. (King's Hospital)—A strong, muscular forward, always on the ball.
Corker, T. M. (Wanderers and Cork)—A capital half-back, but hardly careful enough; good drop.

Corrigan, J. (Cusack's Academy)—A hard-working forward; follows up splendidly.
Cox, J. (Dundalk)—A good forward; works hard.
Cox, R. (Dundalk)—A good forward for his weight.
Crawford, Andrew G. (Lansdowne)—Hard-working and strong forward.
Crawford, Henry C. (Lansdowne)—Very good forward.
Crawford, J. (Armagh Royal School)—Fast though light forward; good collar.
Crawford, W. (Armagh Royal School)—A steady though light forward; improving.
Creegan, James (Ordnance Survey)—A fair, full back; good collar; should practise drop-kicking.
Crick, P., Rev. (St. Columba's College)—A powerful quarter-back and good collar.
Croker, Charles B. (Lansdowne and Wanderers)—Heavy, hard-working forward; always one of the first in a scrummage.
Cronin, A. (Cork Bankers)—Good back; collars and drops well.
Cronyn, A. P. (Dublin University and Wanderers)—Once the best quarter in Ireland; played last season on his return from abroad, and showed much of his old form, but was not quite up to his prestige; played for Ireland v. England, 1875, and v. Scotland, 1880.
Cummins, W. A. (Cork and Wanderers)—A splendid forward; has played for Ireland v. England, 1878-79-80.
Cunningham, J. R. (Lon. Acad. Inst.)—A fast forward or half-back.
Cuppaidge, E. (Wanderers)—A hard-working forward, or can play well behind; a most promising player.
Cuppaidge, J. Loftus (Dublin University, Wanderers, and United Hospitals)—A heavy, powerful, hard-working forward; sure place-kick; has played for Ireland v. England and Scotland, 1879 and 1880.
Curragh, J. (Banbridge Academy)—A promising half-back; tackles well.
Curell, J. (North of Ireland)—A very strong, hard-working forward.
Currey, T. (Cusack's Academy)—An improving forward.
Curtis, H. (Cork)—An energetic forward.
Cusack, M. (Cusack's Academy)—A heavy, hard-working forward.

Daine, R. (Portarlington School)—A first-class forward; always on the ball.
Dalton, Wm. (Clanwilliam)—A good strong forward.
D'Arcy, — (Wesley College)—An energetic forward; lots of dash.
Darley, A. E. (Wanderers)—A powerful forward; played seldom last season.
Darlington, B. (Phœnix)—A valuable forward; improving daily.
Davoren, H. W. Vesey (Lansdowne)—Good forward.
Dawson, W. J. (Portadown)—A very hard-working forward; plenty of dash; uses his weight well.
Deane, George (Lansdowne)—Heavy forward; plays with great spirit.
De Burgh, W. (St. Columba's College)—A steady forward; has much improved.
Delap, A. H. (Kingstown School)—A hard-working forward from start to finish.
Denning, F. (Merrion Square Rovers)—A very useful forward, following up with plenty of pluck.

Denning, J. (Dublin University)—A very good forward; always on the ball; uses his feet well.
Denning, W. (Merrion Square Rovers)—A steady, useful forward, using his weight well.
Dennis, T. (Monkstown, Co. Dublin)—A good fast quarter-back.
Dill, A. H. (Royal Acad. Inst., Belfast)—Very smart on his feet; dribbles well; is a good tackler; plays well quarter-back.
Dimond, J. F. (Phœnix)—A very fast quarter-back; first-class tackler and dodger.
Dobbin, — (Rathmines School)—An excellent half-back; sure collar.
Dobbin, G. (Dungannon Royal School)—A good forward and excellent drop.
Dobbin, S. (Kingstown and Kingstown School)—A good hard-working forward.
Dockrell, — (United Hospitals)—A heavy, active forward.
Donaldson, C. (North Wexford)—A determined forward and tackler.
Donaldson, R. (Portadown)—An admirable forward, playing with great dash, and dribbling well; always on the ball.
Dorman, H. (Cork)—A young, but good back.
Douglas, John (Lurgan)—A good all-round player.
Downing, A. (Dublin University and Nomads)—Plays a genuine forward game, works hard, and always on the ball.
Draper, G. (Santry School)—A young and very promising forward.
Drennan, M. A. (North Down)—A safe back; tackles splendidly.
Drought, A. (Monkstown, Co. Dublin)—Very fast forward, and a good tackler.
Drought, G. A. (Phœnix)—A steady half-back; displays much adroitness in passing.
Dunbar, V. J. R. (Wanderers)—With more practice would make a good player.
Dwyer, Henry H. (Lansdowne)—Heavy, useful forward.
Dill, A. (Knock)—Excellent wing-forward, sure dribbler, and passes well.
Dill, J. (Knock)—A sure tackler and strong kick.
Donnachie, J. (Cliftonville Association)—An old Kilmarnock man; splendid centre forward, dodges and dribbles to perfection, passes judiciously, and is a capital shot at goal.
DuNoyer, G. (Knock)—A rising wing-forward.

Eaton, Wm. (Clanwilliam)—A good hard-working forward; always on the ball.
Eccles, G. M. (Kingstown)—A very fast forward; always on the ball; collars well.
Edgeworth, C. (Wanderers)—Plays well behind the scrummage.
Ekin, Edward (Queen's College, Galway)—A good heavy forward, working hard, and a good tackler.
Elliott, J. (Rathmines School)—A heavy forward; follows up hard.
Ellis, R. (Merrion Square Rovers)—A capital back; a good drop at goal.
Ervin, K. (Banbridge Academy)—A hard-working forward, but lacks speed.
Ervin, R. J. (Banbridge Academy)—A good forward; will improve with practice.
Evans, F. (Cork Bankers)—Good half-back; picks up and runs well.
Evans, J. (Cork Bankers)—Good quarter-back; runs well.

Evans, J. (Wesley College)—A hard-working forward; uses his weight splendidly in the scrummage.
Evans, L. (Wesley College)—A capital quarter-back; drops well with either foot; a most promising colt.
Exham, A. (Cork)—A promising forward.
Exham, J. S. (Wanderers)—A good half-back or forward.

Fahy, T. (Santry School)—A useful forward, with weight and strength, knowing the game well.
Falkner, F. (Dungannon Royal School)—A good half-back; runs well; fair collar.
Faris, E. (King's Hospital)—A good quarter-back; plays with much pluck; good drop at goal.
Farrell, Thomas (Ordnance Survey)—A reliable forward; fair tackler, and good drop; should follow up quicker at times.
Farrelly, P. (Queen's College, Galway)—An active hard-working forward.
Fausset, Thomas (Dublin University)—A hard-working and powerful forward.
Fayle, G. (Galway Grammar School)—A reliable half-back, with great speed and judgment; a splendid tackler.
Fayle, H. (Galway Grammar School)—Good quarter-back; fine tackler.
Ferguson, J. S. (North of Ireland)—A fair half-back; fast; good punt; might tackle better.
Finch, T. (Santry School)—A very energetic forward; follows up the ball well, and of great service in a scrummage.
Findlater, A. (Monkstown and Kingstown, County Dublin)—Fast and dodgy runner; good quarter-back.
Finlay, W. (North of Ireland)—A good hard-working forward. Played for Ireland v. England.
Finny H. (St. Columba's College)—A brilliant runner and sure collar.
Fitzgerald, A. O. (Lansdowne)—A strong, energetic forward.
Fitzgerald, H. (Wesley College and Monkstown)—Good back, and can play well forward; good collar.
Fitzgerald, J. (Wanderers)—A strong hard-working forward.
Fitzgerald, R. (Wesley College)—Dribbles and drops well; swift, but not sure.
Fitzgerald, R. (Cusack's Academy)—A good drop; lacks coolness.
Fitzgerald, R. L. (Monkstown, County Dublin)—Good forward; can drop and run well.
Fitzmaurice, H. (Armagh Royal School)—A very steady forward.
Fleming, A. G. (Wanderers)—A light man behind the scrummage.
Fleming, A. J. (Wanderers)—An A 1 half-back; splendid drop; plays with much judgment; sure collar.
Fleming, H. (Rathmines School)—A hard-working plucky forward.
Fleming, T. H. (Wanderers and Lansdowne)—A heavy forward and good worker; can play well behind the scrummage.
Fletcher, W. P. (Kingstown School)—Captain. Good quarter-back; excellent collar; good drop and punt.
Foley, — (Wesley College)—A good hard-working forward; always plays up with the greatest spirit.
Foley, J. M. G. (North Wexford)—Heavy weight; swift; very useful in a scrummage.

Foley, W. (Portora Royal School)—A reliable forward ; tackles well.
Ford, C. H. (Cusack's Academy)—Can play well behind the scrummage.
Ford, H. (Cusack's Academy)—A most promising player.
Forrest, A. J. (Wanderers, Kingstown, and Lansdowne)—No better forward in Ireland. Played for Ireland v. England and Scotland, 1880.
Forrest, T. (Cusack's Academy)—A good hard-working forward, with plenty of dash.
Forsythe, J. (Hibernian)—A good and promising forward.
Fosberry, F. (Wanderers)—A good player, of much promise.
Fowler, R. (Wanderers)—A hard-working forward ; generally manages to get scraped.
Freeman, H. G. (Dundalk)—A good forward.
Freyer, J. (Queen's College, Galway)—An active and good quarter-back.
Fry, J. (Galway Grammar School)—A hard-working forward.
Furlong, J. (Phœnix)—A hard-working young player of skill and promise.

Galbraith, J. (St. Columba's College)—A most promising forward ; plays well on the ball.
Gamble, R. (Merrion Square Rovers)—A very good back, running and dropping well with either foot.
Gamble, W. (Dublin University)—A good full-back ; promises well ; did not play much last season.
Gardner, T. (Armagh)—A very useful forward, sticking to the ball and dribbling well.
Garside, E. (Queen's College, Belfast, and Ulster)—Very dodgy quarter-back ; lacks pace, but promises well.
Gaussen, A. (Dungannon Royal School)—A fast forward and good drop.
Gavin, M. W. (Ordnance Survey and Hibernian)—Can play with distinction in any postion behind the scrummage ; most difficult to pass ; might drop better ; good tackler and runner.
Gibb, Albert (York Road, Belfast)—An improving forward, and a good drop-kick.
Gibb, B. (Lauriston)—A good heavy forward, but lacks energy.
Gibb, John (York Road, Belfast)—A very sure quarter or half-back, never losing a chance ; a good drop, and sure place-kick.
Giddis, Andrew (Lurgan)—A good forward for his weight ; follows up hard and dribbles well.
Girvan, W. J. (Wanderers)—A very powerful half-back ; strong runner.
Girvin, W. J. (Armagh)—A good half-back ; runs and tackles well, but fails in kicking and picking up.
Glenn, H. (Dublin University)—A good forward ; dribbles well.
Godkin, T. (North Wexford)—A very determined opponent, especially useful in a scrummage.
Gorman, James (Lurgan)—A very fast and good quarter.
Goulding, J. (Queenstown)—A hard-working, quick forward.
Goulding, W. J. (Wanderers)—A quick quarter-back and fair drop ; good collar. Vice-President, Irish Rugby Football Union.
Graham, M. T. (North Down)—A light forward ; runs and dribbles well.
Greene, E. (Kingstown, Monkstown, and Kingstown School)—A fast runner, good drop and place-kick ; a rising player.
Greer, James (Lurgan)—A light active forward, and plays very pluckily.

Gribben, E. (Knock)—A forward of great promise.
Gribben, R. (Knock)—An effective centre forward; kicks with judgment.
Griffiths, Thomas (Clanwilliam)—A fast forward, follows up well, and is a good drop. Played for Ireland and England, 1878.
Guèrin, V. (Phœnix)—A light active forward.
Guerini, A. (Ordnance Survey and Hibernian)—An excellent forward; makes a good quarter-back, being a good runner and sure tackler.
Guy, F. (Cork)—A hard-working forward.

Hackett, Edward A. (Queen's College, Galway)—An active forward; sometimes plays quarter-back.
Haines, C. (Cork Bankers)—A good forward; can run well.
Hallaran, W. (Portarlington School)—A hard-working forward.
Haltigan, John (Ordnance Survey)—A fair forward; sure tackler, and good place-kick.
Hamilton, H. (Wanderers)—A good player, but does not play often enough.
Hamilton, J. N. (Knock)—A sure back; very fast; strong kick.
Hamilton, W. J. (Lurgan)—Plays back fairly, but is a better forward.
Hammond, T. (Ordnance Survey)—A strong heavy forward.
Hanna, James (Lurgan)—An energetic forward.
Hannay, D. (Cliftonville Association)—A hard-working reliable half-back; good tackler; displays admirable judgment in placing the ball to his forwards.
Hannay, D. (Ulster)—Plays a fast following up game.
Hardy, S. C. (Lauriston)—A fast player, but uncertain.
Harpur, H. S. M. (Galway Grammar School)—A capital kick, whether from place or drop.
Harpur, S. (Phœnix)—A good forward.
Harris, S. G. (Cork Bankers)—Good forward or half-back; runs well, and works hard.
Harrison, C. F. (Clanwilliam)—A fair drop; has speed; a good half.
Harrison, Thomas (Lurgan)—Is possessed of great strength and speed, and plays forward or quarter well.
Harrison, T. (Cork)—One of the best full-backs in Ireland; magnificent drop, and sure tackler.
Hartley, A. H. (North of Ireland)—A hard-working unselfish forward.
Harvey, B. C. (North Wexford)—An excellent drop; plays up in good style.
Harvey, D. (North Wexford)—A useful half-back; good drop.
Harvey, W. Leathem (Royal Academical Institution, Belfast)—A most hardworking forward; always on the ball; an excellent drop, and sure tackler.
Haslem, G. E. (Rathmines School)—A fast quarter and sure collar.
Hemsworth, H. (Wanderers)—An industrious forward, but wants practice.
Henderson, J. (Ulster)—Captain. An energetic forward, plays up hard, and dribbles well.
Herdman, A. (Lauriston)—A strong forward; uses his feet well.
Heron, James (North of Ireland)—An A 1 quarter-back; had great pace; good tackler.
Heron, S. (Portadown)—A fairly useful forward, with weight and strength.
Heron, Wm. (North Down)—A promising forward, heavy and useful in the scrummage.

Heron, W. T. (North of Ireland)—Very fast quarter-back. Played for Ireland v. Scotland, 1880.
Herrick, J. E. H. (Galway Grammar School)—A steady forward.
Herrick, R. (Galway Grammar School)—An active forward.
Heuston, F. S. (Clanwilliam)—A useful back or forward; collars and drops well; has speed.
Heuston, F. T. (Clanwilliam)—A useful half; runs strongly; collars well; a good fast forward.
Hickson, J. (Dundalk)—A capital forward, always on the ball.
Hickson, R. (Kingstown)—Works well in the mauls, and follows up hard.
Hickson, S. (Kingstown)—A powerful forward; very useful on the touch-line.
Hill, S., jun. (Banbridge Academy)—Fairback; tackles well, and plays with determination.
Hill, W. K. (Banbridge Academy)—A hard-working half-back; kicks well, and plays an unselfish game.
Hillas, T. (St. Columba's College)—Plays well quarter-back; excellent collar; good drop-kick.
Hodges, H. P. (Monkstown, County Dublin)—Good forward; can play quarter.
Horner, A. L. (Lon. Acad. Inst.)—Captain; a strong fast half-back, and splendid drop.
Hornybrook, H. (Queenstown)—Generally plays behind the scrummage, and can be relied on.
Howard, S. (Dungannon Royal School)—A strong hard-working forward.
Howe, E. A. (Wanderers)—A light quarter, but seldom plays.
Howell, A. (Cliftonville Association)—A most promising back; powerful kick; shows excellent judgment.
Hughes, E. (North of Ireland)—A good forward; fast in the loose; follows up well.
Hughes, George (Queen's College, Belfast)—Heavy forward; very hard-working and conscientious player.
Hughes, R. W. (Queen's College, Belfast, and Ulster)—Hard-working and plucky forward; always does his best; plays really good game with his feet, as well as making good use of his weight. Played:—v. England, 1878 and 1880; v. Scotland, 1880.
Hunter, R. J. (Banbridge Academy)—A promising forward and excellent goal keeper; is certain to come to the front.
Hunter, W. (Albion and Lauriston)—A very useful half-back; quick dodgy runner.

Inman, C. A. (Wanderers)—A good forward; sure collar.
Inskipp, J. (Hibernian)—A good forward.
Ireland, R. (Lauriston)—A hard-working forward, but lacks speed.
Irvine, John (Queen's College, Belfast)—Plucky forward; young, and one of the most promising players in the Club.
Irwin, J. (Wesley College)—An energetic forward; always on the ball.
Irwin, M. (Wanderers)—A very fast forward, or good man behind.

Jackson, G. (Monkstown, Co. Dublin)—Good forward, following up and dribbling well.

Jackson, James (Lurgan)—An excellent forward, playing a sound game and dribbling well.
Jackson, W. (Ulster)—A plucky forward, with good judgment; uses his feet to advantage.
Jackson, W. J. (Queen's College, Galway)—A fine, heavy forward; works well, especially in scrummages.
Jellett, M. H. (Dublin University)—A neat and quick half-back and good drop.
Johns, C. M. (Armagh Royal School)—A good full-back, very sure collar, and fair kick.
Johnston, J. (Ulster)—A dashing forward; plays most unselfishly.
Johnston, M. (Dublin University)—A most reliable quarter-back; certain collar; very fast. Played for Ireland, 1880. Winner of D.U.F.C. Cup for drop-kicking, 1880.
Johnston, W. K. (Rathmines School)—A reliable half-back; has pace; good drop.
Johnstone, W. (Mountpottinger)—A good, plucky forward, with great perseverance; excellent tackler.
Johnson, W. (Cork Bankers)—Very good forward; always on the ball.
Johnson, W. (Kingstown)—A light, fast forward; collars well.
Jones, E. (St. Columba's College)—Plays in good style; promises well for next season.
Jones H. (Cork)—A fast, useful forward.
Jones H. (St. Columba's College)—A heavy, hard-working forward.
Jones, M. S. C. (Armagh)—Useful either as a forward or quarter; passes well, but does not pick up enough.
Jones W. H. (North Wexford)—A smart and exceedingly useful forward.
Joyce, B. J. (Queen's College, Galway)—A good drop-kick; useful full-back.
Joyce, Patrick (North Wexford)—A strong runner; very useful in a scrummage.
Joynt, A. E. R. (Portora Royal School)—Hard-working forward; good collar.

Kearney, F. H. (Phœnix)—Plays well as forward or half-back.
Keillor, G. (King's Hospital)—A steady full-back.
Kelly, H. C. (North of Ireland)—Captain Irish XV., 1879-80. Plays well forward; works energetically; capital dribbler.
Kelly J. (Phœnix)—A reliable forward, but plays too little.
Kelly, M. (Cusack's Academy)—An improving forward.
Kelly, W. (Wanderers)—An energetic, powerful forward; follows up well.
Kennedy, F. (Wanderers)—Always on the ball; sure collar. Played for Ireland v. England, 1880.
Kennedy, G. (Wanderers)—A good forward; seldom plays.
Kennedy, H. (Armagh and Armagh Royal School)—A very hard-working forward; keeps well on the ball.
Kennedy, J. (Wanderers)—A good, energetic forward.
Keon, J. J. (Wanderers)—A most energetic forward. Played for Ireland v. England, 1879.
Kidd, F. W. (Dublin University and Dundalk)—A first-rate half-back; drops magnificently; sure collar. Played for Ireland v. England, 1877-8-9.

Killen, E. B. (North Down)—Plays well behind the scrummage, and runs well.
King, H. (Armagh and Armagh Royal School)—A very long drop and good tackler; dribbles well.
Kingston, H. J. (Wesley College)—Knows how to use his feet in a scrummage; an energetic forward.
Kennedy, R. M. (Cliftonville Association)—Right wing forward; fastest man in the team; fair dribbler, but rather deficient in passing, and inclined to carry the ball too far into the corner.

Lalor, J. (Phœnix)—Can play well forward or half-back; skilful dribbler; can drop with either foot.
Langford, J. (Lansdowne)—Hard-working and useful forward; sometimes plays half-back.
Larkin, Patrick (Lurgan)—A safe and good back; drop and tackles well.
Lavery, P. (Armagh)—May with practice make a good forward.
Lawson, H. A. (Wanderers)—A good player; promises well.
Lee, — (Wesley College)—An exceedingly plucky light weight.
Lee, F. (Kingstown)—An excellent full-back; runs well, sure kick, and certain tackle; steadily improving.
Lee, H. F. (Armagh)—A splendid forward, very fast dribbler, and tackles well; is useful also behind the maul, but wants coolness and judgment.
Lee, J. (Queen's College, Galway)—A light, active forward.
Lee, R. C. (Monkstown, Co. Dublin)—A good full-back, especially at picking up and tackling.
Leeds, H. (Cork Bankers)—Plays a good but uncertain game; can run well.
Lehane, D. M. (Phœnix)—A magnificent drop-kick with either foot; a certain collar, and, owing to weight and pace, difficult to be tackled; ranks as one of the best half-backs in Ireland.
Lemon, G. G. (Clontarf)—A fair quarter or half-back.
Leonard, T. R. (Wesley College)—A reliable half or full-back; swift, and dodges well, but met with accident at close of last season, which has since prevented him playing.
L'Lestrange, G. (Armagh Royal School)—Fast quarter-back, but, owing to want of practice, a little uncertain.
Levis, F. (Cork)—An active and hard-working forward.
Lewis, George (Rathmines School)—A light, active forward.
Lewis, J. (Monkstown, Co. Dublin)—A good runner and drop-kick.
Lindsay, J. C. (North of Ireland)—A good all-round man; doubles well; sure drop.
Lindsay, R. M. (Portadown)—A good quarter; promises well.
Littledale, R. W. W. (Armagh and Armagh Royal School)—A magnificent back, being a sure tackler and unfailing drop with either foot; as a place kick is A 1.
Livingstone, J. (Armagh)—Is fast becoming a good forward, and promises well for next season.
Loane, A. (Cork)—Always on the ball, and follows up hard.
Loane, E. W. (Queenstown)—An energetic forward.
Lowes, J. (Lansdowne)—A most useful player; can play a fair game as full-back, half-back, or forward; is a very good drop-kick.
Lowry, W. B. (Cliftonville Association)—Very promising player as forward or half-back; should come well to the front next season.

Lowry, R. H. (Phœnix)—A capital half-back, and not a bad forward.
Lucas, R. (St. Columba's College)—Plays a fast game; not steady enough on the ball; a good kick.
Luckman, A. G. (St. Columba's College)—An active quarter-back, with plenty of dash.
Lyden, Michael A. (Queen's College, Galway)—A fine, heavy forward; makes some very good runs.
Lynam, Joseph (Queen's College, Galway)—A good forward.
Lynch, T. (Hibernian)—A good, hard-working forward; keeps well on the ball.
Lyttle, J. (Wesley College)—A reliable half-back; an excellent drop-kick.

Macartney, R. (Knock)—Good half-back; very fine tackler.
Macdonald, J. A. (Cliftonville Association)—The International Rugby player is a hard and determined worker, either forward or half-back, dribbles splendidly, and passes with judgment; with practice would undoubtedly excel at the Association Game.
Macrory, C. A. (Wanderers)—A neat player; hurt early in the season.
Madden, J. B. (Lansdowne)—Very good forward.
Magee, F. (Lauriston)—A light but hard-working forward; always on the ball; good tackler.
Magee, J. R. (Lauriston)—Good all-round; neat dribbler and sure tackler.
Mageean, W. (Albion)—Captain; a good untiring forward; dribbles well.
Maguire, H. (Cork)—With more practice will make a good forward.
Maguire, T. (Cork Bankers)—Good half-back, but should drop more; fast on his feet.
Mahon, H. L. (Lansdowne)—First-rate forward; strong and fast half; is a good drop and sure tackler.
Main, D. (Banbridge Academy)—A very promising centre forward; good dribbler, but rather slow.
Main, W. (Banbridge Academy)—A promising and cool young forward.
Malcomson, R. (Phœnix)—An energetic, careful, and effective forward.
Manders, G. (Wanderers)—A powerful forward.
Manly, V. H. (Lansdowne)—Good full-back; long drop; can play very well as half-back.
Mathers, Robert (Lurgan)—A strong hard-working forward.
Matier, A. S. (North of Ireland)—Can play well in any position in the field.
Matier, R. (North of Ireland)—Brilliant half-back; good tackler; runs and drops well.
Maturin, D. C. (Wanderers and Clontarf)—A good player; splendid drop.
Maunsell, E. L. (Clontarf)—A useful forward.
Mayne, R. H. (Albion)—A plucky fast forward.
Mecredy, R. J. (Portora Royal School)—Captain; good half-back; sure tackler.
Meyer, G. R. (Wanderers)—A hard-working forward with great dash; always to the front.
Millington, F. (Clontarf)—A hard-working forward.
Miller, A. (Kingstown and Kingstown School and Wanderers)—A powerful and energetic forward; always on the ball; follows up hard, and dribbles well. Played for Ireland v. England and Scotland, 1880.
Miller, E. (Kingstown and Monkstown)—A strong forward; good kick; greatly improved during the season.

Miller, George, (Dundalk)—A good forward; works hard.
Miller, R. (Kingstown)—A very promising young player, works hard, and is a good dribbler.
Miller, W. (Monkstown, Co. Dublin)—Good forward; dribbles well.
Minchin, W. (Galway Grammar School)—A useful forward.
Minhear, J. (Cork Bankers)—Good heavy forward; works hard; always on the ball.
Molineux, F. (Dublin University)—A powerful forward; good collar.
Monsell, — (Wesley College)—A very useful quarter-back; dodges remarkably well. Played on the County Dublin Fifteen.
Montgomery, R. S. (King's Hospital)—A reliable half-back; good collar and kick.
Montgomery, R. S. (Wanderers)—A good player; sure collar and fair drop.
Moore, D. F. (Wanderers)—A fair full-back; good long drop.
Moore, F. (Hibernian)—A good tackler, and one of the most promising players in the Club.
Moore, F. W. (Wanderers)—A most hard-working keen forward.
Moore, Hamilton (Queen's College, Belfast)—Good half-back; drops well with either foot, and tackles fairly.
Moore, J. (Dungannon Royal School)—A hard-playing forward.
Moore, J. B. (Lansdowne)—Strong and dodgy quarter; very good drop and place-kicker; sure tackler.
Moore, J. W. (Monkstown, Co. Dublin)—Good back-kick, and runs fairly.
Moore, R. C. (Queen's College, Belfast)—Light, but hard-working forward.
Moore, S. J. (Queen's College, Belfast)—Fairly fast quarter-back; watches opposite quarter well; good and safe man; tackles well.
Moore, Thomas (Lansdowne)—Very useful forward.
Moore, W. (Hibernian)—Plays a steady quarter-back game; punts and runs well.
Moore, W. (Rathmines School)—An excellent quarter-back.
Moore, W. C. (Lansdowne and North Wexford)—A heavy energetic forward.
Moore, W. R. (Lansdowne)—First-rate forward; always on the ball in the scrummage.
Moorhead, J. (Kingstown)—A light, fast forward; always on the ball; doing a great deal of work for his weight. Leinster v. Ulster, 1880.
Morell, H. B. (Dublin University and Nomads)—A hard-working forward and good drop.
Morgan, A. H. (Kingstown)—A lively man, who always keeps up the spirit of the game.
Moriarty, G. J. (Kingstown School)—A good forward; works hard, and is always on the ball.
Morris, James (Clanwilliam)—A light active forward.
Morrison, Hugh S. (Queen's College, Belfast)—Useful forward; does good work when ball gets loose; doesn't utilize his weight in the scrummages.
Morressy, P. (Clanwilliam)—A very useful smart light forward.
Morrow, F. A. J. (Phœnix)—With more experience will make a good forward.
Morrow, R. W. (Queen's College, Belfast, and Albion)—A safe half-back; good runner; can drop with both feet; excellent tackler.
Morrow, W. J. (Ulster)—A heavy useful forward.
Morse, S. St. G. (Kingstown School)—A promising back and sure drop.

Morton, Andrew (York Road, Belfast)—An energetic forward and fair drop-kick.
Mosse, C. D. (Wanderers)—A fast forward and good dribbler.
Moynan, — (Wesley College)—A strong runner and sure tackler; a very reliable half-back.
Moyers, L. (Kingstown)—A good forward; collars well.
Mulcahy, Wm. (Clanwilliam)—A useful forward.
Mulholland, C. (Queen's College, Belfast, and Lauriston)—A safe quarter-back; has pace; good punt.
Murray, A. (Kingstown)—A very fair half-back; kicks and tackles well; a very good man on a losing side.
Murray, A. (Ulster)—A powerful forward; works hard.
Murray, W. T. (Monkstown, Co. Dublin)—A good half-back; being a safe kick and very sure tackler.
Murphy, C. (Armagh)—Plays a most unselfish and praiseworthy forward game; passes and dribbles excellently.
Murphy, Jas. (North Down)—An energetic forward; very useful in the scrummage.
Murphy, R. (Cork Bankers)—Good heavy forward, but should play harder.
Murphy, W. (Cork)—A good back, but not sure collar; drops neatly.
Murrow, G. (Ulster)—A hard-working forward and good tackler
Murry, B. (North Wexford)—A very useful half-back; good place-kick.
Myles, H. (Portora Royal School)—An energetic forward.
M'Alery, J. M. (Cliftonville Association)—The father of Irish Association football (the Joseph Taylor of Ireland); splendid back, kicks well with either foot, and is a remarkably good tackler.
M'Alister, E. (King's Hospital)—An energetic quarter-back and good collar.
M'Bratney, R. (Knock)—Promising forward; passes well.
M'Blaine, J. (Merrion Square Rovers and Clontarf)—A brilliant quarter-back, very quick on his feet, and a good drop at goal.
M'Blain, W. J. B. (Wanderers and Kingstown)—A very good hard-working quarter; lacks speed, but dodges well, and is a certain tackle. Played for Leinster v. Ulster, Nov., 1879.
M'Bride, John (Lurgan)—A light plucky forward, and plays quarter fairly.
M'Bride, W. (Mount Pottinger)—A most promising quarter-back; fast, dodges and tackles well.
MacCarthy, J. (Clanwilliam)—A promising quarter.
MacCarthy, St. George (Clanwilliam)—A very active quarter and fair drop-kick; collars well.
M'Carthy, J. J. (Cusack's Academy and Hibernian)—Can play either quarter or full-back; good tackler; fair drop; runs with much dash.
M'Carty, E. A. (Phœnix)—A steady untiring forward; keeps well on the ball, and follows up hard.
M'Cully, S. (Cliftonville Association)—Excellent centre forward, remarkable speed for his weight, good dribbler, passes judiciously, and is a sure shot at goal.
M'Donald, J. (Queen's College, Belfast)—One of best forwards in Ireland; indefatigable player, following up well and being always on the ball. International man. Played Scotland v. England, &c.
M'Donnell, P. (Lansdowne)—Heavy forward.

M'Donough, R. (Queen's College, Galway)—An energetic forward, works very well, and never tires.
M'Dowell, John (York Road, Belfast)—Captain; a strong and quick forward
M'Gee, G. (Mount Pottinger)—Plays well half-back; possesses much speed and drops well.
M'Geown, Patrick (Lurgan)—A fine forward, plays well on the ball, and uses his feet to advantage.
MacGillycuddy, J. (Dublin University)—A hard-playing forward and good collar; has played on Irish Fifteen.
M'Intosh, L. (Wesley College)—Captain; a capital half-back; very quick on his feet; has played well forward.
M'Intosh, M. (Wesley College)—A quarter-back who uses his feet well; a good tackler.
M'Kay, H. (Ordnance Survey)—A steady forward, always on the ball, good dribbler, and sure collar.
M'Kay, M. (Portora Royal School)—Quick collar and good runner; plays well quarter-back.
M'Kay, T. (Hibernian)—A hard-working forward, but lacks dash.
M'Kee, Charles (Queen's College, Belfast)—Fair forward, dribbles well; played only at the end of the season.
M'Kay, Thos. (Ordnance Survey)—A plucky tackler and fair drop.
MacKenzie, A. E. (Clanwilliam)—A smart quarter; runs and drops well.
M'Kenzie, A. L. (Phœnix)—Plays a plucky half-back game.
M'Kinney, Thos. (Portadown)—A first-rate quarter; very fast; will be of good service next season.
MacKillip, G. B. (Londonderry Academical Institution)—A very fast forward, but somewhat inclined to play quarter-back.
MacLaughlin, J. H. (Londonderry Academical Institution)—A splendid forward; always silent, and always on the ball.
M'Lean, R. (Dublin University and Nomads)—A splendid reliable full-back; splendid drop; has much pace. 1st subs. (full-back) on Irish XV. 1879-80.
MacMahon, W. H. (Lansdowne)—Very useful and plucky forward.
M'Mahon, J. (Hibernian)—A strong and promising forward.
MacMullen, J. N. (Londonderry Academical Institution)—Sure tackler and good drop; promises to make a good half-back.
M'Mullen, A. (Cork)—A fast forward; dribbles well.
M'Quade, J. (Santry School)—A heavy and determined half; runs well, making good use of his weight; collars well.
MacVicker, A. S. (Londonderry Academical Institution)—A good forward.
MacVicker, C. G. (Londonderry Academical Institution)—A good dribbler and tackler; plays well forward.
M'Wha, W. B. R. (Knock)—Very fast forward; unselfish in passing.

Nally, W. R. (Cusack's Academy), Captain—Plays well half-back; has much pace; might drop more.
Nash, L. (Lansdowne)—A very plucky quarter; plays an admirable defensive game.
Neil, D. (Cork)—A safe forward; dribbles well.
Neill, J., jun. (Banbridge Academy)—A really good centre forward

Nelson, J. (Mount-Pottinger)—A heavy forward; tackles and dribbles well.

Neville, W. C. (Dublin University and Wanderers)—A first-class forward; Captain of the Irish Fifteen, 1879; President of the Irish Rugby Football Union, 1880.

Newell, — (Wanderers)—A good all-round player.

Newell, F. T. P. (Kingstown)—A very hard-working forward; plays well throughout.

Nicholson, W. (Wanderers)—A fast forward; good dribbler.

Nolan, C. (Dublin University)—A hard-working forward; follows up well; dodgy runner.

Nolan, F. (Armagh)—Has improved most wonderfully, and is now a really good forward; has weight, and uses his head.

Nunn, R. (Nomads)—A hard-working, useful forward; follows up well; good collar.

Nunns, E. H. (Lansdowne)—Captain; first-rate forward; strong and determined; is a good drop, and can play full-back when required.

Nunns, Wm. (Lansdowne)—First-rate forward; good drop and place kick; very satisfactory as a back.

Obre, E. (Cork Bankers)—Good forward or back; sure drop and collar.

O'Connell, W. A. (Cusack's Academy)—A fast forward; follows up hard.

Ogilvie, W. F. (St. Columba's College)—Captain; plays a brilliant quarter-back game; most energetic.

O'Farrell, E. J. (Dublin University)—A first-class forward.

O'Grady, W. (Dublin University and Nomads)—A giant forward; always plays hard.

O'Grady, Waller (Clanwilliam)—Has strength and weight, and uses both to advantage in a scrummage; a capital forward.

O'Hanlon, F. J. (Portadown)—A good plucky forward; follows up well.

O'Keeffe, — Good half-back and sure collar.

Oldham, W. E. (Ordnance Survey)—A hard-working heavy forward.

O'Reilly, E. J. (Phœnix)—A fast and reliable back.

O'Reilly, J. (Clanwilliam)—A light half; picks up well; a good drop.

Orpen, R. (St. Columba's College)—Good full-back; safe drop kick.

Orr, C. (Wanderers)—a hard-working player.

Orr, F. (Kingstown)—A good kick, but wants improvement in tackling.

Orr, Fingall H. (Lansdowne and Wanderers)—good full back; first-rate drop.

O'Sullivan, A. C. (Dublin University and Nomads)—A good forward; plays hard and follows up well.

O'Sullivan, A. C. (Rathmines School)—A useful forward and good runner.

O'Sullivan, A. W. (Dublin University and Nomads)—An honest forward; dribbles and collars well.

Owen, Charles A. (Lansdowne)—Very hard-working and plucky forward.

Owens, R. (Clontarf)—A promising young player.

Oliver, T. B. (Banbridge Academy)—Half-back; a good dodger, but plays a rather selfish game.

Parker, V. (Kingstown)—A very powerful forward.

Parkinson, J. (Santry School)—A very quick quarter and a good runner; tackles well.

Patten, A. (Merrion Square Rovers)—An energetic forward, following up hard and pluckily.

Patten, G. (Dublin University)—A handy forward; follows up and tackles well; a good drop.

Patten, W. (Dublin University)—A fast forward; uses his feet well.

Peacocke, W. J. (Queen's College, Galway)—A good full or half-back; makes a splendid drop kick.

Pedlow, James (Lurgan)—A good half-back, having a fair turn of speed, and playing with great dash.

Peirce, W. (Cork and Cork Bankers)—Excellent half-back, sure drop, and good collar.

Pentland, H. (Armagh)—A most reliable quarter; picks up and tackles very well; plays a losing game safely; makes also a fine forward; is a fair drop.

Perdisatt, P. (Ordnance Survey and Hibernian)—A good all-round man; collars well; fair kick.

Peter, R. M. (Wanderers)—Played for Leinster v. Ulster, 1875; and Leinster v. Munster, 1877. Hon. Treasurer I.F. Union, 1874-9; Hon. Secretary Irish Rugby Football Union, 1880.

Peters, E. (King's Hospital)—A good quarter-back; runs and tackles well; a good drop.

Phillips, R. (Phœnix)—A light though brilliant quarter-back.

Pike, W. W. (Kingstown)—A powerful and fast half-back; punts well; good tackler; played for Ireland v. Scotland, 1879.

Poole, Walter C. (Rathmines School)—An active half-back and good tackler.

Pooler, L. A. (Armagh and Armagh Royal School—A good quarter; gets well away, but does not pass sufficiently.

Porter, H. (Lon. Acad. Inst.)—A heavy, energetic forward.

Pounden, P. C. (North Wexford)—A first-class forward and tackler; makes a good quarter-back.

Price, Walter C. (Rathmines School)—Makes a good forward or reliable back.

Purdon, F. T. (Wanderers)—A heavy, fast forward.

Purdon, H. (North of Ireland)—Works very hard forward; tackles splendidly; played for Ireland v. England, 1880.

Purdon, J. (North of Ireland)—Dodgy runner; drops and punts well.

Potts, R. M. (Cliftonville Association)—Right wing forward, and occasionally half-back; hardest workingman in the team; excellent dribbler; splendid tackler; most reliable for his pluck and determination; never tires.

Quin, J. (Lansdowne)—Fair average forward.

Rambaut, D. F. (Armagh Royal School)—A very hard-working forward.

Raphael, H. (Merrion Square Rovers)—A steady and uniformly good forward; knows how to dribble.

Redmond F. (Santry School)—A light active quarter; plays a hard game; runs well; uses a good deal of dodging in running.

Reid, W. B. (Royal Academical Institution, Belfast)—A heavy and reliable forward.

Reilly, A. (Cork)—A heavy forward; dribbles and follows up well.

Reilly, H. (Armagh)—An excellent forward; always playing on the ball, following up, and tackling well.
Reynolds, W. (North Wexford)—A very useful forward.
Rich, — (Dundalk)—A good half-back, and a difficult man to tackle.
Ridgeway, — (Wesley College)—A very promising colt; a dead shot at goal; drops well.
Ringwood, R. F. (Dungannon Royal School)—An honest, hard-working forward.
Ritchie, D. C. (Cliftonville Association)—Very promising back; kicks well and tackles admirably.
Robb, C. (Royal Academical Institution, Belfast)—A hard-working forward and good long drop.
Roberts, A. (Portarlington School)—A reliable half-back; good collar and kick.
Robertson, J. (Kingstown and Wanderers)—A good half-back; has not quite enough pace, but makes up for it by his knowledge of the game.
Robertson, W. (Cliftonville Association)—Left-wing forward; plays with great determination and dash; dribbles well and passes judiciously; most energetic when near goal.
Robinson, H. L. (Wanderers)—A dashing half-back, with great pace and sure collar. Has been picked for Ireland v. England.
Robinson, J. (Armagh Royal School)—Quarter-back; quick but uncertain.
Robinson, R. (Queenstown)—A fair collar and dashing forward.
Robinson, Samuel (Lurgan)—A very fair forward.
Robinson, W. G. (Armagh)—A useful, hard-working forward; fairly fast; dribbles and follows up well; always close to the ball.
Rooke, J. M. (Phœnix)—A first-class forward.
Ross, J. F. (North of Ireland)—A very dodgy runner; drops well with both feet; rather weak in tackling.
Ross, S. (Cork)—A hard-working forward, but too fond of the ball.
Ross, W. (Kingstown and Wanderers)—A splendid forward; very fast, and always on the ball. Leinster v. Ulster, 1880.
Rountree, F. (Santry School)—A heavy and useful forward; plays well in the scrummages.
Rowand, A. (Queen's College, Galway)—A good kick.
Russell, W. A. (Lon. Acad. Inst.)—A heavy forward; hard to collar.
Russell, W. F. (Phœnix)—A light but effective forward.
Rutherford, Wm. (Clanwilliam)—A good forward, with weight and speed; plays a good game.
Ryan, J. (Galway Grammar School)—Very useful in any part of the field; a good runner and tackler, and a fair kick.
Ryan, J. (Queen's College, Galway)—A strong forward.
Ryan, T. (Clontarf)—Fast half or quarter-back.

Schute, F. (Wanderers)—A heavy, hard-working forward; suffered much from a strained knee last season. Played for Ireland v. England, 1878-9.
Scogings, J. (Cork)—A fast quarter-back; fair collar and neat drop.
Scogings, T. W. (Queenstown)—Generally plays behind the scrummage; fair drop and good collar.
Scott, J. A. (North Wexford)—A watchful quarter-back; quick passer; good drop.

Scott, W. (Wanderers)—A light, fast forward.

Scriven, G. (Dublin University)—One of the best forwards in Ireland; uses his feet well, and is very fast; Captain of his Club and Leinster, 1879-80. Played for Ireland v. England and Scotland, 1879 and 1880.

Scroope, Fred. (Clanwilliam)—Plenty of weight and speed to make a good forward.

Seabrooke, C. (Ordnance Survey)—An excellent forward; always on the ball; silent but determined.

Searight, Frederick S. (Lansdowne)—Very good half or quarter; fast runner and drops well.

Searight, G. Lempriere (Lansdowne)—Very good "quarter;" tackles well and plays a very plucky game.

Seaver, H. (Lauriston)—Captain 1876-7-8-9-'80; a useful forward; runs strong and fast; dribbles well; fair drop and good pace.

Seaver, R. (Dublin University)—A very fast half-back.

Seddall, A. (Rathmines School)—A very good back; fair drop.

Seerif, Wm. (Ordnance Survey)—A plucky quarter-back; good tackler; should practice drop-kicking.

Semple, J. (Armagh)—A heavy forward, but does not use his weight.

Shaw, T. H. (Lansdowne)—Very good forward or quarter.

Shannon, Wm. (Lansdowne)—Hard-working, useful forward.

Shelock, A.—A fair forward; lacks weight; drops well.

Sheridan, P. J. (Ordnance Survey)—A powerful forward and fair tackler.

Shillington, T. A. (Portadown)—A light, active forward; works very hard in the scrummages.

Shuter, J. (Dungannon Royal School)—A splendid drop and place-kick; runs well; reliable full-back.

Shuter, W. (Dungannon Royal School)—A good half-back; excellent runner and tackler.

Sibthorpe, J. (Lansdowne and Wanderers)—A heavy, hard-working forward; always well in the scrummage.

Sidley, H. (Clontarf)—An improving half or quarter-back.

Sims, A. S. (Ordnance Survey)—Will yet make a good quarter-back; has much pace; might study the Rugby Rules to advantage.

Sinclair, D. (Queenstown)—Plays a good forward game.

Sinclair, J. (Knock)—The best player in the Club; centre forward; very sure with his head; always on the alert.

Sinclair, S. (Knock)—Has proved himself a good wing forward or half-back.

Sinclair, T. (Knock)—Brilliant goal-keeper.

Skipworth, P. M. (St. Columba's College)—A good and safe half-back; collars well; an excellent drop.

Smith, C. (Dungannon Royal School)—A hard-working forward.

Smith, E. (Hibernian)—A good half-back; punts well; good tackler; somewhat slow in his movements.

Smith, H. (King's Hospital)—A heavy, strong forward; good drop with both feet.

Smith, H. (Kingstown)—A very fair quarter; kicks and tackles well; rather slow.

Smith, P. (Galway Grammar School)—A heavy, hard-working forward.

Smith, R. S. (North of Ireland)—A light, fast forward; very useful in a loose game.

Smith, W. W. (Santry School)—A fairly useful half-back; plays hard; tackles well.
Smithwick, John (Clanwilliam)—A hard-working forward.
Smyth, Richard C. M. (Lansdowne)—Hard-working, fast forward.
Smyth, Thomas (Lansdowne)—Fair average forward.
Smyth, Thomas (Queen's College, Galway)—Captain; a very good full-back, being a splendid drop-kick and good runner.
Smyth, W. A. (Banbridge Academy)—A fair half-back; should make more use of his weight.
Soady, Collingwood (Rathmines School)—A safe back; good drop with either foot; sure tackler.
Soady, J. (Lansdowne)—First-rate forward; dribbles well and plays with great spirit.
Somerville, T. A. (Wanderers and Clontarf)—Plays quarter-back; has pace; good collar.
Spelman, J. (Queenstown)—Plays well back; sure tackler.
Spelman, S. (Cork)—A fast but rather wild quarter-back.
Spring, A. (Phœnix and Cusack's Academy)—A first-rate back; has great pace.
Sproull, H. C. (North of Ireland)—Has much improved; shows well in the loose.
Spunner, H. (Wanderers)—Can play well behind the scrummage; picks up sharply; good collar and splendid drop.
Stanfield, M. (Santry School)—A painstaking forward, playing well both in and out of the scrummage; dribbles well.
Stanley, C. (Portadown)—A good working forward; plays a sound game; follows hard up.
Stannard, George (North Wexford)—A determined forward and first-class tackler.
Steen, M. (Portadown)—A fair half-back; good dodger; should practice dropping.
Stewart, Henry (York Road, Belfast)—A capital tackler, and very plucky; can kick with either foot.
Stewart, J. (Lon. Acad. Inst.)—Plays well in the scrummage; good dribbler.
Stoker, — (Kingstown)—A fast, hard-working forward, likely to improve.
Stoker, J. (Wanderers)—An able forward.
Stoker, H. (Wanderers)—A good forward of much promise.
Stokes, H. G. (Lansdowne)—Very good forward; runs well when the scrummage breaks up.
Stokes, O. (Cork Bankers)—Captain; a strong, hard-working forward, and splendid collar.
Stokes, William (Clanwilliam)—A very useful, heavy forward; works hard.
Stopford, Hon. G. (North Wexford)—A first-class goal-keeper.
Storey, — (Wesley College)—A fine forward; always on the ball; vigorous and hard-working.
Sullivan, E. W. (Portora Royal School)—Plays well quarter-back; neat runner.
Sutton, F. (Monkstown, Co. Dublin)—Plays well back or forward; is a good kick and plays hard.
Swan, J. (Cork Bankers)—A good, strong, heavy forward.
Swan, W. (Galway Grammar School)—A good half-back.
Swiney, F. (Dungannon Royal School)—A splendid drop and place-kick; plays well behind the scrummage.

Tabuteau, A. O. (Phœnix)—A steady back; runs, drops and collars well, but seems to lack confidence.
Tabuteau, H. (Portarlington School)—A first-rate quarter-back, and excellent kick.
Tarleton, W. F. (Phœnix)—Plays a good game.
Taylor, J. (Albion)—A very strong forward; fast and good tackler.
Taylor, J. W. (Queen's College, Belfast)—Heavy forward; always on the ball; International man. Played v. Scotland '79 and '80; v. England '80. Captain of the Club, and in that capacity has worked hard.
Thomas, C. (Hibernian)—A very promising forward.
Thompson, — (Wesley College)—A vigorous half-back; very swift; plays full-back creditably.
Thompson, C. (Ulster)—A fast forward; not a bad half-back.
Thompson, H. (Lauriston)—A powerful forward, especially in the scrummage.
Thompson, H. B. H. (Clanwilliam)—A heavy forward, with speed; will play a very good game with practice.
Thompson, R. (Cork)—A hard-working forward and good collar.
Thompson, W. F. (Rathmines School)—An active forward and good drop at goal.
Thompson, A. (Cliftonville Association)—Rising left-wing forward; very energetic; good dribbler, but passes rather wildly at times.
Tillie, C. R. (Lon. Acad. Inst.)—Makes a fast quarter or half-back; wants weight.
Todd, J. A. Ross (Wanderers)—A good quarter-back; seldom plays.
Towers, E. L. (Cork Bankers)—A hard-working forward; dribbles well; plays with judgment.
Townshend, R. (Cork)—A very good forward; works hard and follows up well.
Townshend, S. (Cork)—A fast and useful quarter-back; most unselfish in passing.
Tracy, W. M. (Wanderers)—A neat half-back; good drop.
Trouton, F. (Dungannon Royal School)—Good in any position.
Tower, J. C. (Wanderers)—A heavy forward; steady and good worker; not fast.
Truswell, W. (Hibernian)—A good forward; rather tall for his weight; can drop well; will improve by practice.
Tully, H. J. (Lansdowne and Wanderers)—A strong-working, heavy forward; plays a most unselfish game, and is a good drop or place-kick.
Turnbull, J. (Lauriston)—Follows up hard; a sure tackler: fair drop; plays unselfishly.
Turner, Irwin (Dundalk)—A good back, and drops well.
Turner, Samuel (North Down)—A useful quarter-back; fairly fast.
Tyner, D. K. (Wanderers)—A fast full or half-back.

Vereker, J. (Merrion Square Rovers and Lansdowne)—An energetic forward.
Verscoyle, H. (Cork)—A sure half-back; drops well.

Waddell, G. (Albion)—A reliable quarter-back.
Waddell, George (Lurgan)—A useful forward, and plays quarter or half-back fairly.

Walker, R. (Santry School)—A good forward, and occasionally plays a nice quarter; drops and collars well.

Walkington, R. B. (North of Ireland)—Captain; a safe back, sure tackler, and splendid drop and punt. Played for Ireland v. England and Scotland on every match as full-back. Ex-Captain, Irish XV.

Wallace, W. (Lon. Acad. Inst.)—Works well in the scrummage, but wants speed.

Wallis, C. (Wanderers)—A strong forward; lacks dash.

Wallis, W. A. (Wanderers)—A hard-working forward. Played for Ireland v. Scotland, 1880.

Walpole, W. (Wesley College)—A neat quarter-back; plenty of spirit; will make a first-rate player.

Warden, F. W. (Ulster)—An improving forward; good, long drop; runs well.

Warren, J. P. (Clontarf)—A good, hard-working quarter; plays well on the ball.

Waters, H. (Queen's College, Galway)—A fine forward, particularly in the scrummage, where he works most energetically with his head.

Watson, J. (Ulster)—A fair half-back, but lacks pace; punts and tackles splendidly.

Watson, J. R. B. (Dundalk)—A capital quarter-back; tackles splendidly.

Watson, W. (Phœnix)—A hard-working forward; plays with vigour and judgment.

Watt, Wm. (Queen's College, Belfast)—Good half-back; has also played as full-back; drops and tackles well. Only played in the beginning of the season.

Webb, C. (Phœnix)—An energetic, careful forward.

Webb, Gerald (Lansdowne and Merrion Square Rovers)—Hard-working, persevering forward; is a very good place-kick.

Webb, H. (Lansdowne and Merrion Square Rovers)—A good quarter-back, though light; fast, and a good tackler.

Weller, C. H. (St. Columba's College)—A good and sure full-back; his knowledge of the Association Rules causes him sometimes to make mistakes in playing the Rugby game.

Wetherall, James (Lurgan)—Has great strength and weight, and uses both to advantage in a scrummage, but requires to study the game.

White, C. (Santry School)—A young, light, but very quick quarter; plays a sound game.

White, C. G. (Wanderers)—A plucky forward; always on the ball.

Whitelegge, W. (Cork)—A good forward.

Whitestone, A. M. (Dublin University and Lansdowne)—A noted quarter and half-back; splendid collar, and clever drop at goal. Picked on Irish team for last four years.

Whitestone, G. (Wanderers)—A most reliable back; good collar and fair drop.

Whiting, E. (Portarlington School)—An excellent full-back; played well last season.

Williams, J. (Santry School)—A useful man in the forwards, especially in the scrummages.

Williams, W. E. (Lauriston)—A reliable back, splendid drop, and reliable tackler.

Williamson, G. (Kingstown School)—A useful forward and good tackler.

Willis, R. G. (Phœnix)—A forward of no mean order.

Wilson, R. M. (Armagh Royal School)—A light forward; needs more uniform energy.
Wiseheart, J. F. (King's Hospital)—A fast back; dodgy runner and tackler.
Witz, L. (Clontarf)—A hard-working forward.
Wolfe, E. J. (Armagh)—A good half-back; fast, tackles and drops well.
Wolfe, J. C. (Armagh)—Captain; a good forward; has weight, and uses it; dribbles and tackles well, but wants pace.
Woods, J. (Santry School)—Very useful forward; clever at dribbling; keeps well on the ball.
Wright, C. T. Hagberg (Royal Acad. Inst., Belfast)—Captain; a safe half-back of great promise; sharp, but slow pace; a capital dodger and good drop.
Wright, H. B. H. (Royal Acad. Inst., Belfast)—A good quarter-back; plays most unselfishly; punts well.
Wybrants, W. (Portarlington School)—A most reliable half-back; scored thirteen tries in ten matches last season.
Wynne, A. (St. Columba's College)—A genuine forward.
Wynne, J. (St. Columba's College)—A fair forward; lacks energy.

Yeabsley, G. (Hibernian)—A steady and reliable full-back; running, kicking and tackling remarkably well.
Yelverton, J. (Cusack's Academy)—A light, fast forward; good collar.
Young, G. L. (Nomads)—A fair half-back; difficult to tackle; might improve in picking up and collaring.
Young, R. S. (Armagh Royal School)—A heavy forward; but does not use his weight to advantage in the scrummages.
Young, T. G. (Wanderers)—A good forward, but should play more.

THE ASSOCIATION GAME.

As the Association Game of football has now been introduced into Ireland, and as there is every prospect of it, ere long, becoming a very general winter pastime in at least the northern districts, the history of its introduction may be deemed worthy of record in this the first issue of the IRISH FOOTBALL ANNUAL.

During the years 1876-'77, the Scottish Football Association had been endeavouring to introduce the game by playing exhibition matches in Belfast and Dublin, but the Secretary had been unable to make satisfactory arrangements with the several Rugby Clubs for the use of their grounds, and so the matter had been allowed to drop.

Undeterred, however, by the apparent indisposition of the sons of the Emerald Isle for the dribbling code, several of the prominent members of the Association determined to make another trial, and J. A. Allen, Esq., the popular Captain of the Caledonian F.C., put himself in communication with some of his friends in Belfast on the subject, resulting in an arrangement being completed with the Ulster Cricket Club (a Club whose Committee have ever been foremost in the promotion and extension of every department of athletic pastime) for the use of their grounds for an exhibition match.

This match was played on the 24th October, 1878, between teams selected from the Queen's Park and Caledonian Clubs, and was a decided success, the attendance being larger than at any previous football match in the district. Belfast has always been, and most probably will continue, a stronghold of Rugby football; and although the majority of the spectators evinced a decided preference for the Rugby code, still there were not a few who were much impressed with the scientific beauty of the dribbling game, as exhibited by some of its very ablest exponents.

As, however, the larger number of football players had become connected with Rugby Clubs for that season, no definite steps were taken for the formation of an Association Club; occasional practices, however, were indulged in by those most favourable to the game; and when the Lenzie F.C. (from Stirlingshire) signified their intention of paying a visit to Belfast in the spring of 1879, no difficulty was found in raising a team to meet them, and although the visitors were victorious after an exceedingly pleasant and well contested game, the ability and skill exhibited by the Belfast men were highly creditable.

All the available playing grounds being already occupied by Rugby Clubs, some difficulty was experienced in obtaining suitable accommodation for the formation of an Association Club; but the Cliftonville Cricket Club having leased a new ground adjoining the Antrim Road, and prepared for the summer of 1879, an opportunity presented itself which was not lost sight of, and several of the members of the C.C.C. being ardent admirers of the Association Game, all obstacles were speedily overcome, and early in the autumn of 1879 the Cliftonville Club was formed, being the first Association Club in Ireland. The Committee of the new Club then undertook the task of the extension of the game throughout the district, and have succeeded even beyond their most sanguine expectations. At the close of the present season there are four thoroughly organized Clubs playing Association rules only, while there are several others occasionally practising them. As yet Belfast can only boast of the one Club, but it is expected others will be formed early next season, and in several of the suburban districts and villages the establishment of the game is almost a certainty.

The report of the Cliftonville Club is exceedingly creditable for a first season. Four matches with Scotch Clubs were engaged in, and the fact of having played a drawn game with the Ardee Club of Ardrossan proves that the members have made rapid strides towards perfection throughout the year. The Knock Club is in a very flourishing condition, and is certain next season to render a good account of itself, while the Banbridge Academy Club possesses several most promising players. The Moyola Club, of Castledawson, County Derry, was only established in the latter part of the season, but the report therefrom is most encouraging. The ground occupied by the Club is one of the very finest in Ireland, situated in the splendid demesne of Major Chichester, who takes a very lively interest in the game. The enthusiasm excited in the neighbourhood by the introduction of the game is almost unparalleled, and it is expected that nearly every town and village in the district will each next season have its representative Club, so that Castledawson, under the fostering care of Major Chichester, will ere long become a celebrated centre of the Association game.

It is contemplated that at the beginning of next season representatives of the several Clubs will be summoned together, with a view to the formation of an "Irish Football Association" for the better extension and development of the game in the several districts. It is also intended to institute a "Challenge Cup," to be competed for annually by the several Clubs, as it is believed that such an arrangement would add considerably to the public interest in the game, as well as be an incentive to constant and assiduous practice among the members, so necessary for the acquirement of that perfection for which the principal Scotch and English Clubs are so justly celebrated.

The game has also found its way into the Midland Counties, as a Club has been formed at St. Stanislaus College, Tullamore, King's County, and there is a prospect of several of the schools and colleges in the Midland and Southern Counties adopting the code next season. Dublin, Cork, and Limerick are now only needed to join issue to make the Association Game a fairly representative one throughout the island.

LAWS OF THE FOOTBALL ASSOCIATION.

1. The limits of the ground shall be: maximum length, 200 yards; minimum length, 100 yards; maximum breadth, 100 yards; minimum breadth, 50 yards. The length and breadth shall be marked off with flags; and the goals shall be upright posts, eight yards apart, with a tape or bar across them, eight feet from the ground.

2. The winners of the toss shall have the option of kick-off or choice of goals. The game shall be commenced by a place-kick from the centre of the ground; the other side shall not approach within ten yards of the ball until it is kicked off, nor shall any player on either side pass the centre of the ground in the direction of his opponent's goal until the ball is kicked off.

3. Ends shall only be changed at half-time. After a goal is won, the losing side shall kick off, but after the change of ends at half-time, the ball shall be kicked off by the opposite side from that which originally did so; and always as provided in Law 2.

4. A goal shall be won when the ball passes between the goal-posts under the tape or bar, not being thrown, knocked on nor carried. The ball hitting the goal, or boundary posts, or goal bar, or tape, and rebounding into play, is considered in play.

5. When the ball is in touch, a player of the opposite side to that which kicked it out, shall throw it from the point on the boundary-line where it left the ground in any direction the thrower may choose. The ball must be thrown in at least six yards, and shall be in play when thrown in, but the player throwing it in shall not play it until it has been played by another player.

6. When a player kicks the ball, or it is thrown out of touch, any one of the same side who at such moment of kicking or throwing is nearer to the opponents' goal-line is out of play, and may not touch the ball himself, nor in any way whatever prevent any other player from doing so until the ball has been played, unless there are at least three of his opponents nearer their own goal-line; but no player is out of play when the ball is kicked from the goal-line.

6. When the ball is kicked behind the goal-line by one of the opposite

side, it shall be kicked off by any one of the players behind whose goal-line it went, within six yards of the nearest goal-post; but if kicked behind by any one of the side whose goal-line it is, a player of the opposite side shall kick it from within one yard of the nearest corner flag-post. In either case no other player shall be allowed within six yards of the ball until it is kicked off.

8. No player shall carry or knock on the ball, and handling the ball under any pretence whatever, shall be prohibited, except in the case of the goal-keeper, who shall be allowed to use his hands in defence of his goal, either by knocking on or throwing, but shall not carry the ball. The goal-keeper may be changed during the game, but not more than one player shall act as goal-keeper at the same time, and no second player shall step in and act during any period in which the regular goal-keeper may have vacated his position.

9. Neither tripping nor hacking shall be allowed, and no player shall use his hands to hold or push his adversary nor charge him from behind. A player with his back towards his opponents' goal cannot claim the privilege of Rule 9, when charged from behind.

10. No player shall wear any nails, except such as have their heads driven in flush with the leather, iron-plates, or gutta-percha, on the soles or heels of his boots.

11. In the event of any infringement of Rules 6, 8 or 9, a free kick shall be forfeited to the opposite side from the spot where the infringement took place.

12. In no case shall a goal be scored from any free kick, nor shall the ball be again played by the kicker until it has been played by another player. The kick-off and corner-flag kick shall be free kicks within the meaning of this rule.

13. That in the event of any supposed infringement of Rules 6, 8, 9, or 10, the ball be in play until the decision of the Umpire, on his being appealed to, shall have been given.

DEFINITION OF TERMS.

A PLACE KICK is a kick at the ball while it is on the ground, in any position in which the kicker may choose to place it.

HACKING is kicking an adversary intentionally.

TRIPPING is throwing an adversary by the use of the legs.

KNOCKING ON is when a player strikes or propels the ball with his hands or arms.

HOLDING includes the obstruction of a player by the hand or any part of the arm extended from the body.

TOUCH is that part of the field, on either side of the ground, which is beyond the line of flags.

A FREE KICK is a kick at the ball in any way the kicker pleases, when it is lying on the ground; none of the kicker's opponents being allowed within six yards of the ball, but in no case can a player be forced to stand behind his own goal-line.

HANDLING is understood to be playing the ball with the hand or arm.

BANBRIDGE ACADEMY FOOTBALL CLUB.

Club Ground—B.C.A.C. Grounds.   *Colours*—Dark Blue, White Star.
President—H. J. Cooke.
Captain—J. Neill, jun.
Hon. Secretary—Samuel Hill, jun., Banbridge.
Hon. Treasurer—Fred. Woods.
Committee—J. Neill, jun., R. J. Ervin, J. Curragh, W. K. Irvin, W. K. Hill, and R. J. Hunter, President, Hon. Secretary, and Treasurer *ex-officio*.

The above Club, formed under the auspices of the old Academy of this town, was established to meet a want long felt by both present and past pupils; although rather late in starting operations, the members have no reason to be ashamed of the result of the season's work. Our first match, arranged shortly after the Club had been started, against the Cliftonville F.C., could hardly be considered a match, but rather a "tuition," as none of the "Academicals" had ever witnessed the Association game—dribbling and passing being things of which they had yet to learn—we, therefore, suffered defeat by two goals.

In our next match against the Knock, on the Knock grounds, we were again defeated; the Academicals falling off greatly in the last half, during which time all the goals were secured. In our return match against the Knock the play was greatly improved, as after an unusually fast game a draw was declared, neither side having gained any advantage. The concluding match of the season, against the Cliftonville, was played on their ground. Owing to the unavoidable absence of A. M. Buchanan, we had recourse to our own goal keeper, who proved a good substitute, his play being greatly admired and frequently applauded; but, in spite of our most strenuous efforts to avert defeat, we were again obliged to submit to the weight of the Premier Club.

CLIFTONVILLE ASSOCIATION FOOTBALL CLUB.

Club Ground—Cliftonville.   *Colours*—Red and White.
Captain—J. M. M'Alery.
Hon. Secretary—J. M. M'Alery, 6 Donegal Street, Belfast.
Assistant Secretary—R. M. Kennedy, 6 Brookvale Terrace, Antrim Road, Belfast.
Hon. Treasurer—D. C. Ritchie, 4 Duncairn Terrace, Antrim Road, Belfast.
Committee—D. Hannay, R. M. Kennedy, J. A. Macdonald, J. M'Ellery, S. M'Cully, R. M. Potts, W. Robertson, D. C. Ritchie.

The first annual report of the first Association Club in Ireland cannot be expected to record a very brilliant season, but under the circumstances the present report of the Cliftonville Club must be considered highly satisfactory.

During the season fourteen matches have been played (thirteen by the 1st XI. and one by the 2nd XI.), of which eight have been won, four lost, and two drawn; and, singular to relate, the number of goals lost and the number obtained are exactly equal, viz., thirty each.

The Club was formed early in September, and after some little trouble succeeded in obtaining permission from the Cliftonville Cricket Club to play on their ground. Considerable difficulty was at first experienced in obtaining a sufficient number of players to engage in the practice matches, but by degrees the number of members gradually increased, and several of the practices produced really good contests. As, however, matches against teams of players not connected with the Club were considered more conducive to the better acquirements of the game, arrangements were endeavoured to be made for matches against teams of Rugby players, and the first match the Club was engaged in was against a Rugby team under the name of the "Quidnuncs," in which it was unfortunately defeated, owing to several of the best players being unable to take part in the game. Towards the latter part of the season another match was played against a Rugby team selected from the Queen's College and Ulster Clubs (the greater number of whom had been occasionally practising the Association game throughout the season), and after an exceedingly well-contested game resulted in a draw. (In considering the merits of these matches, it must be remembered that the majority of the Cliftonville men had not previous to this season played any game of football.)

The second match of the season was against the Caledonians of Glasgow, in which the Scotchmen proved easy victors; but the home players received a lesson from this match which stood them in good service throughout the season. In the return match, played at Glasgow, the Cliftonville rendered a somewhat better account of themselves, as, up till within about fifteen minutes of time, only two goals had been scored against them; but the wearying effects of their long journey then began to tell on their staying powers, and they seemed almost powerless in the hands of their more formidable opponents, who succeeded in scoring four other goals before call of time; however, when the Caledonians next visit Belfast a really good contest is expected.

The match with the Portland of Kilmarnock was *the* match of the season, and afforded the large number of spectators who assembled an excellent opportunity of witnessing a really good Association game; and, although the home team was badly beaten, the members look forward with pleasure to the return match with this Club. The most creditable match of the season, however (looking at the matter from a Cliftonville point of view), was the closing one, when the Club managed to play a draw with the Ardee Club of Ardrossan, and it certainly shows that there is a decided improvement in the play of the members since the beginning of the season.

The Committee of the Club had in the intervals of the Scotch visits been alive to the necessity for the formation of local Clubs for the extension of the game throughout the district, and the matches with their Scotch friends serving as an impetus to this movement, they have succeeded beyond their highest expectations. The matches with the Knock, Banbridge Academy, and Moyola Clubs during the season have resulted in most interesting and enjoyable games; and although the Cliftonville has for so far succeeded in asserting their superiority, it is expected when next season comes round, these Clubs, as well as others now in progress of formation, will prove most formidable rivals; and should the proposed arrangement of the "Challenge Cup" be completed, some fine contests are anticipated.

MOYOLA FOOTBALL CLUB.

Club Ground—Moyola Park.   *Colours*—White and Blue.
Captain—G. Hewison.
Hon. Secretary—Percival C. Gaussen, Shanmullagh House, Castledawson.
Hon. Treasurer—H. Kelly.
Committee—Major Chichester, J.P., D.L.; W. J. Morrow, Esq.; Campbell Gaussen, Esq., J.P.; O. H. N. Bruce, Esq.; John A. Clarke, Esq., J.P.; John Moorhead, Esq.

As this is the first season of our Club, and a number of our members having never played before, we have had some of the usual difficulties to contend with, but, notwithstanding, we have had some good play, and fair progress has been made for the time. We were only able to play one match with the Cliftonville Club, in which we lost by three goals to nil. Major Chichester, who from the beginning has taken the greatest interest in our Club, has given us liberty to play in the beautiful grounds of Moyola Park. The Major himself thoroughly understands the game, and we find him in every respect a worthy patron and supporter. We hope by commencing early next season, and practising diligently, to make a good appearance in the various matches in which we are engaged.

KNOCK FOOTBALL CLUB.

Club Ground—At Knock.   *Colours*—Black, Yellow, and Red.
Captain—J. Sinclair.
Hon. Secretary—J. N. Hamilton, Knock, Belfast.
Hon. Treasurer—S. Sinclair.
Committee—J. Sinclair, J. Dill, R. Macartney, S. Sinclair, J. N. Hamilton, E. Gribben, R. Campbell, R. M'Beatney.

The Knock F.C. was formed from among the members of the Knock Lacrosse Club, which is the holder for the present year of the Irish Champion Lacrosse Flags. Considering that a large proportion of the members had not previously played football of any kind, it is remarkable that during their first season they should have won more matches than they lost. This was principally owing to the first-class organization which characterizes this Club, but also, doubtless, to the similarity which exists between the Association game and Lacrosse, in both of which a great deal depends upon unselfishness in passing.

There are at present twenty-seven members enrolled on the Club books, and this for the first year promises well for the future.

BANBRIDGE ACADEMY FOOTBALL CLUB.

Matches played, 4—lost, 3; won, 0; drawn, 1. Goals scored, 0.
Goals lost, 10.

1879.
Nov. 22, at Banbridge—v. Cliftonville. Lost by 2 goals.
1880.
Feb. 14, at Knock, Belfast—v. Knock. Lost by 3 goals.
Mar. 13, at Banbridge—v. Knock (return). Drawn.
„ 20, at Cliftonville, Belfast—v. Cliftonville. Lost by 5 goals.

CLIFTONVILLE ASSOCIATION FOOTBALL CLUB.

Matches played, 14—lost, 4; won, 8; drawn, 2. Goals scored, 30.
Goals lost, 30.

1879.
Oct. 11, at Cliftonville—v. Quidnuncs F.C. Lost by 2 goals to 1 goal.
„ 18, at Cliftonville—v. Caledonian F.C. (Glasgow). Lost by 9 goals to 1 goal.
Nov. 1, at Cliftonville—v. Knock F.C. Won by 2 goals to nil.
„ 22, at Banbridge—v. Banbridge Academy F.C. Won by 2 goals to nil.
„ 29, Cliftonville—v. Knock F.C. Won by 2 goals to nil.
1880.
Jan. 3, at Cliftonville—v. Portland F.C. (Kilmarnock). Lost by 9 goals to 1 goal.
„ 24, at Knock—v. Knock F.C. Won by 7 goals to nil.
„ 31, at Glasgow—v. Caledonian F.C. Lost by 6 goals to nil.
Feb. 14, at Castledawson—v. Moyola F.C. Won by 3 goals to nil.
Mar. 13, at Cliftonville—v. United Ulster and Queen's College Rugby Clubs. Drawn; 1 goal each.
„ 20, at Cliftonville—v. Banbridge Academy F.C. Won by 5 goals to nil.
April 3, at Cliftonville—v. Knock F.C. Won by 1 goal to nil.
„ 21, at Cliftonville—v. Ardee F.C. (Ardrossan). Drawn; 2 goals each.

2ND XI. MATCH.

Feb. 28, at Cliftonville—v. Knock F.C. 2nd XI. Won by 2 goals to 1 goal.

KNOCK FOOTBALL CLUB.
1ST XV.

Matches played, 10—lost, 4; won, 5; drawn, 1. Goals scored, 12.
Goals lost, 13.

1879.
Nov. 1, at Cliftonville—v. Cliftonville. Lost by 2 goals to nil.
„ 29, at Cliftonville—v. Cliftonville. Lost by 2 goals to nil.
1880.
Jan. 24, at Knock—v. Cliftonville. Lost by 7 goals to nil.
Feb. 7, at Knock—v. Albion. Won by 2 goals to 1.

Feb. 14, at Knock—v. Banbridge. Won by 3 goals to nil.
„ 21, at Knock—v. R. A. Institution. Won by 3 goals to nil.
Mar. 13, at Banbridge—v. Banbridge. Drawn.
„ 20, at Knock—v. Albion. Won by 2 goals to nil.
April 3, at Cliftonville—v. Cliftonville. Lost by 1 goal to nil.
„ 10, at Knock—v. Albion. Won by 2 goals to nil.

2ND XI. MATCHES.

Matches played, 4—lost, 2; won, 2; drawn, 0. Goals scored, 6; Goals lost, 4.

1880.
Feb. 25, at Knock—v. Wandsworth. Won by 2 goals to nil.
„ 28, at Cliftonville—v. Cliftonville. Lost by 2 goals to 1.
Mar. 3, at Knock—v. Wandsworth. Won by 3 goals to 1.
„ 13, at Dundonald—v. Dundonald. Lost by 1 goal to nil.

ALBION FOOTBALL CLUB v. KNOCK FOOTBALL CLUB.

[PLAYED FEB. 7, '80.—SCOTTISH ASSOCIATION RULES.]

(From the Northern Whig.)

This match was played on Saturday, on the Knock ground, where a good attendance of spectators showed the advance in public favour which this game has made since its introduction. The Knock Captain, having won the toss, elected to play with the wind, and Magean (Albion Captain) put the ball in motion at five minutes to four o'clock. The passing of the visitors from the first was good, and the playing of M'Wha and Jenkins being conspicuous. The Albion team, although one man short, played with much spirit, and it was principally owing to the sure play of the Knock forwards that the result was a win for them. Shortly after the start J. Sinclair obtained the first goal. The Albions now kicked off, and the forwards, following well up, kept the ball in the Knock territory, till J. Dill, by a timely kick, sent the ball to the half-way flag, where it was secured by Macartney and Richards on the right wing, and they were only prevented scoring by Munce. Half-time was now called, and, after the usual interval, the ball was again started. Some loose play took place in the centre of the field, till the Knock left wing carried the ball close up to the Albion's posts, when S. Sinclair added a second goal to their score. This, instead of discouraging the visitors, only stimulated their forwards, who played well together, and J. Black, after a splendid piece of play, secured a goal just before the call of no-side. The score then stood two goals to one. Besides those already mentioned, the play of J. M'Lean, J. W. Taylor, and R. Mayne, for the Albions, and A. Dill and D. A. Main, for the Knock, deserves special notice. The following were the teams:—Albion F.C.—W. Watts (goal), A. Jenkins and A. Munce (backs), W. M'Wha (half-back), W. Magean (captain), J. W. Taylor (centre), J. M'Lean and R. Mayne (left wing), J. Black and S. Taylor (right wing). Knock F.C.—R. M'Bratney (goal), J. Dill and J. Hamilton (backs), D. A. Main and Du Noyer (half-backs), J. Sinclair (captain), H. Lowery (centre), M. Richards and R. M'Cartney (right wing, A. Dill and A. Sinclair (left wing). Mr. Kennedy (Cliftonville A.F.C.) officiated as umpire.

FOOTBALL STATISTICS.
(ASSOCIATION RULES.)

Name of Club.	Matches. Played.	Won.	Lost.	Drawn.	Goals. Won.	Lost.
Banbridge Academy	4	3	0	1	0	10
Cliftonville	14	4	8	2	30	30
Knock	10	4	5	1	12	13
Moyola	1	0	1	0	0	3

STRANGE, BUT TRUE!

RULES

Amongst the novel rules in Gaelic football was one which saw teams required to start the match by holding hands with a member of the opposition team over the half-way line. This gave each side an equal start, but also symbolised the friendship and camaraderie in which games were meant to take place.

Until 1912 soccer goalkeepers were allowed to handle the ball anywhere in their own half of the pitch. Only in this year were they limited to the penalty area.

The first international rugby match to take place between two sides each of 15 players was that between the Irish and English sides at the Oval in London in February 1887. Previously teams had contained 20 players, with 14 generally playing as forwards.

CLUBS

Especially during the early years of football in Ireland, clubs switched regularly between the country's three codes. For example, the Ulster Club in Belfast began as a rugby club, but took up the soccer game in the mid-1880s. It then switched back to rugby in 1898, before going out of existence in the 1930s. The Cookstown Swifts club began as a Gaelic football club in 1888, but was unable to find any opposition locally and switched to playing soccer after one season. They then turned to rugby in the 1890s, after losing an appeal to the IFA over a contested cup tie. The famous Laune Rangers Gaelic Football Club was initially founded as a Rugby club. Other clubs had their origins in

		PRIZES:		
1st Prize	—Diamond Necklet, Bracelet, or Ring, or an Artisan's Dwelling-house, or their value in cash,		value	£100 0 0
2nd "	—Fine Onyx Drawing room Clock, with Bronze Figure on top, 2ft. 10in. high,		"	21 0 0
3rd "	—Engine Working Clock,		"	18 0 0
4th "	—Gent.'s Gold Keyless Lever Watch, No. 5828,		"	15 0 0
5th "	" " " " " 5825,		"	15 0 0
6th "	" " " " " 6431,		"	15 0 0
7th "	" " " " " 5819,		"	15 0 0
8th "	—Tea and Coffee Service and Tray,		"	9 0 0
9th "	—Pair Large Bronze Figures,		"	8 0 0
10th "	—Dining-Room Clock and Ornaments,		"	8 0 0
11th "	—Lady's Gold Keyless Watch, No. 16848		"	8 0 0
12th "	" " " " " 253134		"	8 0 0
13th "	" " " " " 11655		"	8 0 0
14th "	" " " " " 253136		"	5 0 0
15th "	—Drawing-room Clock,		"	5 0 0
16th "	—Gent.'s Silver Lever Watch,		"	4 10 0
17th "	—Pair Bronze Figures,		"	3 0 0
18th "	—Lady's Silver Watch,		"	2 0 0
19th "	—Case Steel Carvers,		"	2 0 0
20th "	—Set Gent.'s Links and Studs,		"	2 0 0
21st "	—Pair Field Glasses,		"	2 0 0
22nd "	—Lady's Silver Watch,		"	2 0 0
23rd "	—Gent.'s Gold Signet Ring,		"	1 10 0
24th "	—Lady's Gem Ring,		"	1 10 0
25th "	—Gent.'s Gold Scarf Pin,		"	1 10 0
26th "	—Biscuit Box,		"	1 10 0
27th "	—Pair Opera Glasses,		"	1 10 0
28th "	—Butter Dish,		"	1 0 0
29th "	—Case Fish Carvers,		"	1 0 0
30th "	—Case Two Fruit Spoons,		"	1 0 0

TICKETS ONE SHILLING EACH.

N.B.—*Each Ticket entitles the holder to Thirty Chances for above Prizes.*

The only Prize for which the value in Cash will be given is the First.

Prizes are now on view in Messrs. WM. GIBSON & CO.'s Window, and full value of all Prizes are guaranteed by them.

The Ballot will be public, and Winning Numbers will be published in Belfast *News-Letter* and *Evening Telegraph* of Feb. 8th, *Irish Times* and London *Standard* of Feb. 11th; also in other papers which will be advertised at a later date.

The running of a football club required considerable funds, even in 1890. The idea of raffles and ballots to raise money was quickly seized on. The total prize fund for this draw in aid of the Distillery soccer club was £300, with the option of a house as first prize.

Ulster Football and Cycling News

Jack Reynolds, pictured in the colours of the Ulster club in 1891.

Ulster Football and Cycling News

quite different sporting pastimes. The Wellington Park soccer club, who were runners-up in the 1884 Irish Cup competition, were formed from the members of a lacrosse club, while several members of the Cliftonville club were members of the cricket club of the same name. Other clubs were formed by groups and organisations with no prior sporting links. Windsor Rugby Club, once one of the leading Belfast sides, was founded by medical and theology students from the Queen's University. Bellinaleck GAA club in Fermanagh was formed by members of the local Gaelic League Irish language classes; and the Freebooters soccer club in Dublin, Irish Cup runners-up in 1901, were composed of young Irishmen who had attended boarding schools together in England.

PLAYERS

Many players have been said to have had unique careers, but that of the soccer player Jack Reynolds was truly so. Between 1890 and 1891 he won five caps for Ireland, even scoring a goal against England in the latter year. However, following his transfer to the English West Bromwich Albion side in the summer of 1891, he subsequently made eight appearances for England, including one against Ireland in Belfast in 1894. He remains the only man to have played soccer at full international level for both England and Ireland.

Amongst many political notables who were to play Gaelic football at club level was one Michael Collins, who was active in the London branch of the GAA. His eventual rival in politics Eamonn de Valera, was said to have preferred the Rugby code however, even playing a trial for the Munster provincial side. A fellow member of de Valera's Fianna Fail party was Oscar Traynor, who served as Eire's Minister of

IRISH FOOTBALLERS IN ENGLAND.

William McCracken was born and raised in Belfast, but made his name as a soccer player in Newcastle-upon-Tyne. A dispute over payments for playing for Ireland, and the intervention of the Great War, led to him gaining only 16 Irish caps over more than two decades. He is perhaps best remembered as the man who perfected the off-side trap.
Ireland's Saturday Night

Defence during the Second World War. This was perhaps a very fitting job for a man who had previously been the professional goalkeeper of the Belfast Celtic soccer side.

When the Irish Rugby team arrived in Cardiff in 1884 to play the Welsh national side, it was three men short of a full team. As a result the IRFU's honorary secretary took to the field, and two players were borrowed from the opposition to make up the Irish numbers. Perhaps unsurprisingly, the Irish went on to lose the match.

PITCHES

The first attempt to stage an international Rugby match at the Lansdowne Road pitch was in 1875. However the ground was rejected as 'quite inadequate' and the match against England was eventually played at a cricket field in Rathmines.

Sam Maguire, a keen player and supporter of Gaelic games of all sorts.
Private Collection

Before being purchased by the GAA, the sports ground at what is now Croke Park was used for various games and amusements. The then Jones's Road stadium in fact provided a home for the Tritonville Association Football Club for several seasons, as well as hosting a number of cricket matches.

Until 1904 major soccer games in Dublin, such as cup finals and internationals, were played on the Lansdowne Road pitch as no soccer team had a large enough stadium to cope with the crowds that attended. The establishment and improvement of the Dalymount ground by the Bohemians club solved this problem, if only temporarily.

TROPHIES

Despite the fact that the Sam Maguire trophy is presented in Gaelic football each year in Ireland, the Cork man after whom it was named actually spent the majority of his life living and working in London. He was also one of the few Protestants to be actively involved in the GAA.

Making contributions to good causes was looked on as a duty by all early football clubs, and many matches were played for charitable purposes.
Belfast Weekly Telegraph

A Charity Cup competition, intended to raise money for good causes in the Belfast area was first begun under the IFA in 1883. However, in 1895 it was withdrawn by its trustees following a dispute over whether professional players should be paid for playing in the final. The trophy was subsequently given over to the Ulster branch of the IRFU, but eventually melted down during the Great War.

An IRFU Challenge Cup, along the lines of the Irish Cup in soccer, was proposed in 1882, but never proceeded with. The rumour circulated that 'pot hunting' was regarded as contrary to the spirit of the game by the IRFU's members.

CROWDS

In 1904 the Honorary Treasurer of the IRFU was ridiculed in the Dublin press for saying that although soccer games could attract larger crowds than Rugby matches, those who attended the former were 'not of the same class' and would in fact lower the tone of Rugby if they attended. Despite his comments, and the protests of the Northern Branch of the Union, he held his office for another two years, and the IRFU continued in a very healthy financial state.

Following crowd trouble at some matches the previous season in Belfast, in September 1913 the Secretary of the Glentoran club issued a series of handbills to spectators. These asked members of the crowd to desist from 'unsportsmanlike conduct', which included using 'revolvers and explosive material to intimidate players and referees.'

Following the imposition of an Entertainment tax by the United Kingdom government in 1916, the price of tickets to all sporting events was required to include a government levy. However the GAA refused to collect the tax, primarily on the grounds that they were a cultural and not a sporting organisation. With the establishment of the Irish Free State, the GAA was legally exempted from the tax. This placed Gaelic football in the same class of pastime as opera, ballet and making a visit to an art gallery.

Would-be soccer spectators force their way aboard a tram in Belfast in 1911.
Ireland's Staurday Night

TRAMS AND TRAINS

The emergence of cheap and reliable public transport, by way of trams and trains, was essential in the development of football in Ireland. It allowed teams to travel long distances quickly to take part in games, and made it possible for large crowds to attend games at the new stadiums in city suburbs. However, the relationships between the transport and sporting authorities were not always easy ones. In 1900 the advertising of all soccer and rugby matches was banned on Belfast's trams, as all such games were reckoned to be 'political' events. By 1908 the manager of the Great Northern Railway, a strict sabbatarian and evangelical Christian, had banned excursions to sports events on Sundays, with the effect that the GAA in some areas of Ulster found it hard to attract spectators to its events. In 1913 a rowdy crowd on a tram outside the ground of the Shelbourne soccer club in Dublin was only brought to order when the tram's conductor drew a revolver, and fired a shot into the air.

NEWSPAPERS

The press was important in Ireland, as elsewhere, for disseminating sporting information and popularising games and their players. Ireland's first purely sporting paper was the *Irish Sporting Chronicle* which began publication in 1840. It was concerned primarily with shooting, hunting and bloodstock however. The first Irish paper to give extended coverage of football matches and athletics meetings was *Sport*, which began publication in Dublin in 1880. The next major contribution came in 1887, when *The Ulster Football and Cycling News*, later *The Football News*, was published in Belfast. Within a decade *Ulster's Saturday Night*, subsequently known as *Ireland's Saturday Night*, was appearing and giving those interested match reports and results within hours of the completion of games. Today only the last mentioned is still being published. Although several attempts were made in the 1880s to launch a newspaper dealing exclusively with Gaelic games, it was not until 1912 that *The Gaelic Athlete* first appeared. It continued publishing until wartime pressures forced its closure in 1916.

FOREIGN TOURS

In 1912 the Belfast Celtic club became the first Irish soccer side to tour Europe when they arranged a visit to the city of Prague and Bohemia. At an after match dinner the entertainments included a display of Irish dancing, as well as recitations of poetry in Irish. The party included the Belfast writer and performer Cahal O'Byrne, who acted as the team's mascot, complete with Irish pipes and saffron kilt.

The combined English, Irish, Scottish and Welsh team which toured South Africa in 1896 included eight Irishmen in its party. Amongst these were Thomas Crean and Robert Johnston, members of the Wanderers club. Both were to return to South Africa within a few years as volunteers during the Boer War. Both were also awarded Victoria Crosses for their bravery while fighting with the Imperial Light Horse.

During the first four decades of the GAA's existence Gaelic football was rarely played outside Ireland. However, in the summer of 1896 a number of demonstration games were played at the Stamford Bridge stadium in London, now the home of Chelsea Football Club. Despite attracting comparatively large crowds, the game was not widely taken up in the imperial capital.

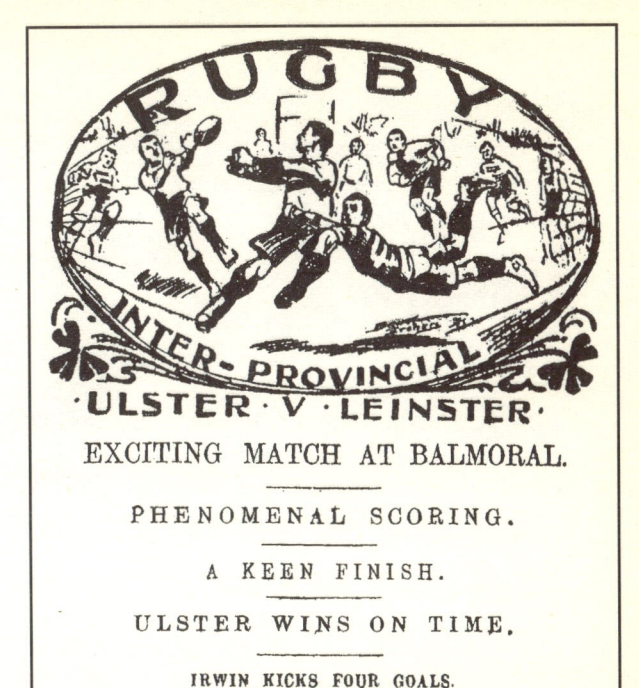

FOREIGN VISITORS

The visit of a team of New Zealand Maori rugby players to Ireland in 1889 aroused a great deal of interest in the game. The actual match was not a very edifying spectacle however, and reportedly included a walk-off by the visitors who were enraged at several of the referee's decisions.

In 1899 a team of mixed race players from the Orange Free State, known as the 'Kaffirs', visited Belfast during a short tour of the United Kingdom. Their opponents in the city were Belfast Celtic, and the visitors were given a rapturous welcome around their ground in the west. One spectator later suggested that it was the only time that Orange flags had been waved so enthusiastically by the residents of the Falls Road.

In 1896 a controversy broke out in the Dublin press after a number of visiting Welsh rugby players attended a Gaelic football match in Dublin, and roundly

Interprovincial matches were an integral part of the Rugby game in Ireland long before the official start of the Interprovincial.

Belfast Telegraph

Prior to the outbreak of war in 1914 three Rugby internationals were played in Cork, including this one against France in 1911.

Ireland's Saturday Night

177

These scenes from the Irish soccer match against the Scots in Dublin in 1913, include the presentation of a gold medal to Val Harris the Irish captain, to commemorate the first ever Irish defeat of England two weeks earlier. The medal was sponsored by the Belfast sports newspaper *Ireland's Saturday Night*, and presented by the earl of Aberdeen, the then Lord Lieutenant.

Ireland's Saturday Night

criticised the whole nature of the game. Despite various challenges being issued by GAA, IRFU and IFA officials as a result, the expected match between players of the various codes never took place.